American Prince, American Pauper

Recent Titles in
Contributions in Political Science
Series Editor: Bernard K. Johnpoll

The Liberal Future in America: Essays in Renewal
Philip Abbott and Michael B. Levy, editors

A Change of Course: The West German Social Democrats and NATO, 1957-1961
Stephen J. Artner

Power and Policy in Transition: Essays Presented on the Tenth Anniversary of the National
Committee on American Foreign Policy in Honor of Its Founder, Hans J. Morgenthau
Vojtech Mastny, editor

Ideology and Soviet Industrialization
Timothy W. Luke

Administrative Rulemaking: Politics and Processes
William F. West

Recovering from Catastrophes: Federal Disaster Relief Policy and Politics
Peter J. May

Judges, Bureaucrats, and the Question of Independence: A Study of the Social Security
Administration Hearing Process
Donna Price Cofer

Party Identification, Political Behavior, and the American Electorate
Sheldon Kamieniecki

Without Justice for All: The Constitutional Rights of Aliens
Elizabeth Hull

Neighborhood Organizations: Seeds of a New Urban Life
Michael R. Williams

The State Politics of Judicial and Congressional Reform: Legitimizing Criminal Justice
Policies
Thomas Carlyle Dalton

With Dignity: The Search for Medicare and Medicaid
Sheri I. David

AMERICAN PRINCE, AMERICAN PAUPER

The Contemporary Vice Presidency in Perspective

MARIE D. NATOLI

Contributions in Political Science, Number 134

GREENWOOD PRESS
Westport, Connecticut • London, England

Library of Congress Cataloging in Publication Data

Natoli, Marie D.
 American prince, American pauper.

(Contributions in political science, ISSN 0147–1066 ;
no. 134)
 Bibliography: p.
 Includes index.
 1. Vice-Presidents—United States. 2. United States
—Politics and government—1945–   . I. Title.
II. Series.
JK609.5.N38 1985   353.03'18   84–28965
ISBN 0–313–24750–1

Library of Congress Catalog Card Number: 84–28965
ISBN: 0–313–24750–1
ISSN: 0147–1066

First published in 1985

Greenwood Press
A division of Congressional Information Service, Inc.
88 Post Road West
Westport, Connecticut 06881

Printed in the United States of America

10 9 8 7 6 5 4 3 2 1

Copyright Acknowledgments

Permission to reprint from the following sources is gratefully acknowledged.

Harry S. Truman, Years of Decisions, Doubleday & Co.,
Inc. Publishers, 1955, used by permisison of Margaret
Truman Daniel.

Oral History Interview, Milton S. Eisenhower, Eisenhower
Administration Oral History Collection, Columbia University,
New York, New York, used with permission of Milton S.
Eisenhower.

Every reasonable effort has been made to trace the owners of copyright materials in this book,
but in some instances this has proven impossible. The publishers will be glad to receive information
leading to more complete acknowledgments in subsequent printings of the book and in the meantime
extend their apologies for any omissions.

To my two sets of parents:

Carmela and Frank Natoli, my mother and father
and
Mary and Ferro Mingardi, my aunt and uncle

Contents

Preface

The Vice-Presidency is a unique institution and has long been a focal point of constitutional concern. Its functions are unclear and ill-defined, yet as the institution "a heartbeat away" from the Presidency, it is pivotal in maintaining continuity and stability. Since World War II, the power of the United States has expanded rapidly, and its government has been buffeted by many grave challenges, both foreign and domestic. Presidential continuity and stability have been seriously challenged on more than one occasion, and political turmoil has heightened controversy regarding the second highest office in the land.

Political scientists and historians generally acknowledge that the end of the Roosevelt years marks the beginning of the "modern" Presidency and Vice-Presidency. As proof, they point to the enormous social and political changes emanating from that period:

1. The abandonment of an isolationist foreign policy which contributed to the growth of the Presidency inasmuch as the President had the inherent power to deal with the heads of other nations and to suggest the agenda for relations with those nations.
2. The technological advances within the mass media—particularly broadcasting—and President Franklin D. Roosevelt's use of them which marked the development of the "personal" Presidency and its corresponding growth.
3. The development of atomic weapons during the Roosevelt years, which made the Presidency the advocate of weapons use as the ultimate decision-maker.
4. The increased role of the federal government as a whole, which brought with it an expanded Presidency.
5. The Congress's "abdication" to the Presidency of the initiative in problem-solving and program development as a result of the Depression, beginning the growth of the institutionalized Presidency.

It is logical that, as the Presidency grew, that growth would extend to the Vice-Presidency.

This study probes the nature and development of the modern Vice-Presidency by focusing on the period from the end of World War II to the present and following a thematic rather than a chronological approach. Among the areas examined are the selection of vice-presidential candidates, the development of the Vice-Presidency as a stepping stone to the Presidency, the contemporary usages of the Vice-President, and the double-edged sword of disability and succession to the Presidency. This work places the functioning of the Vice-Presidency as a constitutional institution within the framework of personalities and circumstances as well as structural development. A salient characteristic of the Vice-Presidency is that, while it is the only nationally elected office besides the Presidency itself, it is simultaneously void of any significant ongoing constitutional function and is almost entirely subject to presidential whim for its activity and growth. Certainly, circumstances have from time to time focused renewed attention on the second office, as has been true in the three instances of succession since World War II: Harry S Truman in 1945; Lyndon B. Johnson in 1963; and Gerald R. Ford in 1974. Delving into each of these instances, this study reveals the particular patterns which these Vice-Presidents have followed in succeeding to the Presidency, both in terms of problems encountered and policies followed. Because the approach in this study is thematic rather than biographical or chronological, occasional repetition of points and issues occurs. Similarly, *selective* case studies are used.

Attention has also been focused on the Vice-Presidency as a source of presidential aspiration. Beginning with the development of the second office during Richard M. Nixon's incumbency, the Vice-Presidency has consistently been in the national limelight of presidential politics. Each Vice-President since that time has either become a presidential candidate or been the object of speculation for such a candidacy. Yet a peculiar dilemma has become associated with this aspect of the office's development: two incumbent Vice-Presidents (Nixon and Humphrey) who served as their party's standard-bearer suffered defeat primarily because of their association with the programs and policies of the President under whom they served. And in the 1984 election, former Vice-President Walter Mondale—despite almost a four-year period since he was a member of the Carter Administration—found it almost impossible to dissociate himself from negative images of that Presidency.

As more prominent individuals have accepted nomination to the second office and as more and more duties, especially within the areas of foreign affairs and domestic campaigning, have been assigned to the Vice-President, a new role has emerged, that of administration spokesman. This role reached its zenith with Spiro Agnew, but all modern Vice-Presidents have had to fulfill it to varying degrees. Richard Nixon provided such a service for President Eisenhower, and Hubert Humphrey, in his defense of President Johnson's Vietnam War policies, served this function as well.

The office, then, has evolved in terms of both statutory changes (for example, the Vice-President is a member of the Cabinet and the National Security Council) and contemporary events and exigencies. Until the middle of the twentieth century, the office offered little more than ceremonial responsibilities, and the President determined what duties a particular Vice-President had. The twentieth century has been kinder to Vice-Presidents, and yet whatever duties a Vice-President assumes remain up to the President. Nonetheless, nine Vice-Presidents have succeeded to the Presidency upon the death or resignation of a President, and several others have come close to succeeding. In these respects, the Vice-President is both a prince and a pauper: the heir apparent and yet a person who often goes "begging" for a role. Subsequent chapters explore the paradox of these roles and concentrate on the modern Vice-Presidency since 1945.

Acknowledgments

Any successful work has a great variety of people behind its author. Some of my early influences are among the most important and deserve considerable thanks: Dr. Nancy Dean, of Hunter College's English department, who not only taught me how to write (even though I still use more dashes than she would probably like) but who has also always been a role model and friend; Professor Robert S. Hirschfield, of Hunter College's Political Science Department, with whom I first studied the American Presidency and who is responsible for instilling in me my continuing excitement about the subject; and the late Professor Robert R. Dobbins of Tufts University's Political Science Department, who guided my early studies of the Vice-Presidency and was one of the most loving and genuinely caring individuals anyone could know.

Supportive friends are essential in both the highs and lows of the many stages of research and writing, and I am fortunate in having more than my fair share of them. Especially important to this work have been (in no order other than alphabetical): Bill Adams; Peter Cohen; Jean Cummiskey; Curt Martin; Lenore G. Martin; Elizabeth Moesel; Janet Morahan; Page Morahan; Nancy Sandman; Jennifer Tebbe; and Rosemary Tobin. A special thank you is due Dr. Maximilian Steiff, whose tireless wit, witicism, and advice (often unsolicited) sustained me in many moments.

I am also grateful for the help provided by the archivists at the presidential libraries I had the opportunity to visit, especially Jo August and Donna Smerlas of the John F. Kennedy Library and Mike Gillette of the Lyndon B. Johnson Library.

Many colleagues at the Center for the Study of the Presidency and on the Editorial Board of the Center's publication, the *Presidential Studies Quarterly*, have encouraged my work on the Vice-Presidency. Special thanks go to Dr. R. Gordon Hoxie, President of the Center; Ambassador Ruth Farkas (ret.), Chairman of the Board of Trustees of the Center; and Dr. Ken Davison, Book Review Editor of the *Quarterly*.

Finally, I thank the people at Greenwood Press who gave invaluable assistance in the production of this book: Dr. James T. Sabin; Susan Costanzo; Douglas J. Gall; and Maureen Melino.

American Prince, American Pauper

"His Superfluous Excellency": An Introduction

Our first Vice-Presidents were actually runners-up for the Presidency. From 1788 until the adoption of the Twelfth Amendment in 1804, the Electors of each state cast *two* votes for the office of President and none for the office of Vice-President, since the Framers of the Constitution had provided that the second highest vote-getter would serve as Vice-President. A Vice-President was necessary, they felt, in the event of the President's death or disability.

In a sense, then, the Electors ignored the office of Vice-President—and the qualifications necessary to hold it. Each Elector voting for his candidates was unable to designate which he preferred to be President, although the method insured that a man of high calibre and reknown would be selected for the second office. But a negative outcome was also possible, and this occurred with the election of 1800, which marked a crucial turning point for the Vice-Presidency.

In that election, Thomas Jefferson and Aaron Burr, both of the Republican party, received an equal number of electoral votes for the Presidency. This, according to the Constitution, sent the election to the House of Representatives. The Federalists attempted but failed to have Burr or a Federalist elected to the Presidency by soliciting a few Republican votes. Jefferson, however, was chosen President, and Burr, as provided by the Constitution, became his Vice-President.[1]

Even though Jefferson and Burr had received the same number of electoral votes, members of the Republican party did not consider Burr a desirable choice for the Presidency; in fact, he was considered dangerous. Thus, what was perceived as a narrow escape revived interest in separate votes for each office, and by May 1802 an amendment had been passed in the House of Representatives.[2]

By no means were opinions unanimous for either the necessity or the virtue of the change, and the opinions of the opponents contained a good deal of prophecy. The two major arguments in opposition were that, first, contrary to the intentions of the Framers of the Constitution that the Vice-Presidency go to someone qualified for the Presidency, the Twelfth Amendment did no such thing, but merely gave it to someone specifically chosen for the inferior spot. Clearly, the argument ran, this would not ensure the election of "fit men" and would "degrade the Vice Presidency."[3]

The second objection was based on fears that residents of the smaller states would be discriminated against in seeking the office of the Presidency. The debate became so heated that at one point an amendment was introduced (but defeated) for the abolition of the Vice-Presidency. When the opposing sides finally lined up, fears for the stature of the Vice-Presidency and for the influence of the smaller states were far outweighed by fears of a repetition of the crisis and near calamity of 1800.[4] The vice-presidential election was established.

To a large extent, the fears of those who opposed the Twelfth Amendment were realized, and the calibre of the individuals holding the Vice-Presidency changed considerably. This phenomenon would not change until the period of the modern Vice-Presidency. An additional impact of the electoral change was the subjection of the Vice-Presidency to the bartering of the political marketplace.

The early (pre-Twelfth Amendment) Vice-Presidents possessed much more independent energy than did their obscure successors. As the next highest vote-getter for President, the Vice-President was obviously a rival of the top vote-getter. As Vice-President, this rivalry continued, and the Vice-President often assumed the leadership of the President's opposition.

It is little wonder, then, that President George Washington chose to exclude his Vice-President, John Adams, a highly prestigious, eminent figure, from Cabinet deliberations. Both in spite of and because of the Vice-President's role as an opposition party leader and administration critic, the executive role of the Vice-President was insignificant, even when performed by men like Adams. The Vice-Presidency was regarded as so insignificant that Adams once dubbed the incumbent of the office "His Superfluous Excellency," and Daniel Webster refused to accept the nomination as Zachary Taylor's running mate, saying, "I do not choose to be buried until I am really dead."[5] Henry Clay, resenting being chosen for second place, twice turned down offers of the nomination, first on the William Henry Harrison ticket and later with Taylor. (Ironically, both Harrison and Taylor died in office.) And one Vice-President, John C. Calhoun, resigned the office in favor of a Senate seat.[6]

In one respect, little changed after the adoption of the Twelfth Amendment. Although the Vice-President was now voted for as Vice-President, it usually happened that the position, as the Framers had feared, was parceled out to a member of a competing faction within the presidential nominee's party. But one important element must be noted. Unlike pre-Twelfth Amendment elections, the vice-presidential nominee, chosen for second place (and, with the development of the party system, running in "partnership" with the presidential nominee), was more bound up with and indebted to the number one man on the ticket. And he was subject as ever to presidential whim in terms of the jobs to which he would be assigned.

The Framers viewed the Vice-Presidency as the solution to numerous controversies in the Convention: namely, the need to provide someone fit to take over for a dead or disabled President; to alleviate the smaller states' fears that they might be discriminated against in the election of a President (the solution of having Electors cast two ballots, one of which *had* to be for a candidate from a state other than their own, was a compromise); and, lastly, to have an objective presiding officer of the Senate who would decide a question in the event of a tie. With these considerations uppermost, little thought was given to what the Vice-President's day-to-day functions would be. The Framers chose to leave the Vice-President with only two constitutional duties: waiting to be President and presiding over the Senate. This latter function nonetheless created constitutional controversy at the Convention, for many delegates feared that the executive branch would thereby gain a foothold in the legislature. Judging from some of their strong misgivings about the Vice-President's role in the Senate, it is evident that they had expected him to be quite active in it. On the contrary, the history of the office has revealed that the Vice-President as President of the Senate has never presented any serious threat of executive infiltration of the legislature.

One function of the Vice-Presidency which the Framers undoubtedly did not foresee was its use as a graveyard to which competitors or troublesome creatures might be relegated. Probably the most blatant instance of this use was in the selection of Theodore Roosevelt as William McKinley's running mate; McKinley, as far as the party bosses were concerned, was to see to it that Roosevelt behaved himself. They might have tried it on a less dynamic individual. Needless to add, Teddy Roosevelt succeeded to the Presidency upon the assassination of McKinley. There is some speculation (as Chapter 1 explores) that Lyndon Johnson was chosen as John F. Kennedy's running mate for precisely this reason—that Johnson as Vice-President might have appeared far less dangerous to Kennedy than as Majority Leader of the Senate. As with the Roosevelt succession, the irony is that Lyndon Johnson became President.

NOTES

1. Louis Clinton Hatch, *History of the Vice-Presidency of the United States*, revised by Earl L. Shoup (Westport, Conn.: Greenwood Press, 1934, 1970), p. 157.

2. Ibid., pp. 5–6.

3. Ibid., pp. 45, 47.

4. Ibid., p. 9.

5. Marcus Cunliffe, *American Presidents and the Presidency* (New York: McGraw-Hill, 1968, 1972), pp. 213–14.

6. Wilfred E. Binkley, *The Man in the White House: His Powers and Duties* (Baltimore: Johns Hopkins University Press, 1958), p. 268.

1

The Vice-President's Constitutional Functions

"TWO LEFT FEET"

Most observers would suggest that the most crucial function of the office of Vice-President is to succeed to the Presidency. While increased awareness of the Vice-President as "a heartbeat away" from the Presidency has occurred as a result of the nine instances of vice-presidential succession, the Founding Fathers were actually more concerned that there be a presiding officer of the Senate who would serve to break a tie vote. The Framers did not want to vest this power in a member of the Senate, since that would give that particular senator two votes. Thus, since the Vice-President seemed to be "without employment," that office was available.

The first Vice-President, John Adams, apparently became far more involved in Senate debates than would most of his successors. Adams saw his role as an activist one, and he often "played the schoolmaster."[1] Later Vice-Presidents tended to limit their involvement to parliamentary questions, although John C. Calhoun occasionally sent correspondence to senators regarding his point of view.[2]

Few incumbents of the early Vice-Presidency were the likes of Adams and Calhoun, and this was particularly so following the enactment of the Twelfth Amendment. Incumbents of the second office soon learned that a Vice-President must conform to the nature and personality of the U.S. Senate. Few statements capture this fact as well as that made by Calvin Coolidge, who had been Vice-President:

Presiding over the Senate was fascinating to me. That branch of the Congress has its own methods and traditions which may strike the outsiders as peculiar, but more familiarity with them would disclose that they are only what long experience has demonstrated to be the best methods of conducting its business. It may seem that debate is endless, but there is scarcely a time when it is not informing, and . . . the power to compel due consideration is the distinguishing mark of a deliberative body. If the Senate is anything it is a great deliberative body.[3]

The unanticipated development of the Vice-President's role as president of the Senate has produced an anachronism. Very little of any Vice-President's time is spent in the Senate. Although he or she is entitled to preside over the Senate without vote "unless they be equally divided," the President Pro Tempore of the Senate is the usual presiding officer. Furthermore, it might well be regarded as an impertinence should a Vice-President attempt to utilize influence on and off the Senate floor, especially within the confines of his or her own party. In recent decades, Presidents and Vice-Presidents have come increasingly from the legislative branch rather than from the governors' mansions, the earlier source. This might suggest that the flow of influence between a Vice-President and his or her former colleagues in the Senate is significant—but quite to the contrary, for the environment in which the Vice-President moves militates against such operations.

In recent years, as the Vice-President has received more and more assignments from the President, the second office has moved more fully into the executive branch. The original constitutional job of the office has atrophied and has little significance today. There may, for example, be an occasional tie vote or a parliamentary ruling advantageous to the administration. Business of this sort makes very little demand on the Vice-President to spend time on Capitol Hill.

Vice-Presidents suffer from being subject to both the *nature* of the institution over which they are intended to preside and to the exigencies of the Presidency and its staff. Straddling the executive and legislative branches, the Vice-President is regarded as an outsider in the Senate which has had no choice in his selection as presiding officer.[4] And even if the Vice-President is a former member of the upper house, it matters little how strong or lengthy a legislative background he has had or how well liked he has been as a legislator. A "once you're out, you're out" rule is long established and pervades the Senate's attitude toward the Vice-President, a reflection in part of the institutional conflict between Congress and the White House.[5]

At the other end of Pennsylvania Avenue, the Vice-President who attempts to arm twist on behalf of the administration's legislative program finds himself dealt with sternly by a legislative body that prides itself on its independence. Spiro Agnew, the first Vice-President in recent years without legislative experience, had to discover this and never recovered from the blow.

Agnew knew little of the Senate—its style, its customs, its view of acceptable behavior. In his early days in the Vice-Presidency, he attempted to compensate for his legislative ignorance by spending a good deal of time on Capitol Hill, mingling and talking with senators, eating with them in their dining room.[6] Early on, however, he made a critical mistake. At the request of the White House in July 1969, Agnew attempted to solidify what was feared to be waning Republican support of the administration's surtax extension. His timing was faulty; ignorant of Senate custom, he tried to buttonhole potentially recalcitrant senators just as a roll call was about to be taken. This prompted one senator, Len Jordan of Idaho, to formulate the notorious "Jordan Rule." He told Agnew he had planned to vote for the extension but that the Vice-President's behavior had convinced him to vote in the opposite direction. At the next Republican senators' weekly meeting, Jordan postulated a rule: always vote the other way if the Vice-President dares to lobby a senator on the floor.[7] Jordan later remarked, "It worked, too."[8]

The Jordan incident marked the end of Agnew's attempt to have a positive role in the legislature, and thereafter he spent considerably less time on Capitol Hill.[9] As Agnew became increasingly vocal in lashing out at administration critics, he again ran up against Senate form, especially in his attempt to purge the Senate of liberals in both parties. His success in ridding the administration of Senator Charles Goodell during the campaign of 1970 continued to evoke hostility from even his fellow Republicans in the Senate.[10] The November 1969 *Economist* quoted Republican senators as saying, following Agnew's New Orleans speech in which he had lashed out against "an effete corps of impudent snobs," that "effete is what Spiro puts in his mouth."[11] Agnew did not have the long-standing relationships that former Senator Hubert Humphrey had had. Moreover, he had trampled on established codes of behavior.

Lyndon Johnson, in moving from the legislative to the executive branch, might well have appreciated how strongly his former colleagues in the Senate felt about executive intrusion into the legislature when the "clubbishness" of which he had been such a vital part in the past was about to backfire on him. Johnson, it seems, had fully expected to continue to play a significant role in the inner workings of the Senate Democratic party.[12] In January 1961, as the Democratic senators caucused in order to set up the machinery of government, Johnson expected to participate, and possibly preside, as was suggested by the new Majority Leader, Mike Mansfield. The senators, much to Johnson's surprise, reacted hostilely: Johnson would be permitted to sit in on the caucuses, but by no means would he be allowed to run the show with the new Majority Leader as merely titular leader.[13] Johnson thus experienced the application of the "once you're out, you're out" rule, and this hostility on the part of fellow Democrats came as a blow to him.[14] "He could no longer snap his fingers," remarked one senator.[15] Although he "got some things done, he wasn't able to crack the whip. . . . He didn't have as much to trade as Vice President as he had had as Majority Leader,"[16] and he found himself "walking an awful [sic] thin tightrope."[17]

Following his "defeat" in the Democratic caucus, Lyndon Johnson did not attempt very much legislative work. A very sensitive man, despite outward appearances, he preferred not to attempt an active legislative role. LBJ aide Walter Jenkins commented that everyone had expected Johnson to be errand boy, but Johnson shied away from a liaison role with Congress. Johnson, reported Jenkins, would probably never have refused a Kennedy request, but he did not really want to be liaison man.[18] Arthur Schlesinger, Jr., in discussing Johnson's rejection by the Democratic caucus, has maintained that "the incident reduced his usefulness on the Hill. Once the necromancer had left his senatorial seat, the old black magic evidently lost some of its power."[19]

Kennedy's own predisposition worked against a legislative role for a Vice-

President who had been the most powerful man in Congress shortly before assuming the Vice-Presidency. Kennedy viewed the relationship between Congress and the White House differently than President Johnson would. Kennedy took much more of a "separation of powers" attitude than Johnson who, as Jenkins has said, believed in a "hit 'em over the head" approach. Other observers close to the scene have pointed to other motivations on Kennedy's part. To have given Johnson a major legislative role would have meant losing "control over his own program . . . something no sensible President would do."[20]

Johnson attended legislative breakfast meetings[21] and would occasionally but quietly offer advice on legislative matters, especially on the question of civil rights legislation and the best approach toward the likely recalcitrant senators involved,[22] but he did relatively little in the way of pushing the administration's legislative program. Instead, he took on as much travel as possible as well as other administrative duties assigned to him both statutorily and by the President. Hubert Humphrey reports that Johnson once told him that President Kennedy had made a mistake in choosing him as his vice-presidential running mate; he would have been more effective in the Senate. Added Humphrey, "He was really a trapped animal in terms of all of his energy, all of his ego, everything else being sublimated."[23]

The much-respected and well-liked Senator Hubert H. Humphrey described the uncertain role of the Vice-President in the Senate and the straddling position anyone in that office must maintain because of his or her constitutionally assigned role:

The Vice Presidency can work to strain the relationship between old friends—even with the old friends in the Congress because you're no longer a member of the Club, and you're not quite out. . . . And you're the President's man, but you know just by the nature of the office that the President is looking over his shoulder at you, wondering, "What's he up to?"

So you live in the forest of suspicion and doubt—that is your cultural environment. You really do.

You walk a very—not fearsome—but a rather uncertain course all the time. You're never quite sure what's going to happen.[24]

Humphrey did not deny that a Vice-President can and does play a role in pushing the administration's legislative program. Depending on legislative expertise and rapport with the legislators, the Vice-President may be very successful. Truman, Vice-President for only three months before assuming the Presidency, had similar recollections:

The Vice-President . . . may have considerable status as a party member. He is considered as the No. 2 man in the party setup, and this may—or may not—give him influence in the Senate. It depends upon the man. If the senators find him likeable, he has considerable influence, and this was true of Garner and Barkley, both of whom were outstanding vice-presidents. If he is not liked or is not familiar with politics or with the Senate approach to things, he is left on the outside. . . . Barkley, as Vice-President, was in a class by himself. He had the complete confidence of both the President and the Senate. He had been majority leader longer than any other senator in the history of the Senate.[25]

Alben Barkley himself pointed out:

Many times I have been asked what influence the Vice-President may have over legislation pending in the Senate or even in the House of Representatives. The answer depends considerably upon the man himself. If he has been a member of both, he may undoubtedly within proper limits exercise some influence in the guiding principle of legislation. . . .

Undoubtedly a Vice-President who is well liked by members of the Senate and by the corresponding members of the House in charge of legislation can exercise considerable power in the shaping of the program of legislation which every administration seeks to enact.[26]

The "proper limits" Barkley mentions include the very nature of the legislature itself—its sense of pride and independence as well as its suspiciousness of executive interference.

In this context, the "sense of the Senate" and of the average senator's self-image which Donald Matthews has described in his popular study, *U.S. Senators and Their World* (1960), is apt: "The greatest deliberative body in the world"[27] frame of mind which pervades the Senate takes its toll on what an outsider, in this case the Vice-President, can do, and the traditional suspiciousness of the executive branch, of course, extends to the Vice-President. The senators' first and foremost loyalty is to their own "aristocratic" legislative body.

These and other "rules" of behavior form what have come to be known as the "folkways," "the clubbishness," of the Senate.[28] They affect the Senate's relationship with its "competitor," the executive branch. Former Senator Herman Talmadge of Georgia has pointed out that the Vice-President technically belongs between two branches.[29] While he suffers from association with the legislative branch, the senators view him as an alter-ego of the President. When asked whether there was any inevitability to the Vice-President's relationship with the Senate, Hubert Humphrey responded,

Inevitable—because of the separation of powers. First of all, who are you? You're not the President, and yet you preside over the Senate. You're not a Senator; you don't have a vote. What are you doing around here? I *know* what you're doing—you're spying. And even your best friends, while they'll be very sociable with you and they like to have you around, they never really confide in you like they did as a Senator. You never feel quite as free to walk back in the cloakroom or the reading room as you did as a Senator. And also they know it's a little different office. The fact is, while it's been downgraded by the pundits, it's the second highest elective office in the history of the American people. And the Senators who are elected know that. And yet it's a peculiar [office]—it's an *awkward* office. You've got two left feet, most of the time trying to walk a straight line— not getting into the President's hair, or getting into the business of the Senate, and yet you are in both of these. On the one hand—I was over here trying to get legislation through without looking too obvious, reporting back to department heads and the President what was going on—the problems we had. If I became too popular or too effective, whoever the Vice President, the President says, "What's he up to?" Not so much the President, but his staff. . . . This office is filled with all the uncertainties of human emotion—unbelievable.[30]

The success any Vice-President has in the legislature will be spotty, at best; there is little guarantee or regularity to it. He must know how and when to act. Johnson had an excellent sense of timing. He reportedly told Humphrey, following their 1964 landslide, "Hubert, I figure we have got about nine months to get our way in Congress, no more." And Johnson was right.[31] A former Humphrey aide has pointed out that a Vice-President has to decide when to use up his credibility, "because he is a political animal and wants to preserve that and develop whatever his known ambitions are."[32] Humphrey grasped the sense of the Senate and of his feasible legislative role as Vice-President. He knew when and how to persuade and that the art of persuasion was critical.[33] Because he had this understanding, he had a measure of success in the legislative arena enjoyed by few Vice-Presidents, notably in his efforts for the Great Society programs to which he had been committed for years and which he could work for as part of his continuing personal goals. In the same manner, he contributed his legislative skills and relationships toward the passage of the Model Cities Program, the Youth Opportunity Program, Medicare, the 1965 Voting Rights Act, the development of the Department of Housing and Urban Development, housing and rent supplement bills, increased aid to education—all of which were consistent with his past legislative interests and record.[34] As noted elsewhere in this work, Johnson in selecting Humphrey as a running mate in 1964 was well aware of Humphrey's major assets, notably his legislative record and expertise. Moreover, the two men worked well together on legislative matters.[35] Humphrey also knew and understood his President and was very careful in his legislative efforts to let it be known that it was *LBJ's* legislative program he was pushing.[36] Again, Humphrey knew where he could act, when he could act, and, above all, how to do so quietly. Humphrey recalled,

I also was many times able to mediate between the times when the President had a difficult assignment—for example, one time when the President just could not permit a postal wage bill, for the postal workers, to go through as high as they wanted it—yet the President did not want to be on record as having to veto that bill. So he put me to work with the postal workers because I was supposed to be able, and he got me to negotiate it out so that he wouldn't have the difficulty of a veto or having the President have to express a "no"—a negative. It worked out—because I had the contacts, and I was able to carefully, quietly, work it out.[37]

Other Vice-Presidents have not been as fortunate, skilled, or inclined to devote much time to the Senate. With the exception of Alben Barkley this has been generally true of the modern Vice-Presidency. Relatively little can be undertaken by the Vice-President in the Senate because of so many demands that he spend time elsewhere. Even so able a legislative expert as Hubert Humphrey spent more of his time as Vice-President on nonlegislative chores. As former Senator Gale McGee observed, while Humphrey was "good at buttonholing Senators," the larger portion of his time was spent in the international theater, especially as Vietnam began to dominate the Johnson Administration.[38]

Although fully loyal to administration policies,[39] Richard Nixon, as Vice-President, spent very little time in the legislature, either in presiding over the Senate or in working for administration programs. By his own account, less than 5 percent of his time was spent on legislative matters.[40]

In addition to his short tenure as a senator himself, Nixon did not possess the personal requisites to be a useful liaison with the legislative body over which he was supposed to preside. Besides, as has been increasingly true of all Vice-Presidents during the modern Vice-Presidency, he had weighty tasks in other areas. The growth of the Presidency and its burdens have made this inevitable, as Vice-President Walter Mondale's assumption of extraneous presidential activity during the Iranian crisis in 1979 indicated.

The Vice-President's decreased presence in the Senate is a positive sign of the office's increased functioning in administrative areas. For example, in his early days in the Vice-Presidency Nelson A. Rockefeller received few assignments from President Gerald Ford, with the exception of heading the blue-ribbon commission to investigate the Central Intelligence Agency. Ford's promise of a very active role for Rockefeller began to be fulfilled in February 1975 when the Vice-President was given full supervisory powers over the Domestic Council, the executive body in charge of all domestic legislation and programs.[41] Despite the protest of some of Ford's aides, the President also allowed Rockefeller to appoint his own men to fill senior staff positions on the council.[42] As Rockefeller spent more and more time and exerted more influence in this and other areas in which he had expertise, the time he spent in the Senate diminished accordingly.

A glimpse at the Mondale role in the Senate reveals the Vice-President's potential role in an administration. As the Republicans began to look ahead to the 1978 congressional campaign, the Carter Administration came under attack for its "ineptness." President Carter seemed to be in trouble, particularly with Congress. One of the President's legislative problems revolved around the administration's energy problems. But this was a critical problem, not only because the President himself placed so much emphasis on it, but also because certain facets of the increasing storm over an energy plan were beginning to take on far-reaching dimensions in areas beyond energy.

One facet that emerged was the battle over deregulation of natural gas, with the administration favoring continued regulation of natural gas prices. During late September and early October 1977, the battle took on filibuster proportions in the U.S. Senate, with the traditionally antifilibuster liberal members of the Senate leading in the use of the device in support of the administration's position.[43] Much to the dismay and, sometimes, anger of their colleagues, the liberals seemed willing to persist for as long as necessary. Among those most angered was the Senate Majority Leader, Robert C. Byrd. But then the liberal plan was broken. With the indispensable assistance of Vice-President Mondale, constitutionally the presiding officer of the Senate, Byrd was able to manipulate an end to the protracted debates.

Historically, Vice-Presidents, particularly recently, have tended to avoid the frustrating job of being *in* the legislature but not *of* the legislature—having the "two left feet"'of which Humphrey spoke. This has been true of all Vice-Presidents, regardless of legislative experience. Those with a legislative background generally find that their departure from the Senate for the executive branch places them outside the trusted entourage of the Senate; those without such experience find themselves ignorant of Senate mores. Both the experienced and inexperienced discover that their time can be better spent elsewhere—except when a tie vote may need to be broken or when parliamentary rulings can be strategically used to determine the outcome of a controversial issue.

Early October 1977 was precisely one of those exceptions to the rule that Vice-Presidents avoid the Senate. Ignoring the Senate customs with which he was so familiar, Walter Mondale allied himself with Byrd to break the filibuster and, in effect, to allow a vote to take place which was contrary to the administration's position. The liberal plan, silently supported by the Carter Administration, was to introduce some 500 amendments and to vote on each of them. Mondale's rulings aborted this plan. He simply declared, as presiding officer, that amendments to the natural gas bill were "dilatory," and therefore out of order. In a 50–46 vote, the Senate voted to deregulate the natural gas industry.[44]

The questions that loomed large were, why did Mondale act in this manner? Why, if the liberal filibuster had the support, indeed, the blessings, of the White House, was an attempt not made to push the President's position? Why would the President's Vice-President do this when he had the parliamentary power to allow the filibuster to continue? The questions were especially compelling in view of the fact that Mondale's own political leanings were compatible with the liberal filibuster leaders and that, had *he* still been in the Senate, he too undoubtedly would have been filibustering on the issue in support of the President.

In order to understand Mondale's seemingly strange move, one must be familiar with the larger context in which it took place—to perceive the finest subtleties of the administration's *overall* relationship with Congress as well as its struggle in the specific instance of the gas deregulation controversy.

Most assuredly, the administration preferred to maintain controls. But as the filibuster to that end continued, it appeared increasingly obvious that, despite the stamina of its leaders, the filibuster would not force Senate conservatives to change their position. Only a frustrating stalemate seemed likely.

It was also increasingly apparent to the administration that it had incurred the displeasure of the Democratic Majority Leader, whose good graces were critical to both the party in the Senate and to the President. To continue in a futile filibuster that was evidently very annoying to Byrd, who prided himself on the smooth workings of the Senate under his leadership, would have probably meant not only losing the battle, but also alienating a vital future ally.

Nonetheless, the President remained relatively consistent in his public stand. He had no choice. In fact, the President cried out against the Senate vote as "an injustice" to the people.[45] It was the Vice-President who stuck his neck out. The development of the Vice-Presidency over the years demonstrates that Vice-Presidents can and must very often do things Presidents are unable to do.

In addition, the Vice-President was aware of the White House's knowledge that the House of Representatives—which had dealt with the issue in August and had maintained price controls on natural gas—would not under any circumstances change its mind.[46] In essence, then, no matter how the Senate voted, the administration could always fall back on the House once the disagreeing chambers of Congress met in conference committee, the vehicle that had been designed to iron out the differences between the House and the Senate versions of legislation.

So while it appeared as if Mondale were working contrary to the administration's best interests, he was actually serving them. Forcing a Senate vote ended the futile measure that was delaying the Senate's business at the same time that the administration had the House of Representatives' firm position as a backup.

But what effect would all of this have on Walter Mondale? In a television interview early in his incumbency, the Vice-President had stated what all Vice-Presidents sooner or later come to realize: that his future was dependent on the success of the President's administration.[47]

Vice-Presidents in the past have found themselves in a position where they have very few alternatives: their future is tied to their President, the man responsible for their nomination and for their continuing functioning, for better or for worse. For those like Hubert Humphrey, making the decision to link their fate with that of the administration ultimately meant defeat. Through his action during the natural gas filibuster, Mondale was sticking the vice-presidential neck out by being the administration spokesman in an area where the administration itself had to remain silent. Walter Mondale was now fully out of the Senate and in the executive branch.

Mondale served the administration well in other legislative areas as well, in much the same manner as had his mentor, Hubert Humphrey: quietly, behind the scenes, unobtrusively. Mondale essentially remained the only Washington "insider" in the Carter entourage and his legislative expertise was invaluable within the limits set by both circumstance and Carter's own style. In this regard, for example, Mondale was not able to persuade Carter to approach Congress with greater caution, planning, and selectivity; instead, Carter barraged the legislature with proposals instead of "picking his fights more carefully and giving Congress more time to catch its breath."[48]

Mondale keenly perceived the view Congress held of the President, and it was less than flattering. Mondale's advice to Carter was to veto something—anything—to demonstrate to the first branch of government that the second branch was indeed in control in many respects. It was Mondale, too, who selected the bill to be the example: a defense authorization bill of some $37 billion. Although Carter's advisers argued against this move, Mondale prevailed. Not only did the President veto the legislation, but the veto stuck. Congress's inability to override it was an even greater victory for the President because defense authorization bills are usually considered untouchable by presidential veto.[49] Clearly, the Vice-President's fine understanding of the legislative frame of mind and presidential power vis-à-vis that frame of mind contributed to many of the Carter successes in Congress.

In summary, then, the Vice-President *can* be an effective congressional liaison, but he often finds himself walking a tightrope between the two ends of Pennsylvania Avenue. Hubert Humphrey's observation best captures the position of the Vice-President:

The Vice Presidency . . . is what the man that you work with is willing to let you make of it, because the President can put the damper on you. First of all, you don't have any real staff. Your staff . . . is from the legislative budget over here, and the Senate guards it very jealously; they don't give the Vice President much, whoever he is. I had been Majority Whip over here—a very popular fellow around here—but when I became Vice President, that was different.[50]

"A HEARTBEAT AWAY"

The second constitutional function of the Vice-President is to succeed to the Presidency if need be. The Constitution fails, however, to provide a prescription for training the Vice-President for this possibility. Nonetheless, in the premodern Vice-Presidency, six Vice-Presidents succeeded the President; three others have done so in the modern period (see Table 1).

As the first Vice-President to move up to the Presidency, John Tyler set the crucial precedent for the Vice-President's actions under such circumstances. The constitutional provision, vague and ambiguous, states: "In Case of the Removal of the President from Office, or at his Death, Resignation, or Inability to discharge the Powers and Duties of the said Office, the same shall devolve on the Vice President."

Tyler chose the clause to mean that a Vice-President does not *act* as President but *becomes* President, an interpretation that is symbolically underscored by his decision to take the presidential oath of office. This precedent has been followed by all subsequent Vice-Presidents who have succeeded to the Presidency, but nowhere does the Constitution state this is necessary. Interestingly, a great deal of gravity and ceremony have become attached to the symbolic swearing-in ceremony of the unscheduled transfer of the Presidency.

While the Tyler precedent determined the course of events in the case of the death of a President, his decision had subtler ramifications. The decision set off a great controversy, which, while it did not alter the impact of Tyler's precedent-

Table 1.
Vice-Presidential Succession

President	Vice President	Date of Succession
William Henry Harrison	John Tyler	April 6, 1841
Zachary Taylor	Millard Fillmore	July 10, 1850
Abraham Lincoln	Andrew Johnson	April 15, 1865
James A. Garfield	Chester A. Arthur	September 20, 1881
William McKinley	Theodore Roosevelt	September 14, 1901
Warren G. Harding	Calvin Coolidge	August 3, 1923
Franklin D. Roosevelt	Harry S. Truman	April 13, 1945
John F. Kennedy	Lyndon B. Johnson	November 22, 1963
Richard M. Nixon	Gerald R. Ford	August 9, 1974

setting action, set the stage for confusion regarding the other half of a dual problem, presidential disability.

If, as Secretary of State Daniel Webster argued at the time of the Tyler succession, the *powers* and *duties* of the Presidency could not be separated from the *office* of the Presidency, it became questionable whether a Vice-President could ever *temporarily* assume the office of Presidency upon the disability of a President. Unlike "removal," "death," or "resignation," disability need not be permanent. After the Tyler precedent, was it constitutionally possible for a disabled President, once recovered, to regain not merely his powers and duties, but the office as well? No Vice-President seemed willing to test the question, and during periods of presidential disability the problem lingered. The problem was not solved until the passage of the Twenty-fifth Amendment in the second half of the twentieth century.[51]

The succession of Millard Fillmore in 1850, following the death of President Zachary Taylor, resulted in an administration that "struck about an average in its virtues and faults."[52]

Andrew Johnson inherited not only the Presidency from the assassinated Abraham Lincoln in April 1865, but also the scars of a nation that had been split apart in a bitter civil war. The problems that had to be solved could not be dealt with by the executive, as Johnson attempted to do, and his tenure as President ended in a narrow escape from impeachment.

Of the three remaining accidental Presidents during this earlier time frame, only Theodore Roosevelt headed an administration that would be ranked among the greatest in the history of the Presidency. Both Chester A. Arthur and Calvin Coolidge had mediocre administrations at best. On the whole, then, the early record set by Vice-Presidents succeeding to the Presidency is not an illustrative one, and it remained for the post-World War II Vice-Presidency to demonstrate that the success of the Roosevelt succession was not a unique event in the history of vice-presidential succession. Those instances are traced in a separate chapter.

NOTES

1. Louis Clinton Hatch, *History of the Vice-Presidency of the United States*, revised by Earl L. Shoup (Westport, Conn.: Greenwood Press, 1934, 1970), p. 67.

2. Ibid., p. 68.

3. Ibid., p. 85.

4. Ibid., p. 419.

5. Bill Welch, Interview held at his Washington, D.C., office, March 1974.

6. "A New Kind of Vice President?" *U.S. News* 66 (March 16, 1969): 32–34; "A Look Inside the Nixon Administration," *U.S. News* 67 (October 6, 1969): 32–38.

7. Rowland Evans and Robert D. Novak, *Nixon in the White House* (New York: Random House, 1971), p. 311.

8. Len Jordan in correspondence with author, December 10, 1973.

9. Evans and Novak, *Nixon in the White House*, pp. 311–12.

10. "Spiro Speaks," *Economist* 33 (November 1, 1969): 50.

11. Ibid.

12. Whitney M. Young, Oral History Interview, Lyndon B. Johnson Library, Austin, Texas.

13. Arthur M. Schlesinger, Jr., *A Thousand Days* (Boston: Houghton Mifflin, 1965), p. 706.

14. George Christian, Interview held at his Austin, Texas, office, April 1973; see also "Apprentice President," *Economist* 213 (December 26, 1964): 1423.

15. Senator Gale McGee, Interview held at his U.S. Senate office, Washington, D.C., March 1974.

16. Ibid.

17. Christian, Interview.

18. Walter Jenkins, Interview held at his Austin, Texas, office, April 1973. See also Hale Boggs, Oral History Interview, John F. Kennedy Library, Columbia Point, Massachusetts, pp. 17–18.

19. Schlesinger, *A Thousand Days*, p. 706.

20. Ibid., pp. 706–707.

21. Charles Daly, Oral History Interview, John F. Kennedy Library, Columbia Point, Massachusetts, pp. 34–35.

22. Norbert Schlei, Oral History Interview, John F. Kennedy Library, Columbia Point, Massachusetts, p. 44ff.; Clarence Mitchell, Oral History Interview, Lyndon B. Johnson Library, Austin, Texas, pp. 22–34; Roy Wilkins, Oral History Interview, Lyndon B. Johnson Library, p. 1ff.; Robert C. Weaver, Oral History Interview, Lyndon B. Johnson Library, Austin, Texas, pp. 1–4; George Reedy Papers, (AF) Container 6, Civil Rights, Lyndon B. Johnson Library, Austin, Texas; VP Papers Box 5, Container: Civil Rights, July 13–July 31, 1963, Lyndon B. Johnson Library, Austin, Texas.

23. Hubert Humphrey, Interview held at a U.S. Senate reception room, Washington, D.C., March 1974.

24. Ibid.

25. Harry S Truman, *Years of Decisions* (Garden City, N.Y.: Doubleday, 1955), pp. 57, 196ff.; Senator John Sparkman, Interview held at his U.S. Senate office, Washington, D.C., March 1974.

26. Alben W. Barkley, "The Vice Presidency," Speech File 63M143. Box XXII. 1952, pp. 1–2. Alben W. Barkley Papers, University of Kentucky Library, Lexington, Kentucky. See also Truman, *Years of Decisions*, p. 57.

27. Donald R. Matthews, *U.S. Senators and Their World* (New York: Vintage Books, 1960), p. 101ff.

28. Ibid., Chapter 5 in its entirety; Christian, Interview. Senator Gale McGee has indicated that the high degree of "clubbishness" during the Kennedy-Johnson Senate days has lessened; McGee, Interview.

29. Senator Herman Talmadge, Interview held at his U.S. Senate office, Washington, D.C., March 1974.

30. Humphrey, Interview.

31. James MacGregor Burns, *John Kennedy: A Political Profile* (New York: Harcourt, Brace, & World, 1961), p. 14.

32. Welch, Interview.

33. "I Enjoy It," *Newsweek* 65 (March 15, 1965): 28–29.

34. Albert Eisele, *Almost to the Presidency* (Blue Earth, Minnesota: Piper Co., 1972), p. 235ff.; Louis W. Koenig, *The Chief Executive* (New York: Harcourt, Brace & World, 1964, 1968), p. 162; Welch, Interview; Humphrey, Interview; "The Humphreys: Right Image for '68?," *U.S. News* 65 (September 9, 1968): 17–18; "Vice President of Many Causes?," *Economist* 211 (April 25, 1964): 379ff; and Allan H. Ryskind, *Hubert* (New York: Arlington House, 1968), p. 320.

35. See also "Vice President of Many Causes?"; "The Bright Spirit," *Time* 87 (April 1, 1966): 21–25; "I Enjoy It"; "Happy Understudy," *Saturday Review* 48 (May 8, 1965): 16–17.

36. "Happy Understudy."

37. Humphrey, Interview.

38. McGee, Interview.

39. Richard H. Rovere, *The Eisenhower Years* (New York: Mentor Books, 1960, 1956), p. 297.

40. "Nixon's Own Story of 7 Years in the Vice Presidency," *U.S. News* 48 (May 16, 1960): 98–106. See also Rovere, *The Eisenhower Years*, pp. 298–99. For more on Nixon in the legislature, see Ralph DeToledano, *One Man Alone: Richard Nixon* (New York: Funk & Wagnalls, 1969), p. 163ff.

41. *Time* (February 24, 1975): 15.

42. *New York Times*, October 1, 1977.

43. Ibid., October 5, 1977.

44. Ibid.

45. Marie D. Natoli, "The Vice Presidency: Walter Mondale in the Lion's Den," *Presidential Studies Quarterly* (Winter 1978): 100–102.

46. Ibid.

47. "Walter Mondale," the MacNeil/Lehrer Report, February 1977 (WNET/13, New York City).

48. Finlay Lewis, *Mondale: Portrait of an American Politician* (New York: Harper & Row, 1980), p. 247.

49. Ibid., p. 249.

50. Humphrey, Interview.

51. Vice-President Thomas Marshall refused to pick up the constitutionally ambiguous gauntlet of the gap in the Presidency; the result was a period of no leadership while President Woodrow Wilson lay incapacitated. Earlier, Vice-President Arthur had behaved similarly, assuming the Presidency's powers (and, of course, the office) only when he was certain Garfield had breathed his last breath. And Richard Nixon was the epitome of discretion during the Eisenhower illnesses, even going so far as to symbolize, by presiding from his own chair and not from that of the President, that he was acting in his capacity as Vice-President in carrying out the chores of heading Cabinet and National Security Council meetings, tasks given to him by Eisenhower during his illness.

52. Hatch, *History of the Vice-Presidency*, p. 413.

2

Vice-Presidential Selection: Choosing the Heir Apparent

Every four years since the birth of this Republic, the American electorate has journeyed to the polls to designate its only nationally elected leaders, the President and the Vice-President. Only recently, however, has the electorate begun to appreciate the importance of the second of these leaders. This new development requires a fresh understanding of the vice-presidential selection process, particularly its evolution during the modern period. The analysis provided in this chapter is thematic rather than chronological, and it views the selection process via the categories of criteria that have emerged. Therefore, not all vice-presidential candidates during this period are examined. Table 2 provides a chronological perspective as well as an overview of the "source" of running mates during this period.

An examination of a series of vice-presidential nominations indicates that a number of selection criteria have emerged. In each case, the presidential nominee is seeking to attract more votes for his own ticket.[1] Vice-presidential candidates are chosen:

1. As a "safety valve" for a party that feels the presidential nomination is "predetermined" because an incumbent President is virtually reassured of renomination or, as in more recent development, because the proliferation of party primaries across the states "sews up" the presidential nomination for a candidate well in advance of the convention and the only thing left is the vice-presidential spot on the ticket, for example, Harry S Truman (1944); Alben Barkley (1948); and George Bush (1980).

2. To emphasize a particular issue that is popular with the people, for example, Richard Nixon (1952; communism); Spiro Agnew (1968; law and order).

3. To serve as an internal party unifier: the struggle to achieve party unity often requires the conciliation of a particular party faction of a defeated nominee's followers, for example, Lyndon Johnson (1960); Hubert Humphrey (1964); Robert Dole (1976); and George Bush (1980).

4. To ensure broader electoral appeal by balancing the geographical or personal characteristics of a presidential candidate: state size, region of the country, age, profession,

Table 2.
Presidential and Vice-Presidential Candidates (1944–1984)

		Democrat	Source[a]	Republican	Source[a]
1944	Pres.	Franklin D. Roosevelt[b]	Incumbent	Thomas E. Dewey	Governor
	V.P.	Harry S Truman	U.S. Senate	John Bricker	U.S. Senate
1948	Pres.	Harry S Truman[b]	Incumbent	Thomas E. Dewey	Governor
	V.P.	Alben Barkley	U.S. Senate	Earl Warren	Governor
1952	Pres.	Adlai E. Stevenson	Governor	Dwight D. Eisenhower[b]	Military
	V.P.	John Sparkman	U.S. Senate	Richard M. Nixon	U.S. Senate
1956	Pres.	Adlai E. Stevenson	Governor	Dwight D. Eisenhower[b]	Incumbent
	V.P.	Estes Kefauver	U.S. Senate	Richard M. Nixon	Incumbent
1960	Pres.	John F. Kennedy[b]	U.S. Senate	Richard M. Nixon	V.P.
	V.P.	Lyndon B. Johnson	U.S. Senate	Henry Cabot Lodge	Dipl. (Amb.)
1964	Pres.	Lyndon B. Johnson[b]	Incumbent	Barry M. Goldwater	U.S. Senate
	V.P.	Hubert H. Humphrey	U.S. Senate	William E. Miller	U.S. House
1968	Pres.	Hubert H. Humphrey	V.P.	Richard M. Nixon[b]	V.P.
	V.P.	Edmund S. Muskie	U.S. Senate	Spiro T. Agnew	Governor
1972	Pres.	George McGovern	U.S. Senate	Richard M. Nixon[b]	Incumbent
	V.P.	Thomas Eagleton (resigned from ticket)	U.S. Senate	Spiro T. Agnew (resigned from office; replaced by Gerald R. Ford)	Governor
		R. Sargent Shriver	Private	1974–1976 Ford-Rockefeller (Nelson A.) Administration	
1976	Pres.	Jimmy Carter[b]	Governor	Gerald R. Ford	Incumbent
	V.P.	Walter F. Mondale	U.S. Senate	Robert Dole	U.S. Senate
1980	Pres.	Jimmy Carter	Incumbent	Ronald Reagan[b]	Governor
	V.P.	Walter F. Mondale	Incumbent	George Bush	Dipl. (Amb.)
1984	Pres.	Walter F. Mondale	V.P.	Ronald Reagan[b]	Incumbent
	V.P.	Geraldine Ferraro	U.S. House	George Bush	Incumbent

[a]last public office prior to running as a candidate.

[b]successful ticket.

and, as a newer trend, religion and ethnic background. Virtually all tickets are balanced geographically; a particularly popular combination pairs candidates from large states (with more electoral votes) in different regions. Examples of balancing personal characteristics include Richard Nixon (1952; age); Spiro Agnew (1968; profession—governor); Edmund Muskie (1968; ethnic background and religion); Thomas Eagleton/Sargent Shriver (1972; religion); Walter Mondale (1976; profession—senator); John Bricker (1944; profession—senator); John Sparkman (1952; profession—senator); and Estes Kefauver (1956; profession—senator).

Any one or any combination of these criteria have been and can be used in selecting a running mate for the national ticket. Indeed, the vice-presidential candidate who manages to satisfy several of these criteria, especially if he or she does not seriously negate any of the others, is well sought after. Obviously, these criteria are overlapping, and the selection process becomes a composite of as many of them as possible. Which particular criterion(ia) will prevail in a given election year is largely dependent on the environmental factors of that year: the issues, a presidential candidate's assets and liabilities, the state of the party, the state of the other party. Ultimately, a "framework of acceptability" emerges that is unique to that time and place.

Pervading all of the criteria is a very critical elimination process. The selection of a suitable running mate frequently involves screening out individuals who do not meet a sufficient combination of criteria for circumstances of the moment or who do not satisfy the presidential candidate's personal predilections. The very nature of the political parties—they are heterogeneous and disparate—makes it seem that the convention itself must "forfeit" the selection of the vice-presidential nominee to unify the party. With the exception of the open Democratic National Convention of 1956, the trend has been increasingly toward rubber stamping the choice of the presidential nominee.[2]

THE ROLE OF THE PRESIDENTIAL NOMINEE

Although the ultimate choice of a running mate belongs to the presidential nominee, it would be a mistake to assume that his choice is an entirely autonomous one. The presidential candidate has *restricted* free choice: he must work within the framework of acceptability, both of his party and of the times at hand. The criteria important to the election are shaped by forces that are largely beyond his control.

It follows that the presidential nominee's freedom will vary from one candidate to another and will take in the full range of possibilities, from the nominee who is able to "handpick" a running mate to one who is virtually backed into an inescapable corner. The history of the office repeatedly demonstrates that the necessity of working within a framework of acceptability frequently requires that personal intimacy or even compatibility be abandoned. This in turn may seriously affect the role the Vice-President will play in the administration. Among recent incumbents, Lyndon Johnson's own nomination and Vice-Presidency are probably the most striking example of this possibility. Kennedy and Johnson, while cordial and friendly toward each other, were not intimates, either personally or professionally. The Johnson nomination had unforeseen ramifications for the Kennedy Administration. Kennedy accepted Johnson as a running mate in an effort to unify a fractured party. As far as the Kennedy staff was concerned, however, the memories of the preconvention fight were bitter ones, and Lyndon Johnson was an unwanted outsider.[3]

One consequence of the central role played by the presidential nominee is that little attention centers on the vice-presidential slot until a presidential nominee has been chosen. Add this to the rather negative image the office has had, and it is little wonder that its choice is oftentimes anticlimatic.

Crucial, too, is the fact that so much focus is placed on capturing the party's presidential nomination that the competing candidates themselves frequently give little thought to the selection of a running mate. Indeed, they are sometimes caught unaware. This was the case with the McGovern nomination victory in 1972 and the resulting scramble for a vice-presidential running mate ending with the hasty and ill-fated choice of Senator Thomas Eagleton. McGovern obstinately held on to his belief that his first choice for Vice-President, Senator Edward M. Kennedy, would eventually relent and agree to run on the McGovern ticket. Despite repeated telephone calls and pleadings by the presidential candidate, however, Kennedy remained steadfast in his refusal to run. What impact a Kennedy acceptance and victory would have had on the Vice-Presidency is a matter of speculation. Could any President who had virtually pleaded for his vice-presidential running mate have refused him a significant, and possibly a dominant, role in the administration? Or would his Vice-President have suffered the usual fate and gone the route of other Vice-Presidents?[4]

An electoral system that forces all attention to be placed on the number one spot creates another necessity. Only after a contender for the presidential nomination has run the gamut and seen the lineup of the opposition, only when he has seen the issues and divisions as they develop (and they frequently develop right there on the convention floor in his attempt to persuade delegations to cast their ballots for him), can he begin to see what type of running mate might best satisfy the rigors of the forthcoming general election. Only then can the presidential candidate envisage and assess what deals may have to be struck and which of the criteria may weigh most heavily in his selection of a running mate. This grave responsibility is most often handled within the space of a few hours.

An entirely different situation emerges when an incumbent President is up for renomination. He is virtually assured of his party's label, and he can think of his running mate long in advance. Two possible situations are apparent. The first-term Vice-President might command such a segment of the electorate's loyalty, as was the case with Spiro T. Agnew in 1972, that dropping him from the ticket would be politically dangerous, if not impossible. As in the Agnew case, the Vice-President may also represent a wing of the party that would feel trod upon if he were to be replaced. This doubtless was the case regarding Lyndon Johnson's Vice-Presidency and the speculation in 1963 regarding whether he would be dropped from the 1964 ticket.[5] A similar situation existed in 1944 with regard to the Henry Wallace Vice-Presidency under FDR, although in that case there were considerable forces against Wallace as well that ultimately prevailed. FDR, however, avoided alienating the staunchest Wallace supporters (especially labor) by nominating Harry S Truman, a candidate well respected by Wallace supporters.[6]

Thus, even an incumbent President may find himself operating within a framework of acceptability as far as his running mate selection is concerned. Indeed, if the only alternative left him is to stick with his first-term Vice-President, his framework of operation has narrowed and is much *more* restricted than if he were a first-term presidential candidate.

President Eisenhower found this to be his situation in 1956. Despite denials from his associates to the contrary,[7] Eisenhower's actions seem to point to an attempt to edge Nixon off the second-term ticket. Eisenhower did not go so far as to ask Nixon to leave the Vice-Presidency; he did suggest, however, that perhaps a Cabinet post would give Nixon the executive experience needed if he were to contemplate the Presidency. In addition, although the President announced his intention to seek reelection on February 29, he steadfastly declined to commit himself on Nixon's future, preferring to take refuge in talk about an "open" convention. Meanwhile, a "Dump Nixon" movement, led by Harold Stassen, had begun to roll. The President said little to discourage Stassen's efforts. Eisenhower found, however, that, although opinions within the Republican ranks were divided, one thing was clear: dumping Nixon from the 1956 ticket would take its toll within the right wing—the Taft wing—of the party, unless Nixon were replaced by a candidate more pleasing to the right (which would have meant someone with even more conservative views).[8] In this case, it was considerably less detrimental to let the status quo prevail than it would have been to engineer Nixon's exit. Eisenhower's personality itself was crucial to this episode. Preferring not to fight, the President gave in to the desires of the Republican National Committee and kept Nixon on the ticket.[9]

In this connection, an incumbent President who is reluctant to "dump" his Vice-President may sometimes appear to be the victim of irresistible forces. In 1944 Roosevelt did not wish to see Henry Wallace renominated, but he did not want to remove him openly since he had backed Wallace so strongly only four years earlier. But as Vice-President, Wallace was outspoken, advocating extreme liberal policies that were not in keeping with the times. This had caused considerable dissension within the party and even produced the threat of a Southern revolt.[10] Clearly, Wallace had to be dropped, and the most pragmatic solution was to have the President's decision made by "uncontrollable forces." Finesse was required to regiment the forces which Roosevelt called upon and utilized to his advantage in the "consultations" then taking place regarding the next vice-presidential nominee. Meanwhile, the President gave lukewarm support to Wallace—a far cry from the position he had taken in 1940—while the Vice-President was out of sight and circulation, having been sent on a mission to China.[11]

THE VICE-PRESIDENTIAL NOMINATION AS A SAFETY VALVE

When FDR's advisors so skillfully engineered the removal of Vice-President Wallace from the 1944 ticket and in his place vested Harry Truman, they did so with an understanding that the next Vice-President of the United States— should the Roosevelt ticket move on to its expected victory in the general election—

would probably succeed to the Presidency. Wallace was far too controversial a figure to permit him to remain a heartbeat away from the most powerful institution in the world. Some observers have maintained that because of fatigue and failing health or perhaps other reasons, the President himself did not really much care who was Vice-President. Even if FDR might have wished things to remain as they were, he could neither ignore the handwriting on the wall nor push in any direction. In this regard, the 1944 Democratic vice-presidential choice also came to serve as a safety valve for the party.

In 1940, the controversial third-term nomination of FDR had caused internal dissension within Democratic ranks, and the vehement opposition to liberal Henry Wallace was, in part, a venting of resentment against the President himself.[12] By 1944, the fourth-term candidacy was not the issue, but by that time the opposition to Wallace had come full circle. Now, the President would let "forces" take their course, and he would ultimately acquiesce "reluctantly."[13] The nomination appeared to have been "taken" from the President's hands; the myth of party control made it impossible to blame FDR for Wallace's rejection. The vice-presidential issue in 1944 supplanted any questioning of FDR's nomination for a fourth term and served to pacify the convention as well as to enhance its self-esteem as a body with the capacity to make decisions.

The ability of the party to "let off steam" through the vice-presidential nomination was also demonstrated in the 1948 Democratic nomination of Senator Alben Barkley—the one moment of exhilaration for a party (mistakenly) resigned to impending disaster at the polls with the incumbent President, Truman.

The safety valve may operate in another direction. The 1976 "dumping" of Vice-President Nelson Rockefeller by President Gerald Ford is a clearcut example of an incumbent President, facing opposition to his own renomination, seeking ways to appease recalcitrant segments of his party. Rockefeller had to be sacrificed to maximize the security of the number one spot for the President. In this regard, too, the early fall 1979 (prior to President Carter's announcement that Vice-President Walter Mondale would indeed be his running mate again) White House staff criticism of Mondale perhaps sought to have the Vice-Presidency serve as a safety valve, thus reducing pressure on the presidential nomination.

ISSUE EMPHASIS: THE NIXON SELECTION OF 1952 AND THE AGNEW SELECTION OF 1968

Issue emphasis—the selection of a running mate who is identified with an issue which the presidential nominee wants to or must focus on—has become a major criterion for selecting the vice-presidential running mate. The issue, if any, is determined by the broader social and economic contexts in which the selection and campaign are taking place. The selection of Richard Nixon as Dwight Eisenhower's running mate in 1952, Hubert Humphrey as Lyndon Johnson's in 1964, and Spiro Agnew as Richard Nixon's in 1968 all bear this in common. The Humphrey selection included other criteria as well and will be treated in a separate section of this chapter.

Both Nixon in 1952 and Agnew in 1968 were chosen as vice-presidential running mates in order to conciliate potentially troublesome segments of the Republican party as well as to emphasize particular issues in the upcoming campaign.

The political climate of the 1950s has been well documented. Fraught with the renewed fear of communism at home and abroad following the end of the world war, this climate provided the arena for the 1952 campaign. Richard Nixon, former Representative from California's Twelfth Congressional District, had clearly emerged as a beneficiary of this national paranoia. By 1952, Nixon's meteoric public career was inextricably linked to the search for the enemy within.

In 1946, Nixon had waged a successful congressional campaign against an incumbent Democrat of many years. Once elected, he had served as a member of the much-publicized House Un-American Activities Committee. Nixon was perhaps the most influential agent in the actively followed Alger Hiss-Whitaker Chambers case; the young congressman's name rapidly became well known. In 1950, Nixon grasped the opportunity to win a seat in the U.S. Senate and waged a successful campaign against Helen Gahagan Douglas using a campaign technique that had been so effective in 1946: the innuendo. Through this technique, Nixon had very cleverly placed his opponents on the defensive, largely in terms of the issue of the day, communism. The technique and the issue fit the climate of the times, and by the time the Republican party met to select its 1952 presidential and vice-presidential candidates, Richard Nixon's name was prominent.

Once General Dwight D. Eisenhower had secured the nomination as the party standard-bearer, the task remained to select a suitable running mate. Eisenhower, who prided himself on not being particularly political, consulted with his advisers and drew up a list of some half-dozen "younger men, that I admired that seemed to me to have made a name for themselves."[14]

In addition to Nixon's youth, Eisenhower was impressed by the Californian's nationwide reputation on the issue of communism as well as by his political maturity.[15] Nixon might be useful to Eisenhower in the event Joe McCarthy, the crusading senator from Wisconsin, might have to be dealt with.

In retrospect, it is not surprising that Eisenhower placed Richard Nixon at the head of the list of eligible running mates. To counterbalance his own candidacy, Eisenhower virtually *had* to have a young, energetic, and political running mate. What better choice than a candidate who had rallied all of these characteristics in a fight against the major issue of the day?[16]

Years later, in 1968, an unpopular war 6,000 miles away hit home at its hardest; Lyndon Johnson, who had been very popular in 1964, was forced not to seek reelection; the nation's foremost civil rights leader, the Reverend Martin Luther King, Jr., was assassinated in Memphis; and a young, vibrant, popular presidential candidate bearing the Kennedy name was shot down moments after a victorious primary battle in California. In short, this country seemed to be in a tailspin.

While these critical events were occurring, another storm was brewing that ultimately relegated the war in Vietnam to second place in the voters' minds. Issues of law and order: crime in the streets, ghetto riots, burning cities, especially following the assassination of King, all hit white America hard and produced an outcry for solutions. The "Social Issues" were in "full flower," as the noted observers of American elections, Richard Scammon and Ben Wattenberg, have suggested.

Richard Nixon was the center candidate in 1968—the position of power in American politics—and won because he had a profound understanding of what the real issues in that campaign were. His selection of Spiro Agnew as his running mate was, in large measure, a product of that understanding.

The Spiro Agnew of 1968 was just what Nixon had in mind: a candidate who was strong on domestic issues and who had struck a chord on the critical question of law and order. Nixon, meanwhile, planned to devote the major portion of his own time to the foreign arena.

As governor of Maryland, Agnew had had occasion to demonstrate his position on what would come to be the critical issue of the 1968 campaign. A year prior to that campaign, in July 1967, following riots in Cambridge, Maryland, Governor Agnew issued a statement entitled "Civil Rights and Rioting," which demonstrated his reaction to immoderate black leaders. The occasion was Agnew's response to H. Rap Brown, who had delivered a scathing antiwhite speech in Cambridge, which contributed to the later riots.[18]

In March 1968, trouble was building up on Maryland's predominantly black Bowie State Campus. Dr. Samuel Myers, president of the college, had pleaded with Agnew to make a personal appearance so that the students could air their grievances. Agnew declined, choosing instead to send a representative. Unfortunately, the representative chosen, Charles Bresler, was not especially noted for tact or diplomacy. Meanwhile, Agnew, believing that militants were inciting the students, began to grow more and more rigid, refusing to give in under pressure.[19] Instead, state police were sent to the campus, and Governor Agnew threatened the students with forcible removal if necessary. Myers, however, was able to come to an agreement with the students, but several days later Agnew made the mistake of choosing to make a personal appearance at Towson State College for the purpose of hearing student (predominantly white) grievances. The Bowie State students were incensed; when they decided to go en masse to the State Capitol, Bowie State was closed and they were arrested.[20]

To make matters worse, this incident occurred on the same night as the assassination of Martin Luther King, Jr. On April 7, in declaring a state of emergency in Baltimore, Agnew once again proclaimed his firm commitment to law and order:

To all those who have been victimized, I pledge to you that all possible power will be exerted to restore order and security to your lives, and to assist those made homeless by fire.

To those few who loot and burn we shall have no sympathy, nor will we tolerate those few who would take the law into their own hands.[21]

Agnew's message was clear: above and beyond all else, law and order must reign supreme.

In a confrontation with black leaders following the Baltimore riots and the looting and pillaging in response to the King assassinaton, Agnew had yet another opportunity to demonstrate his firm position. In a speech on April 11 which would cause approximately seventy out of one hundred of the leaders to walk out while he was speaking, Agnew lashed out against militant leaders (none of whom was present) and criticized those nonmilitants present for giving in to the demands of those leaders.[22]

Agnew had made his point. For him there was no room for softness when it came to law and order. He, as well as the bulk of white America, had had enough. Furthermore, he would not be silent while the Kerner Commission blamed white racism for America's problems. Agnew blasted the commission and its findings just several days before the opening of the 1968 Republican National Convention.

Prior to the convention, Agnew had been an avowed Rockefeller man and had actively engaged in a draft Rockefeller movement, only to suffer the humiliation of hearing, in the company of a roomful of reporters, his candidate declare his noncandidacy (on the very day Agnew had expected Rockefeller to declare himself in the running). The Nixon camp began to court Agnew's support by playing to Agnew's vanity, seeking his advice and ideas. Following Lyndon Johnson's withdrawal from the race at the end of March, and again after Robert Kennedy's assassination in early June, Rockefeller reconsidered his own plans and made efforts to win Agnew back. But Agnew had found his man in Richard Nixon. As for his own future, Agnew typically behaved like the office-seeking politician, engaging in conflicting actions and statements: on the one hand, he disavowed any interest in national politics, and on the other, he sent out clear indications of his position on the crucial issue of the upcoming campaign.

Agnew's speech on the convention floor on August 7 placing the name of Richard Nixon in nomination hinted at what Agnew's role in the campaign and the administration would ultimately be. Again he vigorously voiced the law and order theme:

A nation plagued with disorder wants a renewal of order.
A nation haunted by crime wants respect for law.
A nation wrenched by division wants a rebirth of unity.[23]

Richard Nixon was eminently successful in convincing the leadership of his party that his time had come. The delegates to the convention agreed on him as their presidential choice on the first ballot, moving the choice of a running mate to the fore.

Spiro Agnew more than fulfilled the requirements Nixon sought in a vice-presidential candidate. In addition to his experience and his ability to achieve, he had other appealing characteristics. He was a self-made man, the son of a poor Greek immigrant; he epitomized the Great American Dream. Agnew seemed very much akin to what Nixon viewed himself as being and what would strike a note of empathy among that segment of voters soon to become known as "the vast majority of silent Americans." Nixon's acceptance speech in 1968 itself dwelled on both law and order and the Great American Dream and gave voice to the silent majority; it masterfully captured the heart of the social issue.

CONCILIATION: THE SELECTION OF
LYNDON B. JOHNSON

As amalgams of a diversity of groups and interests, the political parties have the burden of emerging from the national convention with a presidential ticket that alienates as few, if any, of these factions. The period of the modern Vice-Presidency has witnessed the utilization of the second office as a key resource to achieve party harmony at the convention. The 1960 nomination of Lyndon B. Johnson as the Democratic vice-presidential running mate to John F. Kennedy represents such an attempt at party conciliation.

Kennedy's position in 1960 was a particularly vulnerable one. He was young, rich, Catholic, and running for the Presidency against an incumbent Vice-President who had served under an immensely popular President. Faced with such handicaps, it was imperative for him to muster all the resources at his disposal.

Having waged a hard and bitter preconvention fight against Senator Lyndon Johnson of Texas, Kennedy had created animosities that would last throughout his administration and well into Johnson's. The young presidential candidate from Massachusetts had to mend fences if the party was to achieve victory in November. Kennedy's most ardent opponent for the nomination, Johnson was not only "a Protestant with a capital P,"[24] but commanded a wealth of prestige and votes as well. Yet the scars of the nomination fight were deep. Johnson and his followers had to be conciliated; if not, Kennedy's nomination victory would be a shallow one.

Kennedy's position was not enviable. Somehow, he had to pacify the South without alienating his own liberal supporters. Kennedy was further hemmed in by the strong civil rights plank his team had indicated it would support. Moreover, both Bobby Kennedy and Kenneth O'Donnell had been affirming that the vice-presidential candidate would have an ideological position akin to Kennedy's and would probably hail from the Midwest.

There are numerous versions of what lay behind the Johnson nomination for the Vice-Presidency, but a definitive scenario is still lacking. One account (denied by all three Kennedy brothers and their lieutenants)[25] reports that John Kennedy, aware that he had no alternative to making a conciliatory move toward Johnson, decided to do so under the assumption that Johnson would be unwilling to give up the power of the Majority Leadership of the Senate for the relative impotence of the Vice-Presidency and would, therefore, refuse the offer. In his memoirs, Johnson recalls that, "When John Kennedy offered me the Vice Presidential nomination, I asked him to be candid with me. If it was only a courteous gesture, I said, I wanted him to say so. He replied that he needed me to run with him if the ticket was to be successful."[26]

Johnson's comments in the preconvention campaign seemed to indicate that he would not be a candidate for the second office. In a Chicago press conference on July 7, for example, Johnson responded to a question that he was only interested in the Presidency and that he would most assuredly not trade a vote (as a senator) for a gavel (as Vice-President and thus presiding officer of the Senate, who only casts a vote in the case of a tie).[27] He echoed this sentiment three days later in a "Meet the Press" television interview and added: "I have the assignment of Majority Leader of the Senate, and I think every person should seriously consider where he can be most effective and what job he can do best, and bear that in mind."[28]

As this version has it, Kennedy thought he could have his cake and eat it too. Since neither Kennedy nor anyone in his camp had expected an acceptance from Johnson, Kennedy could appear as both a conciliator by making a generous offer as well as a healer of party wounds. Author Hugh Sidey has related a preconvention conversation with Kennedy which underscores Kennedy's perception of where Johnson stood. "I remember once Chalmers Roberts and I were talking with him on the *Caroline* about Johnson," said Sidey, "and we put the question right straight to him . . . : 'Would you accept Lyndon?' Kennedy said he would accept Johnson 'in a minute,' and went on to say Johnson would 'carry the South and that's where we need the strength, and he's a good man. But . . . he [Johnson] won't accept it.' " From this conversation, Sidey speculated that following Johnson's refusal, Kennedy would be able to choose his own nominee, probably Stuart Symington.[29]

Another version of the Johnson nomination holds that the Johnson camp itself, with the aid of Speaker of the House Sam Rayburn, manipulated the vice-presidential nomination and that Johnson had actually forced himself onto the ticket.[30] Johnson discusses this allegation at length and denies it in his memoirs.[31]

The role played by Robert Kennedy remains unclear. The presidential candidate's younger brother had not forgiven Johnson for the disparaging remarks which he and his aides had made about the Kennedy family during the campaign. Once his brother's nomination had been achieved and the name of Lyndon Johnson began to emerge in talks which the two brothers had with their father, Joseph Kennedy, it is reported that Robert Kennedy attached little credibility to a Johnson nomination because it was "so inconceivable."[32]

How Johnson finally made it onto the ticket is beclouded by indistinct events and conflicting versions of what took place. Unclear, too, are the reasons for Johnson's turnabout on his availability for the second spot. It seems that when Kennedy (whether as a gesture toward reconciliation or out of the pragmatic belief that Johnson was necessary for victory in the general election) initially offered Johnson the nomination, as Johnson had expected him to do, the Texan planned in advance to decline it or at least to be very "hesitant to accept."[33] Perhaps the clearest fact that emerges about the Johnson nomination is that Rayburn's advice was critical to Johnson's ultimate acceptance. The Speaker, skeptical about the possibility of a Catholic being elected to the Presidency, was initially hostile to the thought of a Johnson candidacy for the Vice-Presidency. He also had misgivings about Kennedy's age. Johnson, despite the urgings of some, would not accept the nomination without his mentor's approval. Rayburn had been like a father to Johnson. Theirs was a relationship nurtured by the years; Johnson respected his judgment and wisdom. Furthermore, Johnson loved and was satisfied with his work in the Senate. So, when he reported that he might be offered the vice-presidential nomination, Rayburn initially told him not to accept; with this Johnson agreed. However, when Kennedy ultimately made his approach, Johnson at first wavered and then, much to Kennedy's surprise, accepted.[34]

Other observers believe that Johnson very much wanted the Vice-Presidency, and, in fact, that he "was angling for the Vice Presidential nomination."[35] According to this thesis, he was aware that no Southerner at that time could be nominated for the Presidency. The second office could provide an entrance for a Southerner onto the stage of nationwide politics,[36] so that even if he himself could not be President, at least "a Southerner might be President one day."[37] Perhaps too, Johnson was concerned that the role of Majority Leader under a new President might change markedly from what it had been under President Eisenhower. One of Johnson's top aides speculates that Johnson could have had some concern about the strain of continued Majority Leadership on his already weakened heart.[38]

While still undecided, Johnson suggested that Kennedy confer with Rayburn. Thus, Kennedy had to pursue what he had begun. Despite Rayburn's skepticism about Kennedy's chances, as well as his reluctance to have Johnson leave the legislature, one factor loomed large: the prospect of Richard Nixon in the White House.[39] Rayburn's hatred for Nixon was deeply embedded. The Speaker believed, correctly or incorrectly, that Nixon had once deemed him a traitor. And for this he had not forgiven him.[40]

By the time Kennedy made his appeal promising the Speaker that Johnson would enjoy an expanded Vice-Presidency, particularly in the area of foreign affairs, Rayburn acquiesced. According to George Christian, LBJ's press secretary, he did so especially "to save the country from Nixon."[41] Liz Carpenter (Mrs. Johnson's press secretary) told this writer that President Johnson always said that "Kennedy walked down two flight of steps"[42] to invite him to contract what another insider has described as a "marriage of convenience."[43]

The unexpected Johnson acceptance produced a flurry of reactions. The Kennedy staff, already divided in their opinion over the vice-presidential nomination, was stunned—as was Robert Kennedy.[44] It was at this juncture that the younger Kennedy allegedly paid his visit to Johnson in an attempt to get him to change his mind in exchange for the chairmanship of the Democratic National Committee.[45] It was also at this point that the nomination, intended to produce party reconciliation, caused an uproar among liberals and Southerners alike. Liberals felt betrayed; Southerners thought Johnson a turncoat.

In the face of so much adverse reaction, especially the threat of a liberal revolt, Kennedy undertook to reassess his decision and to consider what, if anything, could be done about it. The two brothers, Jack and Bobby, weighed the pros and cons of getting out of the commitment. On the negative side, besides the threat of a liberal revolt, Kennedy was disturbed about what it might be like to work with the temperamental Texan, "a proud and testy man, well known for his sensitivity and his egotism, unlikely to defer to a backbencher nine years his junior."[46] In addition, Robert Kennedy had apparently assured labor that the choice would definitely not be Johnson.

The arguments in favor of keeping Johnson weighed heavily as well. First, Johnson and his backers were too powerful to alienate. Second, Johnson would bring the ticket strength in the South. Kennedy felt the liberal storm could be ridden out and that the benefits of having Johnson on the ticket would far outweigh the disadvantage. Third, the vice-presidential spot would not only heal party wounds; it would also place Johnson in a position where he could be of greater legislative use to the Kennedy Administration.

CONCILIATION: THE SELECTION OF
HUBERT H. HUMPHREY

Although many of the criteria involved in LBJ's consideration of his own vice-presidential running mate in 1964 were of the traditional variety (a candidate who would complement him geographically, "even out" his views and political record, and, at worst, not lose any votes for the ticket), less emphasis had to be placed on these because of the political circumstances of the moment. With one exception, Johnson had virtually the freest hand possible in his vice-presidential options. Ironically, the Kennedy assassination that had given Johnson the Presidency set the scene for his choice of running mate: Johnson had to conciliate the Kennedy and liberal forces in the Democratic party who suddenly found a "Southern conservative" as the party standard-bearer.

With only one year in office behind him, Johnson was immensely popular. He had pulled a grief-stricken nation through a crisis and had demonstrated the workability of the American political system. Although he enjoyed immense flexibility in his choice of a running mate—far greater than most presidential nominees—he nonetheless had to operate within a prevailing framework of circumstances, events, and personalities.

Johnson's main problem from the moment he succeeded to the Presidency was that of overcoming his ideological image, of bridging the gap to the liberals. On November 23, 1963, just one day following the tragic assassination of the President, Johnson's aide and adviser Walter Jenkins transmitted a message from

Secretary Orville Freeman stating that ''the liberal movement needs badly a good clear impact from the President's speech.''[47] Freeman accurately believed that Johnson had to win the confidence of the liberal community in his forthcoming address to a Joint Session of Congress. The speech of November 27, 1963, indicated that Johnson was well along in creating a liberal image, but time was short and the new President needed to reinforce that image as the presidential election neared. His insistence on the immediate passage of civil rights legislation had served as one more building block in closing the ideological gap. He had done all he could to remake his own image; the vice-presidential nomination would provide added strength. He had taken the plunge that had clearly separated him from Southern conservatives. Earlier in his career, as Majority Leader of the Senate, he had found himself with a different constituency and had moved toward a position of greater consensus, especially on civil rights. Indeed, in his home state, he had been viewed as a liberal.[48] As Vice-President, his constituency had changed again but in the direction of a more consensual position. While the plunge toward a civil rights position separated him from the conservatives, it was not enough to bring confidence to the liberals. During his tenure as Vice-President, Johnson had worked as chairman of the President's Commission on Equal Employment Opportunity, and his performance in that role led some observers to believe that Johnson was much more dedicated to civil rights than was Kennedy himself.[49] He had traveled about the country in an effort to achieve business compliance. He had made speech after speech in which he spoke of the distressing conditions in the employment field. He tried desperately to impart his understanding of the South and of Congress to President Kennedy in an effort to deal with the racial crisis during the summer of 1963. He knew that no President in the summer and fall of 1963, especially following the Birmingham bombings, could have done anything else but press for civil rights legislation. Johnson had urged Kennedy, however, to lay the groundwork for this legislation cautiously. The events in Dallas on November 22 thrust responsibility for this crucial legislative leadership on a President with a Southern background who had less than one year in which to prove himself before the next election.

Above and beyond the moral perquisites of the civil rights bill were the political necessities. The new President was cognizant of the delicate situation in which he found himself confronting the burdens of the Presidency and the selection of a running mate with solid liberal credentials.[50]

In the months following John Kennedy's death, Lyndon Johnson, aided by Hubert Humphrey and others, worked feverishly for the passage of the 1964 civil rights legislation. As he approached the summer and fall of 1964 and the forthcoming election campaign, he had done all he could to establish and burnish a liberal image of himself. Someone else now had to lend a hand, someone who would not be accused of changing ideological courses midstream for political reasons, someone who was clearly identified as a liberal yet who would not alienate the conservatives.

Other factors affected the necessity of balancing. An incumbent President is lucky: he has the opportunity to see what cards his opposition holds before placing his bet on a running mate. The nomination of Senator Barry Goldwater as Johnson's Republican opponent further shaped the environment in which Johnson selected his running mate. Goldwater refused to compromise himself by ideologically balancing his choice of a running mate, so he selected Congressman William Miller of New York, also a conservative. This dictated that Johnson place greater store on the liberal than on the conservative vote.

Besides conciliating the liberals of his party, Johnson had another problem as he moved toward the 1964 campaign. The major obstacle to Johnson's free hand in 1964 was the position of the Attorney General, Robert Kennedy, who had been de facto the second most powerful individual in the government under his brother.

Johnson had suffered all the frustration inherent in the office of the Vice-Presidency and more. He had been Vice-President in an administration that had no room for him; he had simply never fit in. Despite President Kennedy's orders to the contrary, he was the odd man out of the administration. He was out of their element, and they were out of his. And he suffered most severely of all in his relationship with Robert Kennedy, a relationship going back to the bitter days of the 1960 convention in Los Angeles.

In the months before the 1964 convention, a groundswell of support arose for Robert Kennedy as a vice-presidential candidate. This presented a dilemma for Johnson because of the emotional and political forces that existed in the aftermath of the assassination. Johnson was a President who had not been elected to that office. To some he seemed a sorry replacement for a young, vibrant leader who was also a handsome, polished, well-spoken man with a Harvard education. In contrast, Lyndon Johnson appeared to many as elderly, somewhat crude—a Southwest Texas State Teachers College graduate and former high school teacher who was not very impressive before an audience. As Vice-President, Johnson had had great difficulty living in Kennedy's shadow and image; trying to follow him in the Presidency was even tougher. To have Bobby Kennedy and his supporters potentially trying to "reclaim" the White House was anathema to him. He was determined to win the White House on his own, to get out from under the Kennedy image. But because of circumstances—because Bobby Kennedy was extremely popular, because so much of the nation's heart longed for a Kennedy in the White House—Johnson had to act gingerly, and the vice-presidential candidate he ultimately selected would have to soothe ruffled feathers. Lyndon Johnson was engaging in a politically volatile process of elimination: solving the "Bobby problem" but emerging with the support of Robert Kennedy's followers.

Eliminating Kennedy from vice-presidential consideration was done with a master stroke: Johnson announced that *no* member of the Cabinet would be eligible for the nomination. Conciliating the Kennedy forces would be more difficult.

Johnson needed both a liberal and a *particular* liberal: one who would be embraced by the Kennedy forces. Johnson thus considered placing a Catholic on the Democratic ticket, and Eugene McCarthy, Hubert Humphrey's Minnesota competitor for the nomination, appeared to be a likely possibility. Johnson liked McCarthy; they were close personal friends. However, when Johnson tossed out the suggestion of McCarthy for Vice-President in a meeting with his advisers soon after his decision regarding the ineligibility of Cabinet members, all but Walter Jenkins were opposed to the idea.[51]

Humphrey emerged as an asset. Following his elimination of all Cabinet members, the President found himself faced with the possibility of a party split. Humphrey, however, was a suitable second choice of those who had wanted Robert Kennedy nominated, and Kennedy himself came out in support of Humphrey. Humphrey carried great weight with important liberal segments of the Democratic party and the electorate—labor, civil rights advocates, and party leaders. Humphrey's identification as a champion of urban area problems as well as the floor manager of the 1964 civil rights bill clinched his liberal credentials, and those credentials were exactly what Johnson needed to emerge from the 1964 Democratic Convention with a united party behind him.

CONCILIATION AND CAUTIOUSNESS: THE SELECTION OF WALTER F. MONDALE

Although Jimmy Carter did not enjoy the full luxury that LBJ had had in selecting a vice-presidential running mate, Carter's early capture of the 1976 Democratic party nomination allowed him considerably greater flexibility than is usually afforded presidential candidates.[52]

Earlier candidates set the stage for the Carter victory, Lyndon Johnson's in particular, since it removed the long-standing taboo surrounding a Southern candidacy. Nonetheless, Carter's candidacy had to be carefully balanced, and the former Georgia governor was up against some of the same constraints that Johnson had faced in choosing a running mate. Carter, too, was considered ''conservative'' by factions in his party and the country, although Carter was perceived as far more liberal than LBJ had been. While not entirely having to overcome the conservative label, Governor Carter still had to counteract his ''Southernness'' and the ideological orientation it implied. And so began the search for a liberal who would bring with him that wing of the party.

Comfortable primary victories behind him and assured of the nomination significantly prior to the opening of the convention, Carter paraded vice-presidential hopeful after vice-presidential hopeful before him and, more importantly, before the national news media. Carter took full advantage of the leverage the early nomination victory had given him and used the vice-presidential search to the media hilt. He did this for two reasons: to guarantee the soundness of his ultimate choice and to benefit from continuous media coverage of the selection process itself.

Mondale, the Carter people increasingly felt, was the clearcut choice. The

Minnesotan's long affiliation with Senator Hubert Humphrey set the stage for the remaining litany of advantages on his side. As Humphrey's protege, long-time associate, Senate successor, and later colleague in the same body, Mondale enjoyed a positive record and image as a liberal champion of many of the causes with which Humphrey had long been associated—civil rights, poverty, minority programs, and labor, whose support Carter needed to solidify. As one commentary noted at the time of the Mondale nomination, "If there is one characteristic that has dominated Mr. Mondale's political life, it is his genuine compassion for the underdog."[53] Indeed, if Hubert Humphrey's qualification for the Vice-Presidency in 1964 had included a long arm extended into the liberal camp, Walter Mondale's arm was equally extended in 1976. Jimmy Carter needed this arm to overcome what Democratic polls were telling him: the liberals were wary.[54]

It was Humphrey who placed Mondale's name in nomination, symbolizing the passing of the torch to the younger Minnesotan, and Senator Humphrey's remarks underscored the essential qualities of the "new generation of leadership" and its political significance. Senator Mondale, said Humphrey, was "a truly good and great American . . . a man who will give of himself for the common good—mind, body, and soul." Humphrey added, "The Carter-Mondale ticket means a significant turning point in the political and social history of this Republic. . . . It represents the final reunification of North and South . . . from Canadian border to the Rio Grande, from the Golden Gate to the Potomac."[55] This reunification also represented a blending of ideologies. In an overall nominating atmosphere of party unity and congeniality that seemed uncharacteristic of the Democratic party in relatively recent times, Jimmy Carter's acceptance speech stressed the need for "a time for healing," "a time for great national deeds." The nomination of Walter Mondale, reconciling the inevitable fears of some liberals within the party in response to the Carter nomination, brought full circle the harmonious aura surrounding this party convention.

The Republican side, equally uncharacteristic, was not quite as compatible. The incumbent President faced a serious ideological challenge for the nomination. As the Mondale nomination unfolded, both President Gerald Ford and conservative challenger Ronald Reagan assessed their positions and shaped their strategies: turn around what Jimmy Carter perceived as the ideological benefits of the Mondale nomination; stress the vice-presidential candidate's extremely liberal record. Ford himself, it will be recalled, had been forced by ideological circumstances to rid himself of a liberal running mate, Vice-President Nelson A. Rockefeller. His assessment now was that a liberal running mate was not only anathema within the Republican party, but would also be so across a country that seemed to be in a conservative frame of mind.

As they prepared to do their own internal battle, both Ford and Reagan, acting independently, determined to portray *both* Democratic candidates as liberals; but the Mondale nomination solidified this determination. Ford, who ultimately won the Republican nomination, found his choice of a running mate shaped by the prevailing framework of acceptability, a framework shaped principally by party and ideological circumstances as well as by the campaign strategy predicated by Mondale's candidacy. As Ford sought to pacify the conservative wing of his party, Senator Robert Dole of Kansas thus became the beneficiary of this framework. Dole, a Midwesterner from the conservative wing of the party and a strong party man, rounded out the Ford ticket. Those Republicans who saw Ford as too close to center rallied around Dole's vice-presidential nomination. Ironically, Dole's candidacy may have cost the Republicans the campaign, for as the campaign unfolded and Dole assumed a "hatchet man" pose, Mondale's temperament and well-spokenness—particularly during the national televised debate in which both running mates squared off—seemed to sway the decision of many an undecided voter in what was ultimately a razor-thin victory by the Carter-Mondale team.[56]

CONCILIATION: THE SELECTION OF GEORGE BUSH. GERALD FORD AS HEALER? GEORGE BUSH AS SECOND BEST?

After leaving the Presidency, Gerald Ford wrote poignantly of "A Time to Heal," a time in which he had been critical of Ronald Reagan's "penchant for offering simplistic solutions to hideously complex problems."[57] During the 1980 Republican National Convention, Reagan would turn to Ford himself as perhaps the one individual who could so dramatically and most effectively "heal" and unify the party by agreeing to serve as Reagan's running mate. There were unprecedented discussions and negotiations regarding a former President as "the second man." Both because of the unusual circumstances surrounding this event and because of what it tells us about the Presidency and Vice-Presidency, the Reagan-Ford-ticket-that-never-materialized merits examination.

As the Democratic party seemed to be torn asunder by internal dissatisfaction and divisions, by a nomination challenge to the incumbent President, and by a threat of a convention upheaval that might result in an "open convention," the time was ripe for Republican presidential candidate Ronald Reagan—the nomination was clearly his—to solidify his prospects of electoral victory. Perhaps it can be aptly said that conditions were so ripe for a Republican victory that only a serious mishap could have lost the election for Ronald Reagan. Just four years earlier, this same Republican party had narrowly lost the Presidency to Jimmy Carter following a challenge by Reagan himself to the incumbent President Ford. Now the tables were turned in more ways than one. The Democrats were even more divided than the Republicans had been in 1976. Now, too, Gerald Ford perhaps stood between victory and defeat, just as Reagan had in 1976. What better way to salve the wounds inflicted on Ford and his wing of the party four years earlier than to offer the still very popular former President the second spot on the Reagan ticket? What better way to appease the more moderate segment of the Republican party, a segment already disgruntled by an extremely con-

servative platform? What better way to appeal to disgruntled Democrats across
the country—many of whom no doubt often regretted having voted for Carter
rather than Ford in 1976?

The analysts all said no; no former President would even consider the second
spot. But there had never been a former President like Gerald Ford. Always true
to his political and personal character, Ford placed party loyalty above all else.
Moreover, he had never suffered from false pride, and his behavior during the
1980 Republican Convention demonstrated just how unassuming and direct he
could be.

Approached by Reagan just hours before the presidential candidate's own
nomination, Ford did not dismiss the possibility of joining the Reagan ticket.
He knew such a conciliation would help his party. But the former President
made clear that his role as Vice-President would have to be forged in advance;
he would be no figurehead. In his usual forthright manner, Ford stated, "If I
go to Washington, and I'm not saying that I'm accepting, I have to go there
with the belief that I would play a meaningful role, across the board, in the
basic, crucial, tough decisions that have to be made in the four-year period."[58]

Ford was equally forthright in stating his hesitation about accepting Reagan's
offer—a hesitation that highlights, incidentally, the basic nature of the presidential-vice-presidential relationship, especially in terms of the inevitable staff
tensions. As Ford said, "I don't have any hang-up on pride," but he realized
that staff tensions might set up an "unworkable, unhealthy situation," exacer-
bated by the fact that the Vice-President had once been President himself.[59]

As speculation mounted and the convention progressed, it became readily
apparent that the Reagan forces were hard at work trying to convince Ford to
take the second spot. It was equally apparent that the Ford forces were not as
resistant as they might have been expected to be. Determined not to settle for a
figurehead Vice-Presidency, Ford reportedly sought many concessions from the
Reagan camp. Perhaps the magnitude of these concessions is what led to speculation that Reagan was considering a "co-Presidency," a move that was clearly
out of keeping with the essence of presidential leadership. Indeed, this notion
of a "co-Presidency" would lead to serious criticism of Governor Reagan and
to charges that he was naive in his understanding of presidential power. In fact,
former Reagan campaign manager John Sears observed, "It doesn't sit well with
people who are looking for a leader. . . . The people want to see one man in
charge."[60] Reagan's naiveté about Washington politics seemed about to undo
the edge he had achieved over President Jimmy Carter, who himself had so often
been criticized on the same grounds.

Contrary to this kind of criticism were the commentaries praising Reagan's
"flexibility," his "openness," his willingness to broaden his ideological base
in his attempt to achieve electoral victory.[61]

It was ironic that, unlike their interaction four years earlier, when Reagan had
perhaps been too lukewarm in his efforts toward the Ford reelection, Ford was
now in the driver's seat.

If the Ford forces had succeeded in their negotiations, the results would have been an unprecedented dismantling of presidential power. As Reagan's Vice-President, Ford would indeed have been a "co-President," sharing in Cabinet, National Security Council, and other important appointments, and having the White House staff report to the President through him. In essence, the Vice-President would have served as the "Chief Operating Officer," with the President in the position of a chairman of the board.[62]

Perhaps nothing more than a twist of fate aborted such a "constitutional coup," as Anthony Lewis of the *New York Times* termed it. Perhaps the television coverage of the convention, which seemed to reach the dimensions of the absurd in this rather unsurprising year, will be credited for so publicizing the negotiations over the Vice-Presidency that the unwanted publicity and mounting speculation forced both Ford's and Reagan's hands. So little was happening at the convention that the media seemed desperate for "news" or anything that might pass as news. This led the television reporters to spend an inordinate amount of time and energy on this one issue of a prospective Ford candidacy and its implications: the powers Reagan would give up in the bargain; its unprecedented nature; and, critically, the potential role of former Secretary of State Henry Kissinger in a Reagan-Ford Administration. Ford was seen as the nice guy, as the unwitting victim of the devious Kissinger who was looking toward his own return to power, undoubtedly as Secretary of State. As the Ford forces dragged their heels, Reagan realized the speculation had to be ended. A decision had to be rendered and rendered immediately, both because "there was a major danger that they [the delegates] were going to draft Ford,"[63] according to a participant in the negotiations, and because allowing the speculation to continue was making Reagan look indecisive and like a poor leader. Ironically, the move that had been geared to solidify Reagan's electoral prospects emerged as a potential handle which the Democrats might grasp. Reagan was therefore prompted to refuse Ford the chance to have one more night to "think on it," and he decided to make an unscheduled appearance at the convention hall a day prior to his own official acceptance of the presidential nomination. Perhaps the essential nature of the Vice-Presidency doomed the Ford negotiations from the outset. After all, no matter who the individual involved, no matter what level of popularity or influence of that individual, the *second* spot is dispensable. So, in his appearance before the Republican delegates, Ronald Reagan announced that George Bush would be his running mate.

George Bush, the candidate who had taken an early lead in the 1980 presidential competition when he had "separated himself from the pack" with his victory in the Republican Iowa caucus, had initially threatened the prospects of an easy Reagan nomination victory. But the California governor made his comeback, and Bush ultimately withdrew from the Republican primaries. Once the Reagan-Ford talks began, Bush seemed to lose hope of winning the second spot on the ticket.[64] But now, with those talks abandoned, Bush was exactly what Ronald Reagan needed to keep the Republican party united as it left the convention site and moved into the electoral arena. Bush's most crucial credentials were his appeal to the more moderate wing of the party, whose support was vital, and his previously held position of Republican National Chairman, to which he had been appointed by Nixon in 1972 as Watergate began to emerge and which had earned him a reputation for helping the party stay together during troubled times.[65] Thus, despite the unhappiness among the party conservatives who had hoped for a clean sweep and a "pure" ideological ticket, Reagan saw the pragmatism in the Bush nomination.

Once nominated, George Bush studiously played down the differences between himself and the presidential candidate: "I'm not going to say I haven't had differences at some point with Governor Reagan. . . . But what I will be doing is emphasizing common ground. I will be enthusiastically supporting this Republican platform."[66] He preferred instead to emphasize what united them. Bush was also studious in squelching a would-be issue: George Bush as second best to Ford.

Clearly, the Reagan choice was principally geared toward party conciliation; either the Ford or Bush candidacy would have met his party's needs.

VICE-PRESIDENTIAL SELECTION: BALANCING PERSONAL CHARACTERISTICS

In a particular election, although one criterion might stand out as most important in the selection of a vice-presidential running mate, in reality a composite of factors needs to be balanced. So, for example, although issue emphasis was the most important criterion Eisenhower had to consider in 1952, Nixon balanced Eisenhower's "Eastern Establishment" identification and could also be an asset with the California delegation over which the Eisenhower camp was troubled, and Nixon was very legitimately a solid Republican.[67]

Lyndon Johnson, following his abrupt succession to the Presidency, was aware that the circumstances that had propelled him into the Presidency drew attention to at least one criterion in the selection of a running mate, namely, the Vice-President's ability to perform in the Presidency—"in case I fall out an airplane tomorrow," Johnson reportedly told his staff.[68] A major strategy of the Humphrey people, therefore, involved presenting the Minnesota senator as a fully qualified successor. In the wake of the Kennedy assassination, this was a strong selling point.

Humphrey had certain assets that were extraordinarily compatible with Johnson's hopes for his administration. The President's plan for a Great Society was, to a large extent, the embodiment of the issues to which Hubert Humphrey had committed himself two decades earlier. If his advocacy of the civil rights bill in 1964, a performance testified to by Johnson in his memoirs,[69] was any indication of his abilities, he would be quite an asset.

Linked to the desire for a running mate who would support the aims Johnson hoped to achieve in his Great Society programs were additional considerations that had more to do with Johnson's personality and convictions than anything else. Johnson had strong, well-defined views of what the Vice-Presidency should be and what he wanted in a Vice-President; namely, he wanted someone with whom he could work, someone who could work well with Congress, and, above all, someone who would be loyal, almost to the point of subservience at times, and who would avoid public disagreements. Johnson sought someone willing to enter into a relationship that would be an "insoluble marriage."[70]

Hubert Humphrey seemed to be satisfactory on all counts. He was very well liked within the legislative chamber. His personal and professional relationship with Johnson extended back many years, and Johnson had rapport with, as well as affection for, Humphrey. Both men shared similar backgrounds with not "much of a gap socially."[71] They had worked closely as Majority Leader and Majority Whip, respectively, in the Senate; indeed, in the Senate, Humphrey had worked subordinately to Johnson, as he would be doing in the Vice-Presidency. This situation was in sharp contrast to that in Kennedy's 1960 selection of Johnson as his running mate, wherein Johnson found it difficult to become subservient to a man much his junior, not only in age, but especially in experience. More importantly, Humphrey *understood* the loyalty Johnson demanded and was willing to accept all the requirements placed on the second spot. Humphrey aspired to win the Vice-Presidency, and he could hope to succeed by demonstrating his helpfulness to Johnson. That Humphrey had been appreciative of the requirements for a vice-presidential aspirant is implicit in the comment of one of his aides who pointed out that when Humphrey looked to Edmund Muskie in 1968 as *his* running mate, he perceived Muskie as a man in whom he "could have complete confidence."[72]

With the aid of James Rowe, Humphrey's West Virgina campaign manager in 1960 as well as long-time Johnson friend, Humphrey had set out to prove himself. Humphrey did this by praising Johnson in television interviews (as did his competitor, Senator Eugene McCarthy); by courting the business community (especially via his publication of *The Cause Is Mankind*); and by demonstrating his talents as the "master of compromise," as he had done as floor manager of the 1964 civil rights legislation.[73] It was Jim Rowe who had transmitted Johnson's demands to Humphrey. It was he who had carefully screened Humphrey's background for Johnson to insure that there was nothing in Humphrey's past that might jeopardize the ticket (in sharp contrast to the lack of investigation that would later occur in the 1972 Democratic vice-presidential selection process).

Nixon, too, wanted to find a candidate who would conform to his view of the Vice-Presidency, someone who would not lose any votes for the 1968 Republican ticket and, moreover, someone who was not a superstar.[74] The party superstars were out. They would not be subordinate enough, and, clearly, this was how Nixon envisioned the Vice-Presidency in his administration.

Despite the protests of his aides who supported a candidate who would be ideologically different from Nixon (who was viewed as a centrist), Nixon wanted a vice-presidential running mate who would encompass and be acceptable to all wings of the party. Agnew, a "conservative liberal," met all of these criteria. Moreover, Agnew had proven that he could appeal to Democrats, which is critical to a Republican candidacy because the Democrats far outnumber the Republicans in voter registration.

The circumstances surrounding Nixon's own nomination as the presidential candidate as well as the anticipated circumstances of the forthcoming presidential campaign need to be recalled. First, Nixon had to rely heavily on the support of Southern and Border state delegations, and he was not their favorite candidate. Second, the spectre of the third-party candidate George Wallace posed a large threat. South Carolina Senator Strom Thurmond and the South had to be placated; George Wallace had to be offset. Thus, while he hoped to avoid leaning either left or right, Nixon had grave concerns that made it difficult to remain in the center.

The so-called Southern Strategy was beginning to take shape. The dictates of circumstance had again meshed with the personality of the presidential nominee to form the criteria for the selection of the 1968 Republican vice-presidential candidate. Governor Spiro T. Agnew of Maryland was the product of that strategy.

As with many a presidential candidate, Nixon's search for a running mate was very much a process of elimination that restricted his freedom of choice. Nixon wanted desperately to avoid many of the names that had been speculated on—the Lindsays, Percys, and Rockefellers of the party. Nixon's efforts not to be outstarred led him on a search for a candidate who would be grateful to be on the ticket. Besides, the polls indicated that Nixon ran better alone than with any name with which he had been paired.[75] Therefore, the selection of a vice-presidential running mate who would not *lose* any votes was critical. "The Vice President can't help you," Nixon told close aides. "He can only hurt you."[76] Moreover, the vice-presidential candidate had to conform to Nixon's view of the second office. Nixon's criteria and Agnew's credentials were well matched. Agnew was no superstar, and he was in agreement regarding the subordination of the Vice-Presidency.

When Jimmy Carter approached the vice-presidential selection process in 1976, he had to conciliate the party liberals. In addition, as with all previous presidential candidates, Carter's choice was also conditioned by the framework of acceptability prevailing at the time.

Ironically, one key liability in need of balancing was a characteristic of the Carter candidacy itself which provided much appeal in the post-Watergate campaign: Carter's lack of association and familiarity with Washington politics. Thus, it was no accident that the parade of vice-presidential hopefuls was limited to members of Congress. In addition to Mondale, consideration went to Senators Frank Church of Idaho, who emerged in the polls as the most popular potential running mate; John H. Glenn of Ohio, allegedly daughter Amy Carter's first choice for the spot; Adlai E. Stevenson of Illinois; and Representative Peter W. Rodino, Jr., of New Jersey, who had gained widespread praise as chairman of the House Judiciary Committee during the Nixon impeachment hearings.[77]

Carter spoke candidly of his need for an insider in his July 12, 1976, news conference in New York City. "I feel a need to know more about the Washington political procedure. This is an aspect of my own experience that is missing," he admitted.[78] (Four years later, Ronald Reagan, also an outsider to Washington politics, would find his vice-presidential choice conditioned by this necessity.)

In 1976, a second liability was indicated by polls taken among Democratic and independent voters prior to the convention. These polls showed concern for Carter's possible lack of understanding of regions outside the South.[79] Thus, the need for regional balance on the ticket emerged.

Lastly, no presidential candidate after the Eagleton debacle of 1972 and the Agnew resignation of 1973 would ever be able to settle on a running mate haphazardly. A thorough investigation of background would henceforth be necessary, and Carter's early primary victories afforded him a comfortable three-month period in which to scrutinize candidates. Thus, not only did Carter benefit from the publicity of his vice-presidential search: he had no choice *but* to focus attention on the thoroughness of his efforts to avoid a mistake.

No stone was left unturned to uncover "the best," as Carter himself put it. For Carter this person meant someone whose competence to assume the Presidency would be obvious, someone with whom he could be politically and personally compatible, and, of course, someone who could balance the ticket for the Democratic party.

In announcing the choice he had made, Carter characterized Senator Mondale as "an uncommon man, terribly gifted, committed, skilled, experienced, ready, but above all a good man." Carter went on to say that he had selected Mondale not only because the Minnesotan was the "best equipped available" but also because this choice would result in "the best politics."[80] Two immediate problems, however, had to be dealt with, and Carter did so with dispatch.

Referring candidly to the fact that Walter Mondale suffered from hypertension, the presidential candidate felt that this relatively minor medical problem did not warrant the elimination of one so highly qualified. The second problem stemmed from statements Mondale had made regarding his dislike of and incompatibility with presidential campaigning. Mondale's book, *The Accountability of Power*, spends a good deal of time on the rigors of presidential politics.

In a November 21, 1975, news conference, following his withdrawal from the race for the 1976 Democratic presidential nomination, Mondale had bluntly stated: "I do not have the overwhelming desire to be President, which is essential for the kind of campaign that is required. I admire those with the determination to do what is required to seek the Presidency, but I have found that I am not among them."

Mondale's perspectives on presidential politicking would thus provide some initial controversy over Carter's choice for the number two spot. But this, too, Carter handled squarely and adeptly. "It was one of the major doubts that I had about him at the beginning," admitted Carter, but he added that his talks with Mondale prior to the decision to nominate him had allayed the presidential candidate's fears.[81] Once these considerations were out of the way, Mondale's credentials readily made themselves apparent.

Four years later, candidate Reagan would also have to turn to a running mate whose background and experience would fill in "gaps" in his own credentials. In addition to being able to conciliate the moderates and liberals of the Republican party, George Bush was experienced in foreign affairs. Bush had served as U.S. delegate to the United Nations under the Nixon Administration, as head of the U.S. liaison office in Peking, and later as the director of the Central Intelligence Agency under President Ford. Thus, he would provide an expertise which Reagan lacked. Moreover, as a former two-term congressman, Bush was in a position somewhat parallel to Walter Mondale's in 1976: a "Washingtonian" paired with a candidate who held a disdain for and an unfamiliarity with Washington politics.

Clearly, the Reagan choice was geared principally toward party conciliation, but his framework was likewise conditioned by several other necessities, necessities met by George Bush: a candidate qualified to succeed to the Presidency; one who balanced Reagan's personal characteristics, particularly his advanced age; and one who could appeal to voters in the Northeast. Thus was the Reagan-Bush team ready for its "coast-to-coast, border-to-border campaign."[82]

While presidential candidates have traditionally sought to maximize their electoral strength by selecting vice-presidential running mates who will unify the national party, the more recent trend has been away from an out-and-out, diametrically opposed balancing of political ideologies. This trend demonstrates the growing realization that the Vice-Presidency is more than just a political plum to be passed around—a fear of the Founding Fathers—and the office has increased in importance as a positive, functioning institution.

Nonetheless, degrees of ideological balancing or ideological sameness remain. The candidate, while perhaps sharing views similar to those of the presidential candidate, simultaneously is either more appealing or at least more acceptable to a potentially troublesome wing of the party or the electorate. So, Nixon was seen as *more* conservative than Eisenhower but still within reach of Eisenhower's views; Humphrey already had the liberalism for which Johnson had been struggling and would not contribute to factionalism; the "New Nixon" of 1968, the centrist candidate, could simultaneously play the Southern Strategy with a non-offensive "conservative liberal," Spiro Agnew. John Kennedy could woo Southern votes while not bringing in a candidate of the extreme opposite but turning, instead, to Senate Majority Leader Lyndon Johnson, who had received the bulk of the Southern delegate votes at the convention. As a Southerner and a less liberal politician than Kennedy, Johnson had nevertheless been moving toward the center, especially on civil rights.

Nixon's choice of Lodge in 1960 avoided a candidate of opposing views at the same time that it added a candidate who appealed to the North. This became especially important once Kennedy had selected Johnson for the Democratic second spot since Johnson would probably take a major part of the Southern vote with him.

In 1968, Humphrey's choice of Maine Senator Edmund Muskie rounded out a moderate to liberal ticket.

George McGovern's choice in 1972 of, first, Democratic Senator Thomas Eagleton of Missouri and, then, following Eagleton's departure from the ticket, Sargent Shriver, represented the selection of a running mate who would balance the ticket ideologically, since neither Eagleton nor Shriver was associated with McGovern's "extreme" views. The divergence from this trend, as noted earlier, was Senator Barry Goldwater's refusal in 1964 to strike a balance ideologically; instead, Goldwater selected the conservative Republican Congressman William Miller. The particular degree of ideological balancing within this trend toward an acceptable range of views hinges on the total political environment in which the balancing takes place; although patterns do emerge, each situation is unique.

THE POLITICS OF TIMING: THE FERRARO SELECTION

Walter Mondale's former incumbency as Vice-President had given him a head start as he sought the 1984 Democratic presidential nomination. Although Mondale was ultimately victorious in the primaries and amassed sufficient delegate support to claim the nomination, the challenges of Colorado Senator Gary Hart and civil rights figure the Reverend Jesse Jackson helped shaped Mondale's "framework of acceptability" in his choice of a running mate.

Had Mondale behaved true to what many perceived as his traditionally cautious style, he might very well have selected Hart, since Hart had emerged as his major opponent in the primaries. Indeed, the Hart forces might have been able to back Mondale into a convention corner by playing to Mondale's hopes of achieving party unity. But the Jackson candidacy had brought other considerations to the forefront. Not only was Jackson the first serious black contender for the presidential nomination; early in his campaign he had also promised to name a woman as his running mate, if nominated himself. Thus, in addition to all of the traditional considerations which go into the choice of a vice-presidential candidate, no presidential candidate in the 1984 season was able to ignore the added consideration of gender. Beyond this, Mondale's considerations were also shaped by the growing "gender gap" seemingly being suffered by the Reagan Administration and the increasingly vocalized demands of women's groups, particularly N.O.W., that the Democratic party take a significant stance in support of women by actually naming a woman to the national ticket. In short, the time was ripe for just such a selection. Indeed, with the dismal Democratic prospects in 1984—Mondale trailed considerably behind the enormously popular incumbent Ronald Reagan—the vice-presidential selection served as a "safety valve" through which the Democratic party, much as it had in 1948, was able to add a moment of hope and excitement to its electoral efforts.

As had Carter in 1976, Mondale used the time between securing sufficient delegate votes in the primaries and the opening of the convention to have the vice-presidential selection become a media event. Ironically, perhaps, Mondale's "public" selection of his running mate, while engendering visibility and media coverage, further limited his freedom of choice. The astute Speaker of the House Tip O'Neill remarked during Mondale's interviews, "It's going to be Hart or a woman."[83]

Besides Hart, among the more "traditional" candidates under consideration were such prominent Democrats as Ohio Senator John Glenn, Texas Senator Lloyd Bentsen, Jr., Arkansas Senator Dale Bumpers, and New York Governor Mario Cuomo. Glenn certainly would have balanced the ticket ideologically; Bentsen would had added strength in the Southwest; Bumpers, generally considered a "liberal Southerner," could have been within the Mondale range of issues at the same time he offered geographical diversity; Cuomo could have attracted the important New York and ethnic votes.[84] But Mondale had to go beyond tradition if he hoped to have a fighting chance against the President. Perhaps if the race had been a closer one, presidential candidate Mondale would have taken a "safer" route and balanced his ticket within the traditional criteria. But circumstances mandated bold and courageous action. His candidacy needed an "energizer" and the hope was that the vice-presidential nomination would be just that.

Mondale's search extended the list of potential vice-presidential characteristics and scored at least symbolic chords of the Democratic party's image as the party of diversity. Mondale's interviewees included Philadelphia Mayor Wilson Goode and Los Angeles Mayor Tom Bradley, both black, and San Antonio Mayor Henry Cisneros, the first Hispanic to ever be considered for a national ticket. Mondale also met with San Francisco Mayor Diane Feinstein, who would have added both a change of gender and religion to a national ticket; Martha Layne Collins, governor of Kentucky; and Congresswoman Geraldine Ferraro of New York.[85]

Mondale desperately needed to give his candidacy a flair that he himself seemed unable to bring to it. Beyond this, Mondale, himself still very much associated with the negativism of the Carter Administration, needed to redirect media and public attention elsewhere. The Ferraro nomination, announced prior to the convention, seemed to give the Mondale candidacy momentum and redirection.

Ferraro, a fast-talking, quick-witted forty-eight year old Congresswoman from Queens, was ideologically very much like Mondale; indeed, had Ferraro not been a woman, she might very well have been eliminated because she and Mondale were so ideologically similar. In addition to gender, Ferraro brought other attributes to the ticket. She added strength in the Northeast and Midwestern industrial states. As an Italian-American, Ferraro, it was hoped, would lure back that segment of voters, one which the Democrats had slowly been losing over the past several presidential elections. Beyond this, her immigrant and working-class roots and her personification of the "American success story" fit in well with the prevailing issues Mondale wanted to develop during the campaign: America as the land of opportunity in which the underdog could rise to prominence and the Democratic party as the party which cared about, and represented, them. Moreover, Ferraro's congressional career had proven she could survive in the "man's world" of politics; early on she had won the respect of her colleagues and her "boss," House Speaker Tip O'Neill. In fact, O'Neill had pushed for Ferraro's candidacy.

The Mondale-Ferraro theme of caring extended into international issues, with Ferraro vociferously speaking of arms control as the "pre-eminent issue."[86] Ferraro, who was also a wife and mother, was able to incorporate those roles to underscore her concern for the issues. During one rally, for example, Ferraro said, "I see little children held up by mothers and fathers. You can't help but wonder what is going to happen to them unless we do something about arms control right now."[87] And she wondered aloud what would happen to her son and to the sons of those in her audience.[88]

Perhaps Ferraro's greatest asset to Mondale was that, as the first woman on a ticket, her candidacy was an unknown, an untested quantity; only the campaign would reveal its effect. Indeed, the Reagan-Bush team initially seemed stymied about how to deal with her as an opponent, since attacking her directly might be perceived as an attack on a woman's candidacy per se. The Republican strategy to a great extent, at least initially, was to ignore Ferraro. But various Ferraro remarks, especially one in which she bluntly questioned President Reagan's "Christianity" in light of some of the consequences for the poor resulting from the administration's economic policies, pitted Mondale's running mate in direct confrontation with the Republican team.

The momentum of Ferraro's candidacy was slowed when controversy began to surround the finances of her husband, John Zaccaro. Ferraro herself proved her mettle under fire as she adeptly and candidly took on a barrage of media scrutiny in this area. Similarly, her candidacy took on controversy when differences of views on the abortion question found Ferraro in confrontation with New York Archbishop John J. O'Connor.[89] Despite these controversies and the fact that the Mondale-Ferraro ticket could not overcome the significant lead of the popular Reagan, Geraldine Ferraro's place on the 1984 Democratic ticket continued the evolution of acceptable criteria in the vice-presidential selection process. Much as John F. Kennedy's 1960 presidential candidacy once and for all laid to rest the unacceptability of a Catholic on a national ticket, so too did Ferraro's presence eliminate the unacceptability of a woman in a national leadership role.

TRENDS AND PROPOSALS FOR CHANGE

Recent events have suggested that our present methods of vice-presidential selection may be inadequate. As a result, a number of reforms have been suggested; a brief overview of both the methods of selection and reforms is presented here.

The criteria for choosing presidential and vice-presidential candidates do change. New factors are added while others are discarded, and once a criterion has been tested it becomes part and parcel of the myriad factors to be considered in the selection process. For example, well into the twentieth century it was widely believed that only a native-born American of Protestant faith could be elected President or Vice-President.

This belief might have been discarded in 1928 when the Democratic party nominated Governor Alfred E. Smith of New York, a Roman Catholic, as its presidential candidate, but the success of the Republican party candidate, Herbert Clark Hoover, tended to cause the idea to persist for another generation.

Once a Catholic became President, however, Catholicism as an obstacle seemed to evaporate rapidly. Developments following the assassination of President Kennedy gave added legitimacy to the desirability of a "Catholic spot" on the national ticket and the need for due consideration in the selection process. This consideration weighed heavily on Lyndon Johnson as pressure developed for selecting the deceased President's brother, Attorney General Robert F. Kennedy, as Johnson's running mate in 1964. Although the President found a way out of his predicament by his shrewd announcement that no Cabinet member would be eligible for the vice-presidential nomination, Johnson felt obliged to give consideration to the selection of another Catholic, Senator Eugene McCarthy of Minnesota, even though he was subsequently rejected.

The notion that only a Protestant was an acceptable national candidate has been thoroughly overturned in recent history. President Johnson's opponent in 1964, Goldwater, chose a Catholic as his running mate. In 1968, Humphrey's choice, Muskie, likewise was a Catholic. At least one of the factors entering into the aborted selection of Senator Thomas Eagleton of Missouri as McGovern's running mate in 1972 was his Catholicism, and this was also a factor when Mayor Kevin White of Boston was considered as Eagleton's replacement and Sargent Shriver ultimately chosen; both White and Shriver are Catholic.

In the rapidly developing political scene in the United States, not only had Catholicism ceased to be the proverbial kiss of death for national candidates, but also the stage was set for inclusion of wider religious and ethnic representation. Senator McGovern extended the horizon further in 1972 when he sought to persuade Senator Abraham Ribicoff, a Jew, to accept the vice-presidential nomination. And ethnic diversity was reflected in Nixon's selection of a running mate: Agnew was of Greek ancestry, the son of poor immigrants. In 1968, the vice-presidential candidate, Muskie, was the son of a Polish immigrant, and he had demonstrated capacity to win in gubernatorial and senatorial elections in the traditionally Republican Maine. On more than one occasion, the name Edward Brooke, the former Republican senator from Democratic Massachusetts and a black, had been mentioned as a vice-presidential possibility. Moreover, today the nation would not be rocked to its foundation by the suggestion that such a distinguished Hawaiian as Senator Daniel K. Inouye, a Japanese-American, be considered for the vice-presidency. Prior to the 1984 vice-presidential selection of New York Democratic Congresswoman Geraldine Ferraro as the first woman on a national ticket, speculation had already begun to surround future vice-presidential candidacies of prominent Republican women, such as Kansas Senator Nancy Kassebaum, Transportation Secretary Elizabeth Dole, and Supreme Court Justice Sandra Day O'Connor. And the 1984 Democratic vice-presidential selection itself had included consideration of other women, such as San Francisco Mayor Diane Feinstein and Kentucky Governor Martha Layne Collins.

THE TWENTY-FIFTH AMENDMENT: THE CASE OF RESIGNATION

Momentous events beginning with the Kennedy assassination and the succession of Lyndon Johnson have pushed the Vice-Presidency to prominence. Concern continued to focus on the office with the casual selection of Senator Thomas Eagleton, with its subsequent embarrassment to the Democratic presidential candidate, his party, and followers. Not long thereafter, during his second term as Vice-President, Spiro T. Agnew, confronted by criminal charges, was forced to resign.[90] The denouement of the "Agnew Affair" was the elevation of Representative Gerald Ford of Michigan to the Vice-Presidency—the first to be chosen to fill that office in accordance with the provisions of Article 25 of the Amendments to the Constitution. This first test of the new amendment, adopted in 1967, added an entirely new dimension to the vice-presidential selection process.

The Twenty-fifth Amendment had been inspired by a quite different set of considerations from those that necessitated its first application, namely, a vacancy in the Vice-Presidency due to the resignation of the incumbent. Rather, the concern had been over the possibility of presidential disability and the lack of constitutional clarity regarding vice-presidential behavior during such a period. Senator Birch Bayh, author and Senate floor manager of the amendment, reflected on the problem of disability as he spoke before the Senate committee considering the nomination of Gerald Ford as Vice-President.

The events of Dallas reminded us of [a] tragic possibility. Had the assassin failed in his primary purpose, the . . . national specter arose of a once energetic President left physically or mentally disabled and unable to perform the powers and duties of his office. We all recall a tragic period of our history when Woodrow Wilson, a once-vigorous leader, was stricken by a stroke and left unable to perform the powers of the Presidency for many months.[91]

The Kennedy assassination had focused attention on the dual problem of presidential disability and a vacancy in the office of the Vice-Presidency. Four years following the assassination, an amendment to deal with these problems finally became part of the Constitution. The vacancy created by the resignation of Spiro Agnew caused the Twenty-fifth Amendment to be invoked and the machinery for its operation to be developed and set in motion. Because of what it says about the evolution of vice-presidential selection, the Ford selection warrants some attention here.

More than ever before in the history of the office, attention centered on the Vice-Presidency, and in particular on concrete issues regarding it. No previous vice-presidential candidate had ever experienced the careful scrutiny Gerald Ford underwent by Congress. Moreover, the review of his credentials for the Vice-Presidency took place within a far wider set of circumstances than the startling ones that led to the Agnew resignation. As the new amendment was being tested for the first time, there was omnipresent a sense that the need for testing it had hung over the nation for more than a year. The Watergate scandals could not be submerged; added disclosure of possible wrongdoings had made the possibility of a presidential impeachment or resignation a matter of time.

Senator Bayh spoke to this point as well: "Is this nominee qualified, not just to be the vice-president, but is he fully qualified to assume the most powerful job in the world—that of President of the United States?" Bayh further stressed recent events by adding: "Who could have imagined the possibility of Vice Presidential resignation as a result of criminal charges. Who could have imagined that at the same time the future of the President would be subject to serious question."[92]

The singular, dramatic circumstances under which the Ford confirmation hearings were being conducted poignantly emphasized the place of the Vice-President within the scheme of American government, as well as the need for a cautious selection. The awareness that Congressman Gerald Ford, if confirmed for the Vice-Presidency, would very likely be President increased both the stature of the second office and the gravity of the investigation for filling it. Throughout the hearings, the underlying question that Ford the vice-presidential nominee was being asked placed him in the hypothetical role of President. "If you were President, what would you do if ———?" Question after question delved into Ford's concept of the Presidency. Ford was being considered on the very grounds which the Founding Fathers mistakenly had thought all the vice-presidential nominees would be considered, namely, their fitness to be President.

Nixon's selection of Ford, as dictated by past vice-presidential selections, was conducted within a framework of acceptability conditioned by circumstance. The troubled times dictated that he take the utmost care in his selection. Mindful of his own predicament with the long shadows it cast, Nixon had to choose someone who would soothe a disgruntled Congress and an increasingly disgruntled and angry public.

The resignation of Vice-President Agnew was a rare event. (John C. Calhoun was the only other Vice-President to resign.) Had it occurred prior to 1967, the nation would not have had a vice-presidential replacement. In deciding to nominate Congressman Ford as Agnew's replacement, President Nixon wisely carried off an exercise in practical politics. Contrary to speculation that he would try to push for confirmation of his very controversial Secretary of the Treasury, John Connally of Texas, he geared his choice to conciliation—not the party conciliation of past nominations, but a conciliation extending to the far reaches of a troubled and disillusioned nation.

The selection of Ford, a congressman of some two decades, a Minority Leader, and a popular man with both parties in the House and Senate, noted one confidential informant, "seemed to be inevitable," and there was a very real practicality to selecting a House leader since "the impeachment business would begin in the House." The selection of a popular member of the House might produce more sympathetic treatment of the President if he were to appear to answer charges. In the past the House has been relatively neglected as a source of candidates. The President's announcement of his selection of Ford was made before a joint meeting of the Congress and prompted a standing ovation. Even before Ford's name was actually announced, Nixon's description of his nominee could only fit the well-liked House Minority Leader.

The confirmation hearings that led to the approval of Nixon's choice tested the effectiveness of the Twenty-fifth Amendment. Because of the times in which they were conducted, they also focused dramatic attention on the office of the Vice-Presidency and the selection of the new incumbent. As noted earlier, no previous vice-presidential candidate had been subjected to so rigorous an examination as Ford had been; his financial status and personal life, as well as his political philosophy, were thoroughly examined. The Ford hearings underscored the need to question seriously the procedure of the national convention. For those who advocate a major overhaul of our entire selection process, perhaps the solution is found in the existing primary system. In many cases the primaries clearly select a presidential candidate long before the convention meets and so in a very natural way can afford greater leisure and greater care in the selection of a running mate.

Other forces have contributed to the new awareness of a more thorough scrutiny of the nominating process. Only a year and a half elapsed between the time Senator Thomas Eagleton left the McGovern ticket and Gerald Ford's nomination was approved by Congress. In addition, two of the past five Presidents had died in office, thrusting the powers and duties of the office on men who, although they rose to the occasion, had been selected rather haphazardly and usually within just a few hours following the presidential nomination. The 1980 nomination and election of Ronald Reagan, at the age of sixty-nine, further highlighted the importance of the vice-presidential selection in three respects: Reagan's advanced age suggested the very real possibility that his Vice-President might succeed to the first office; it was speculated that if Reagan survived his entire first term, it would be uncertain whether he would choose to run for a second term at the age of seventy-three, thus making his Vice-President the heir apparent; and if Reagan in fact sought reelection and won, as turned out to be the case, again the possibility occurred that his Vice-President might succeed to the Presidency or be the heir apparent for 1988.

PROPOSALS FOR CHANGE IN THE SELECTION PROCESS

Numerous proposals, both in the literature and from individuals closely associated with the second office, have been made to change the vice-presidential selection process. Many opinions have been offered, but there is no consensus as to what, if anything, should be done. An overview of the proposals should give a clear indication of how far-reaching the thought has been on the subject.

1. *Select a vice-presidential candidate prior to the selection of the presidential candidate*[93]

This suggestion ignores some basic facts about American presidential politics. Whatever significance a particular Vice-Presidency has depends entirely on the incumbent President. A Vice-President chosen without, at the least, the approval of the presidential candidate might very well find himself at odds with the President. While greater independence would have been gained *within* the confines of the nominating *process*, the functioning of the Vice-Presidency would suffer.

Unless we are prepared to make substantial changes in what a Vice-President is constitutionally and otherwise assigned to do, this proposal would increase the likelihood of a Vice-President who would not be congenial with the President or with whom he could not work. Although theoretically this is possible even with the current nominating process, the likelihood of it would be greater with the prior selection of the Vice-President. It might also create the possibility that a presidential candidate would be chosen to balance the vice-presidential candidate.

2. *Have a separate election of the Vice-President and President*

The worst outcome of this arrangement would be the election of two individuals of different political parties, which would be contrary to one of the underlying intentions of the Twelfth Amendment. Numerous additional problems would ensue.

First, the President would have a Vice-President at his side who would owe him no allegiance whatever. While a Vice-President should not be bound hand and foot to a President, the administration should speak with relative consistency. A separately elected Vice-President raises the possibility of confusion and, quite likely, irreconcilable points of view, each directed to disparate constituencies. An additional problem would occur in the event the Vice-President succeeded to the Presidency. Vice-presidential succession already brings with it problems, as ensuing chapters will indicate. Succession by a Vice-President of a different party would almost certainly produce dramatic policy and staff shifts.

3. *Require that the presidential and vice-presidential candidates seek nomination as a team*[94]

This "package deal" suggestion has numerous drawbacks. For one thing, it ignores the complexities of presidential election politics. The vice-presidential nomination, as has been said, is one of the presidential candidate's most significant resources for achieving party unity. A candidate needs the full duration of the primary battles to see the development of party and electoral lines; requiring the candidate to bind himself or herself to a running mate at the outset would be a disservice to party unification. Were the candidate to make a "mistake" in an early choice, the result might be a divided convention and an ideologically tense election campaign.

Another drawback to this package deal is the remote possibility of finding a top contender who would be willing to settle for the second spot at the outset of a preconvention battle. It is doubtful, for example, that a Lyndon Johnson, Hubert Humphrey, Walter Mondale, or George Bush would have been willing to do so, and thus individuals of high calibre would be lost to the Vice-Presidency.

4. *Expand the pool of vice-presidential potentials by agreeing to allow the Vice-President to retain a previous office*

The adoption of this suggestion would increase what has already been the trend during the past twenty years: that top-notch individuals would be willing to make themselves available for the office. Allowing a Vice-President to continue, for example, as a senator or a governor, would attract individuals who might otherwise be reluctant to trade a substantially busier occupation for much of the frustrations of the Vice-Presidency.

Increasingly, the incumbents of both nationally elected offices are coming from the Senate (particularly the Democratic nominees). Since 1948, few candidates for either office have arrived without previous service in the national legislature, with candidates from the Senate predominating. The Senate's heavy involvement in foreign affairs and its generally more moderate stance than that of the House are no doubt contributing factors in this trend. Furthermore, the state governorships have declined as a source of candidates (despite the victories of the last two Presidents) primarily because governors are easily identified with unpopular policies. (Parenthetically, perhaps the future will see a turning away from the legislature as a source since pursuing the presidential nomination has become a full-time job; the last two Presidents were "unemployed" while seeking the office.) The above suggestion would allow a senator to retain his or her seat while occupying the Vice-Presidency. Members of the Congress could not be excluded from holding the Vice-Presidency, for to do so would be counterproductive; it would eliminate some of the most qualified possibilities.

There are several objections to this proposal. First, it constitutes a breach of the constitutional doctrine of separation of powers. It might be countered that the constitutional position of the Vice-President is already a breach of the doctrine, since it places a member of the executive within the Congress as presiding officer of the Senate. Not only is this *part* of the Constitution, but it assigns to the Vice-President a relatively passive role, with a vote allowed in the rare instance of a tie. To allow a senator to serve in both the executive and legislative branches of the government would be to compromise the separation of powers doctrine. It would allow a legislator representing his or her state or district in the national legislature to have access on an active basis to the executive branch. In addition, it would give the Vice-President two votes in the event of a tie. Unless this suggestion were considered within the framework of an open review of the entire Constitution and many of the principles on which it is based, it would have no validity.

Second, a key goal of any changes in the selection process should be a Vice-President capable of assuming the office of the Presidency if necessity demands it. Reducing the office's workload to enable its incumbent to fill some specific position would make that individual less familiar with the policies and procedures of the administration. If anything, the workload must be substantially increased in meaningful directions. That undoubtedly would increase the attractiveness of the position to qualified individuals.

Third, this suggestion misses the point that the proximity of the Vice-President to the President as heir apparent and successor has already made the office attractive and appealing to individuals of national stature.

5. *Select the vice-presidential candidate via an open contest within the convention*

Few presidential candidates, Adlai Stevenson in 1956 being the most recent, have chosen this existing option. To make an open contest mandatory raises many of the same problems as many other suggestions for change. While increasing internal party democracy, it enhances the possibility of a severely imbalanced ticket and a splintered party, thereby endangering the party's ultimate goal, election to office.

6. *Select the vice-presidential candidate from among the top three contenders for the Presidency*

This suggestion raises the fewest obstacles or objections, the major one being that any of the three individuals might be reluctant to settle for the Vice-Presidency (although recent contenders have seemed quite pleased to do so). A second concern might be what this forced selection might mean for the party in the general election, especially if the candidates available who fit this criterion do not balance the needs of the party. A third possible problem would be, once again, the incompatibility of the two candidates.

7. *Have only the presidential candidate selected by the party's national convention*

Once elected, the successful presidential candidate would submit the name of his vice-presidential choice for congressional approval. While this proposal would allow more careful inquiry into the qualifications of a vice-presidential candidate, it is one more unnecessary departure from the direct, democratic selection and election of candidates. Such a change would mean that the nation's voters would have no hand in the selection of the individual "a heartbeat away" from the Presidency.

8. *Have separate selections for both the presidential and vice-presidential candidates via a national primary*

This proposal has widespread appeal throughout the nation, for it promises a more direct and therefore democratic selection process. There are major flaws in it, however, including the possibility of poorly constructed tickets. While both the presidential candidate and the delegates in a national convention have the opportunity to weigh electoral realities, the random pairing of candidates via a national primary would do no such thing. Thus, neither coalition-building within the party nor conciliation of the party's diverse interests would be very likely. In addition, a national primary system would increase the likelihood that only the better known candidates would have a reasonable chance of winning, thus reducing the possibility of a gradual development of a candidacy, such as occurred in 1972 with the candidacy of George McGovern and in 1976 with that of Jimmy Carter. Beyond all these flaws, such a system would undoubtedly require a runoff primary, which would add to the burden of an already too costly electoral system.[95]

9. *Allow the presidential candidate to select the vice-presidential running mate within a designated time period after the convention has convened and have the candidate approved by the national committee*[96]

Gerald Ford made this suggestion while he was Vice-President. Ford proposed that the vice-presidential nominee-designate be put through a screening process by the party's national committee similar to the one he experienced during his confirmation hearings by the Congress.

This suggestion has obvious merit, for it would allow a presidential candidate sufficient time in which to examine his or her options and would then permit a party organ to serve in an overview capacity. This was the process followed in the aftermath of the "Eagleton Affair" when, following Eagleton's resignation from the ticket, McGovern named a replacement, Sargent Shriver. Shriver's candidacy had to be approved by the Democratic National Committee, since the national convention was over. The major objection to regularizing this process is that it is one more step removed from the people.[97]

10. *Abolish the office of the Vice-Presidency*

The most radical suggestion relating to vice-presidential selection is to abolish the office entirely. Following the Agnew resignation, several legislators and political scientists voiced this notion.

Perhaps Arthur M. Schlesinger, Jr., has given this idea its widest airing. In the second editon of *The Imperial Presidency* (1974), he added material on the Vice-Presidency with a concluding recommendation to abolish that office. Such suggestions overlook the reality that the Vice-Presidency is the symbol of continuity of the executive branch. To claim that the Vice-President does very little of significance is to avoid the real problem: the delineation of vice-presidential functions that would both prepare the occupant of that office to fully assume the Presidency and at the same time make the job more desirable.

While numerous suggestions have been made for revising the vice-presidential nominating process short of abolishing the office, none of them is completely acceptable.

No one has fully considered the nature of the Vice-Presidency and the nominating process. The inherent dilemma is that, while the office is potentially very powerful, it is nevertheless the *second* office. If the paramount consideration is to select a candidate capable of serving as President, the dilemma lies in finding a person who would be willing to settle for the second office. Until the Presidency itself is out of reach, candidates of high calibre are not likely to want to volunteer to spend their days as faithful and loyal troopers.

As has been pointed out, the nominating process itself contributes to the lack of attention focused on the Vice-Presidency, for until a presidential candidate has been selected, the question of filling the second office lies in abeyance.

Finally, all the proposals lack a basic preliminary step: before changing the nominating process, you must decide what the Vice-President is to do.

It is useless to establish a new method for selecting the incumbent of an office unless and until there is a clearcut delineation of his or her chief mission. Only then can a candidate's credentials be fully examined, by whatever process, to determine his or her suitability for the office. The question remains whether such a delineation is politically feasible.

In summary, then, all of the above proposals are attempts to solve a series of related problems:

1. The need for time to scrutinize a vice-presidential candidate.

2. The need for compatibility between the President and Vice-President.

3. The desire for conciliatory or balancing factors in a Vice-President, which may not be recognized until the convention.

4. The need for party and, ultimately, all voters' approval.

5. The time factors involved in the sequence of events.

PARTY EFFORTS TO REFORM THE SELECTION PROCESS

Following the national party convention in 1972 and the subsequent Eagleton Affair, both parties began to examine their procedures for candidate selection. The Democrats responded to the need for change by designating a Commission for Vice-Presidential Selection Reform, chaired by Senator (and former Vice-President) Hubert H. Humphrey.

After much deliberation, the commission issued a majority report, adopted 65 to 1.[98] Included in the report were the following suggestions:

1. The establishment of a fact-finding commission, several months prior to the convention, to screen candidates for the Vice-Presidency. The presidential nominee would then be advised of the findings of the commission.

2. The inclusion of an extra day in the convention so that the presidential nominee would have additional time in which to reach a decision.

3. The ability of the presidential candidate to request a delay of as long as three weeks before a decision on the Vice-Presidency is reached. This delay may be granted by the approval of the convention; the national committee would then have to approve the vice-presidential selection of the presidential candidate.[99]

Former Massachusetts Governor Endicott Peabody issued a minority report to limit "the nomination for Vice President on the first ballot only to those nominees who had run in state Presidential primaries or conventions."[100]

Peabody's suggestion merits further exploration. It is significant that the Democratic party is moving in a positive direction toward recognizing the importance of the vice-presidential selection. The critical factor involved in the disparity between the majority and minority reports is the contrast in views of the role to be played by the presidential candidate. The majority report assumes that a presidential candidate *should* play a significant, if not determining, role in the selection of the running mate with whom he or she will have to work if elected. Peabody's minority report assumes a counterapproach: the Vice-Presidency is an *elected* office, not an appointed one, and therefore justifiably is elected by the people.[101]

The Republican party at the Republican National Convention beginning on August 21, 1972, provided for the appointment by the National Committee chairman of

a committee broadly representative of the Republican party, including members of the Republican National Committee, to review, study and work with the States and territories relating to the Rules adopted by the 1972 Republican National Convention, and the relationship between the Republican National Committee, Republican State Committees, and other Republican organizations.[102] (Rule 29)

The resulting Rule 29 Committee, chaired by Congressman William A. Steiger of Wisconsin, among its many considerations, embarked on an examination of the opinion of party members regarding the method of selecting presidential and vice-presidential candidates (that is, national convention or direct national primary; as for the Vice-Presidency, one other option is included: opinion regarding the abolition of the Vice-Presidency). Although some attention is being given to the selection of the Vice-President, it is at best minimal and in no way approaches the scope of the Democratic party's deliberations. Neither party, however, has to date moved significantly toward actualizing reform to any length; perhaps only another crisis in the selection process will underscore the need in this area.

NOTES

1. Gerald M. Pomper, *Nominating the President: The Politics of Convention Choice* (New York: W. W. Norton, 1966), p. 158ff.

2. Patrick Anderson, *The President's Men* (Garden City, N.Y.: Doubleday, 1968), p. 63; James MacGregor Burns, *The Lion and the Fox* (New York: Harcourt, Brace & Co., 1956), pp. 428–39; Pomper, *Nominating the President*, p. 164.

3. For example, see Charles Roberts, Oral History Interview, John F. Kennedy Library, Columbia Point, Massachusetts; Hale Boggs, Oral History Interview, John F. Kennedy Library, Columbia Point, Massachusetts; Pierre Salinger, *With Kennedy* (Garden City, N.Y.: Doubleday, 1966), p. 40ff.; Arthur M. Schlesinger, Jr., *A Thousand Days* (Boston: Houghton Mifflin, 1965), p. 50ff.; Theodore Sorensen, *Kennedy* (New York: Harper & Row, 1965), p. 162ff.

4. Somewhat of a parallel is the selection of Lyndon Johnson as John Kennedy's running mate in 1960. All of the Kennedy team's efforts had been devoted to getting the presidential nomination; little if any attention had been paid to what would happen once that nomination had been secured. The goal of capturing the presidential nomination causes the vice-presidential nomination to become an afterthought.

5. Regarding the "Dump Johnson" question, see, for example, Tom Wicker, *JFK and LBJ* (New York: Morrow, 1968), p. 158; Boggs, Oral History Interview, John F. Kennedy Library, Columbia Point, Massachusetts, p. 18; G. Gould Lincoln, Oral History Interview, John F. Kennedy Library, Columbia Point, Massachusetts, pp. 22–23; Lyndon B. Johnson, *The Vantage Point: Perspectives of the Presidency* (New York: Holt, Rinehart and Winston, 1971), p. 2; Michael Dorman, *The Second Man* (New York: Delacorte Press, 1968), p. 261; "A Conversation with the Vice President," Interview, ABC News, March 26, 1963, Vice-Presidential Statements, Container 43, Lyndon B. Johnson Library, Austin, Texas, p. 11; George E. Reedy to Lyndon B. Johnson, in folder for ABC Interview (Reedy, in his briefing to Johnson regarding remarks about his political future, cautions Johnson not to mention 1964 so as not to express any doubt); "Bobby Kennedy on LBJ's '64 Ticket?" *U.S. News* 56 (March 23, 1964): 44; Kenneth P. O'Donnell, telephone interview, February 1974; Hobart Taylor, Jr., Interview held at his Washington, D.C., law firm, March 1974.

6. Harry S Truman, *Years of Decisions* (Garden City, N.Y.: Doubleday, 1955), p. 191.

7. Milton S. Eisenhower, Oral History Interview, Eisenhower Administration Oral History Collection, Columbia University, New York, New York, p. 48; Sherman Adams, Oral History Interview, Eisenhower Administration Oral History Collection, Columbia University, New York, New York, pp. 230–34.

8. Herbert S. Parmet, *Eisenhower and the American Crusades* (New York: Macmillan, 1972), p. 173.

9. Ibid., p. 434.

10. Truman, *Years of Decisions*, p. 190ff.; Dorman, *Second Man*, p. 156ff.; Papers of Henry A. Wallace, Franklin D. Roosevelt Library, Hyde Park, New York; manuscript of *This I Remember*, chap. 13, p. 196, Eleanor Roosevelt Papers, Franklin D. Roosevelt Library, Hyde Park, New York. See George Allen, Oral History Interview, Harry S Truman Library.

11. FDR Statement re: Wallace Trip, May 20, 1944, Official File 12, Vice-President, Franklin D. Roosevelt Papers, Franklin D. Roosevelt Library, Hyde Park, New York; Official File 12, April 17, 1944, Vice-President, Franklin D. Roosevelt Papers, Franklin D. Roosevelt Library, Hyde Park, New York.

12. Pomper, *Nominating the President*, p. 164; John Morton Blum, *Years of War, 1941–45* (from the Morgenthau Diaries) (Boston: Houghton Mifflin, 1967), pp. 280–81.

13. Blum, *Years of War*, pp. 280–81; Cabell Phillips, *The Truman Presidency: The History of a Triumphant Succession* (New York: Macmillan, 1966), p. 38; Mrs. Hannegan to Rosenman, undated, Rosenman 25 MS 62--4, Papers of Samuel Rosenman, Franklin D. Roosevelt Library, Hyde Park, New York.

14. CBS Broadcast, 1955, Official File 339–99B, Papers of Dwight D. Eisenhower, Dwight D. Eisenhower Library, Abilene, Kansas, p. 17.

15. Sherman Adams, Oral History Interview; Parmet, *Eisenhower and the American Crusader*, p. 100ff.; Sherman Adams, *Firsthand Report* (New York: Harper & Brothers, 1961), p. 34ff.

16. In 1960, Nixon, now the presidential candidate, selected a vice-presidential running mate who epitomized the central issue Nixon wanted to emphasize—international affairs and the maturity to deal with them. Henry Cabot Lodge, former U.S. ambassador to the United Nations, well exemplified this criterion.

17. Richard M. Scammon and Ben J. Wattenberg, *The Real Majority* (New York: Coward, McCann & Geoghegan, 1970), pp. 43–44.

18. See Appendix A.

19. *U.S. News* 67 (October 6, 1969):32–38.

20. Jules Witcover, *White Knight: The Rise of Spiro Agnew* (New York: Random House, 1972), p. 268.

21. Robert Curran, *Spiro Agnew: Spokesman for America* (New York: Lancer Books, 1970), p. 39.

22. See Appendix B.

23. As quoted in Curran, *Spiro Agnew*, p. 54.

24. Sorensen, *Kennedy*, p. 163.

25. Edwin Guthman, *We Band of Brothers* (New York: Harper & Row, 1971), p. 78.

26. Johnson, *The Vantage Point*, p. 78.

27. Lyndon B. Johnson, Press Conference, Chicago Airport, July 7, 1960, Container 39, July 7, 1960, Vice-Presidential Statements, Lyndon B. Johnson Library, Austin, Texas.

28. Lyndon B. Johnson, "Meet the Press," July 10, 1960, Container 3, July 10, 1960, Vice-Presidential Papers, Lyndon B. Johnson Library, Austin, Texas.

29. Hugh Sidey, Oral History Interview, John F. Kennedy Library, Columbia Point, Massachusetts, p. 45ff.; Sorensen, *Kennedy*, p. 165.

30. Salinger, *With Kennedy*, p. 44ff.; Johnson, *The Vantage Point*, p. 92.

31. Johnson, *The Vantage Point*, p. 92.

32. Guthman, *We Band of Brothers*, p. 77.

33. Walter Jenkins, Interview held at his Austin, Texas, office, March 1973.

34. For more on this point, see Schlesinger, *A Thousand Days*, p. 46ff.

35. Hodding Carter, Jr., Oral History Interview, Lyndon B. Johnson Library, Austin, Texas; Allen J. Ellender, Oral History Interview, Lyndon B. Johnson Library, Austin, Texas, p. 8ff.; Schlesinger, *A Thousand Days*, p. 46ff.; Bill Welch, Interview held at his Washington, D.C., office, March 1974.

36. Ellender, Oral History Interview, p. 8.

37. Ibid., p. 9ff., Bill Welch, Interview.

38. Hobart Taylor, Jr., Interview.

39. Ibid.

40. Boggs, Oral History Interview, pp. 22–23; George Christian, *The President Steps Down* (New York: Macmillan, 1970), p. 154.

41. Johnson, *The Vantage Point*, p. 90.

42. Christian, Interview.

43. Liz Carpenter, Interview held at her Washington, D.C., office, March 1974.

44. Robert Troutman, Jr., Telephone Interview, Atlanta, Georgia, May 1973.

45. For additional material on the reaction of the Robert Kennedy and JFK aides, see Leonard Baker, *The Johnson Eclipse: A President's Vice-Presidency* (New York: Macmillan, 1966), pp. 182–86; Salinger, *With Kennedy*, p. 46; Kenneth P. O'Donnell, Telephone Interview, February 1974. O'Donnell claims Bobby Kennedy was "almost neutral" to Johnson's selection by JFK. See also "Bobby Kennedy on LBJ's '64 Ticket?"

46. Dorman, *Second Man*, pp. 249–50; Guthman, *We Band of Brothers*, p. 252; see Salinger, *With Kennedy*, p. 46, for a contrary view. Salinger claims that it was just "a semantic misunderstanding"; Sorensen, *Kennedy*, p. 166, claims that Bobby Kennedy,

in offering the alternative of the Democratic National Committee chairmanship, was acting on the orders of his brother Jack, and not on his own initiative.

47. Schlesinger, *A Thousand Days*, p. 50.

48. Walter Jenkins to Lyndon B. Johnson, Remarks, Joint Session of Congress, November 27, 1963, Vice-Presidential Statements, Container 5, Lyndon B. Johnson Library, Austin, Texas.

49. See Vice-Presidential Papers on Civil Rights, Lyndon B. Johnson Library, Austin, Texas; Frances Keppel, Oral History Interview, Lyndon B. Johnson Library, Austin, Texas; Fred Lazarus, Jr., Oral History Interview, Dwight D. Eisenhower Library (part of the Columbia University Oral History Project), Abilene, Kansas.

50. Johnson, *The Vantage Point*. Along these lines, Harry McPherson's memorandum of February 18, 1963, is interesting. He wrote:

Yesterday, Berl Bernhard, staff director of the Civil Rights Commission, was at my home. Berl is young, very able, and I think more interested in progress in civil rights than in the politics connected with it.

He talked about the Equal Employment Committee. He said that according to his information you were about to be the target of terrific abuse on this matter. It will come from Republicans, and from some Democrats; it may have help from within the White House. In general it will attack the record of the committee, and its personnel. Its purpose will be to make you look foolish and insincere in your claims of effectiveness for the committee.

Berl said he regards this as "wretched stuff; because it hits somebody I think responds a great deal more sincerely and basically to the underdog than the President does."

He is in my opinion genuinely concerned about this attack, which he says will come in early 1964 (with a prologue in *Newsweek* this week.) Container 7, Civil Rights: Labor-President's Committee on Equal Employment Opportunity, Vice-Presidential Papers, Lyndon B. Johnson Library, Austin, Texas.

51. Johnson, *The Vantage Point*, p. 18.

52. Albert Eisele, *Almost to the Presidency* (Blue Earth, Minnesota: Piper Co., 1972), p. 205.

53. To a large extent, the characteristics Carter was seeking in a running mate paralleled those sought by Johnson in 1964.

54. Ibid.

55. *Time*, July 12, 1976.

56. *New York Times*, July 16, 1976.

57. Inexplicable, incidentally, was Ronald Reagan's announcement that, if nominated in 1976, Pennsylvania Senator Richard Schweiker, a staunch liberal, would be his running mate. Perhaps this was in part attributable to the realistic appraisal of the necessities of ticket balancing, especially if one candidate is clearly identified, as was Reagan, with an extreme ideological position.

58. *New York Times*, July 17, 1980.

59. Ibid.

60. Ibid.

61. Ibid., July 22, 1980.

62. Ibid.

63. Ibid.

64. Ibid., July 18, 1980.

65. Ibid.

66. Ibid.

67. Parmet, *Eisenhower and the American Crusades*, pp. 91–94.

68. Sidney Warren, *The Battle for the Presidency* (Philadelphia: Lippincott, 1969), p. 363; see also *New Statesman* 68 (August 21, 1964): 237 +.

69. Johnson, *The Vantage Point*, p. 159.

70. Eisele, *Almost to the Presidency*, p. 225.

71. Dean Rusk, Interview held at his Athens, Georgia, office, May 1973.

72. Bill Welch, Interview, March 1974.

73. Eisele, *Almost to the Presidency*, pp. 206–12.

74. Jules Witcover, *The Resurrection of Richard Nixon* (New York: Putnam, 1970), p. 350.

75. Witcover, *White Knight*, p. 219.

76. Witcover, *The Resurrection of Richard Nixon*, p. 351.

77. *Time*, July 12, 1976.

78. As cited in Congress, House of Representatives, Committee of House Administration, The Presidential Campaign, 1976, Vol. 1, Jimmy Carter, 2d Session, 1978, p. 317.

79. *Time*, July 12, 1976.

80. *New York Times*, July 15, 1976.

81. Ibid.

82. Ibid., July 26, 1980.

83. "Mondale's Demanding Suitors," *Time* 124:12–17 (July 9, 1984).

84. "Filling the Democratic Pipeline," *Time* 123:28–29 (June 18, 1984).

85. "Mondale's Demanding Suitors."

86. "Ferraro the Campaigner," *New York Times Magazine*, September 30, 1984.

87. Ibid.

88. Ibid.

89. Ibid.

90. Only once before in the history of the nation had a Vice-President resigned during his term of office. The seventh Vice-President, John C. Calhoun, resigned to serve in the U.S. Senate.

91. *Statement of Senator Birch Bayh Before the Senate Committee on Rules and Administration Regarding the Nomination of the Hon. Gerald Ford as Vice-President of the United States.*

92. Ibid.

93. Pomper, *Nominating the President*, pp. 174–75.

94. Ibid., pp. 175–76; Sidney Hyman, *The American President* (New York: Harper, 1954), pp. 190–91.

95. Some of the views held by past Vice-Presidents regarding the use of the national primary are as follows:
Barkley:

I would adopt the same method for nominating a candidate for Vice President that I would favor for President, and that is nominating them by the people, let the people vote on whom they want to nominate. But, as long as the convention system prevails it is difficult to visualize any reform in the method of nominating a Vice President different from that which now prevails. . . .

No convention would want to nominate a candidate for Vice President who was offensive to the nominee for President, or out of harmony with him.

Barkley admits, however, that "it does result in the people themselves having practically no voice in the selection of a Vice President." Sidney Shalett, Interviews with Alben W. Barkley, Harry S Truman Library, Independence, Missouri; Franklin D. Roosevelt Library, Hyde Park, New York, reel 12, side 2, pp. 1–2. Barkley expressed similar views in a 1955 CBS Broadcast with Edward R. Murrow, in which Barkley, Eisenhower, Truman, and Wallace participated. Official File 339, 99B, 1955 CBS Broadcast, Papers of Dwight D. Eisenhower, Dwight D. Eisenhower Library, Abilene, Kansas, pp. 16–21. Truman:

The direct primary is an ideal situation for selecting public officials, but there isn't a man in the world with money enough in the world to put on a direct primary for President and then run for President. It would require an immense amount of money in each one of the States, and I am not so sure that it would obtain the results that we think about. (CBS Broadcast 1955.)

96. Vice-President Gerald R. Ford, Interview held at his U.S. Senate office, March 1974.

97. For a sample of the reaction, see *Washington Star*, August 7, 1972 ("Eagleton Episode Stirs Reform Tide"); *Washington Star*, July 29, 1972 ("Challenge to Selection Procedures"); *New York Times*, August 23, 1972 ("Veeps on Veeps"); *Washington Star*, August 18, 1972 ("How to Choose a Veep"); *Chicago Tribune*, August 12, 1972 ("On Picking Vice Presidents"); *Christian Science Monitor*, August 9, 1972 ("Selecting a Veep"); *Washington Post*, August 5, 1972 ("The Perpetual Whirl Over Veeps"); *Washington Star*, August 4, 1972 ("Taft Hits Vice President Selection Setup"); *New York Times*, August 10, 1972 ("Accidental No. 2 Man"); *National Review* 24 (September 15, 1972): 994 ("How to Pick a Veep"); *Los Angeles Times*, August 17, 1972 ("The Crown Prince"); *New York Times*, September 9, 1972 ("The Three Ways to Reform the Booby Prize"); *Christian Science Monitor*, August 14, 1972 ("Horse Sheds and Reforms"); *Washington Post*, September 1972 ("Why Not Abolish the Vice Presidency?"); *Los Angeles Times*, August 4, 1972 ("One Possible Solution: Abolish the Office"); *Los Angeles Times*, July 25, 1974 ("There Must be a Better Way to Pick Vice Presidents"); *U.S. News* 73 (August 14, 1972): 80 ("The People's Voice in Picking a Vice Presidential Nominee?")

98. Endicott Peabody, Interview held at his Washington, D.C., office, March 1974.

99. Official Report of the Vice-Presidential Committee of the Democratic Party—Majority Report, December 19, 1973.

100. Endicott Peabody, "For a Grass-Roots Vice Presidency," *New York Times*, January 25, 1974; "Thoughts on the Vice Presidency Following the Democratic National Committee Meeting in Washington on March 1, 1974," March 8, 1974, memo; Interview, March 1974.

101. Peabody, Interview, March 1974.

102. Rules Adopted by the Republican National Convention, Miami Beach, Florida, August 21, 1972.

"Civil Rights and Rioting" (A statement delivered by Governor Spiro Agnew, July 1967)

Our country is as much threatened by the lawless rioting in our streets as it is by our enemies abroad. In such a serious time, the people of a State are entitled to a clear and direct statement of their Governor's position. This is such a statement.

In the first place, it is evident that there is ample cause for unrest in our cities. There is still discrimination and, in too many cases, there are deplorable slum conditions. Our Negro citizens have not received, and in many cases are not receiving, equal education, job, and housing conditions. The gains recently made, while good, are not enough.

I believe that responsible militants within the Negro leadership should use every means available to place legitimate pressure on those in authority to break the senseless and artificial barriers of racial discrimination. But legitimate pressure—the power of the vote— the power of organized political, economic and social action—does not give any person or group license to commit crimes.

Burning, looting, and sniping, even under the banner of civil rights, are still arson, larceny, and murder. There are established penalties for such felonies, and we cannot change the punishment simply because the crime occurred during a riot. The laws must be consistently enforced to protect all our people. If an angry man burns his neighbor's house, or loots his neighbor's store, or guns his neighbor down, no reason for his anger will be enough of an excuse.

In Maryland, rioting or inciting to riot, no matter what wrong is said to be the cause, will not be tolerated. There are proper ways to protest and they must be used. It shall now be the policy in this State to immediately arrest any person inciting to riot and to not allow that person to finish his vicious speech. All law-breakers will be vigorously and promptly prosecuted.

Acts of violence will not be later forgiven just because the criminal after awhile adopts a more reasonable attitude. The violent cannot be allowed to sneak unnoticed from the war dance to the problem-solving meeting. No, the problem-solving conference must be reserved for those who shun lawlessness, who win their places at the conference table by leadership that builds rather than destroys.

The problem-solving must be done by constructive militants such as the Wilkinses, Kings, Youngs and Randolphs—not by the Carmichaels, Joneses, and Browns. But it should include the younger responsible leadership as well as older, more established leaders. Responsibility is the yardstick.

It shall continue to be my firm policy to do everything possible to provide jobs, good housing and better educational opportunities for the poor and underprivileged, both Negro and white, in Maryland. I will meet with any responsible leaders to discuss the problems that confront us. I will not meet with those who engage in or urge riots and other criminal acts as weapons to obtain power.

In conclusion, I commend the citizens of both races who have continued to conduct themselves with intelligent restraint in spite of great pressure. I share the sorrow of those who have suffered and who continue to suffer from the reckless acts of a few.

For the confused and weak who seek to excuse, appease and rationalize for the criminals who threaten our society, I have only pity.

As cited by Joseph Albright, *What Makes Spiro Run: The Life and Times of Spiro Agnew* (New York: Dodd, Mead, 1972), pp. 164–66.

(A statement delivered by Governor Spiro Agnew, April 11, 1967)

I did not ask you here to recount previous deprivations, nor to hear me enumerate prior attempts to correct them. I did not request your presence to bid for peace with the public dollar.

Look around you and you will notice that everyone here is a leader—and that each leader present has *worked* his way to the top. If you'll observe, the ready-mix, instantaneous type of leader is not present. The circuit-riding, Hanoi-visiting type of leader is missing from the assembly. The caterwauling, riot-inciting, burn-America-down type of leader is conspicuous by his absence. That is no accident, ladies and gentlemen, it is just good planning. And in the vernacular of today—"that's what's it's all about, baby."

Several weeks ago, a reckless stranger to this city, carrying the credentials of a well-known civil rights organization, characterized the Baltimore police as "enemies of the Black man." Some of you here, to your eternal credit, quickly condemned this demogogic proclamation. You condemned it because you recognized immediately that it was an attempt to undermine lawful authority—the authority under which you hold your leadership position. You spoke out against it because you knew it was false and was uttered to attract attention and inflame.

When you, who courageously slapped hard at irresponsibility, acted, you did more for civil rights than you realize. But when white leaders openly complimented you for your objective, courageous action, you immediately encountered a storm of censure from parts of the Negro community. The criticism was born of a perverted concept of race loyalty and inflamed by the type of leader whom I earlier mentioned is not here today.

And you ran. You met in secret with that demagogue and others like him—and you agreed, according to your published reports that have not been denied, that you would not openly criticize any black spokesman, regardless of the content of his remarks. You were beguiled by the rationalization of unity; you were intimidated by veiled threats; you were stung by insinuations that you were Mr. Charlie's boy, by epithets like "Uncle Tom." God knows I cannot fault you who spoke out for breaking and running in the face of what appeared to be overwhelming opinion in the Negro community. But actually it was only the opinion of those who depend on chaos and turmoil for leadership—those who deliberately were not invited today. It was the opinion of a few, distorted and magnified by the *silence* of most of you here today.

(The reference here is to the appearance of the Baltimore chapter head of CORE, Robert Moore.)

As cited by Joseph Albright, *What Makes Spiro Run: The Life and Times of Spiro Agnew* (New York: Dodd, Mead, 1972), pp. 175–76.

3

The Vice-Presidency as a Stepping Stone

> The Vice President is in a sense a stand-in for the President. He is an alter ego or he is an echo, or he is nothing. . . . It depends upon what the President wishes to give him in terms of responsibility and authority. Remember, this office is vested with all the responsibility in the world but no authority. . . .
>
> You're not the President, and yet you're the Vice President—you *may* be President.[1]

That a Vice-President is indeed a "heartbeat away" from the Presidency is confirmed by the statistical yardstick: eight Vice-Presidents have become President following the death of a President and one has succeeded following a President's resignation. Thus, the Vice-President enjoys a one-in-five chance of entering the Presidency through the "backdoor," and at least in this regard the Vice-Presidency has become a stepping stone to higher office.

The death of a President is a traumatic event in the life of a nation. How the successor deals with this event is crucial to the continuity of and trust in the American Presidency. During the period of the modern Presidency and Vice-Presidency, the American people have learned that their Chief Executive is indeed mortal. In the three instances of succession examined in this chapter—those of Harry S Truman in 1945, Lyndon B. Johnson in 1963, and Gerald R. Ford in 1974—a comparative approach will be taken in exploring both common and divergent themes and actions.

THE TRUMAN SUCCESSION TO THE PRESIDENCY: THE KING IS DEAD

On April 13, 1945, just three months following his inauguration as Vice-President, Harry S Truman, Franklin D. Roosevelt's third Vice-President, was called on to provide national leadership.

In the months preceding FDR's death, Truman had seen the rapidly increasing strain on the President and the deterioration that twelve years in office had wrought. In his memoirs, Truman explained his own reactions to what he knew was unquestionably a steep decline in the President's health, but recalled, "I did not allow myself to think about it after I became Vice President."[2]

The nation as a whole was not fully aware of Roosevelt's condition, nor did it prefer to think about it, and the press seemed mercifully kind and considerate in avoiding discussion of the subject. The effect was a prevailing Roosevelt mystique which is perhaps best summarized by a statement made by one citizen, "I would vote for him even if I knew he was going to die tomorrow. I hope he will stay President as long as he lives."[3]

Polls conducted during the 1944 presidential campaign indicated relatively little concern over the question of Franklin Roosevelt's health,[4] as did the thrust of the Democratic party's major campaign theme—the inadvisability of abandoning Roosevelt's experience.[5] Truman later recalled in his memoirs that his campaign travels during the summer and fall of 1944 made him fully aware of the people's reluctance to change leaders during a war.[6] And as Truman journeyed, he vociferously cautioned the people about the inherent dangers of expecting a new President to be able to learn his job in less than a year. Certainly, argued Truman, this danger was all the more pronounced when the country was at war, and only Roosevelt fully understood "the objectives and the inner thoughts of such divergent personalities as those dominant leaders who have guided the destinies of our courageous allies."[7] Truman, it seemed, could see no further than being FDR's running mate, and yet as the nation's thirty-third President, Truman was faced with the task of finding the time to learn—and learn quickly— all that he had not been told or given the opportunity to learn during his brief incumbency in the Vice-Presidency. The Roosevelt experience and expertise Truman had described in the course of the campaign in reality underscored a Presidency so personal, so individualistic, that the transfer of power was clearly jeopardized; the virtues of the Roosevelt Presidency contained the seeds of its own defects.

Many people shuddered at the thought of Harry Truman being responsible for the future leadership of the country. No one else but FDR had been called "President" since 1932. The June 1945 *Current History* noted that Truman lacked "the magnetic personality of his predecessor." The May 19, 1945, edition of *The Nation* commented that the American public, in reaction to the death of Roosevelt and the subsequent Truman succession, "tended publicly to hope for the best and privately to fear the worst." *Time* magazine on April 23, 1945, reported that Truman's friends seemed to agree "that he would not be a great President," and *Time* itself commented, "Harry Truman is a man of distinct limitation. . . . In his administration, there are likely to be few innovations and little experimentation." *Time* went on to say of Truman, "He is frank with himself as the ordinary, honest politician grown to stature through patience, hard work and luck. He believes in strict party responsibility, a politician's reward for work done, and complete loyalty to friends."[8] (Students of American politics will not fail to notice the similarity of this gratuitous comment to what has been said about the "backdoor" Vice-Presidency and Presidency of Gerald R. Ford.) To many people FDR's third and last Vice-President appeared to be nothing more than a compromise candidate, hardly worthy of succeeding to the Presidency merely because the people around FDR at the 1944 Democratic Convention wanted to avoid Henry Wallace as a running mate and needed a candidate amenable to labor. And now, this candidate himself was having difficulty adjusting to the notion of holding the first office in the land. As Harry Truman faced newsmen during the first hours of his Presidency, he said, "Boys, if you ever pray, pray for me now. . . . I've got the most terribly responsible job a man ever had." And when the newsmen wished him "Good luck, Mr. President," he responded, "I wish you didn't have to call me that."[9]

The prompt and orderly transition from one leader to another is one of the great achievements of the American political system. Under normal circumstances, the transfer is provided for by fixed terms of office and regularly scheduled elections. When the system is disrupted by uncertainties and sudden crises, the transfer of power has added significance. Political circumstances of the moment condition the steps that must be taken by a Vice-President assuming the Presidency.

As Harry Truman succeeded to the office vacated by Roosevelt's death, a world war raged, albeit a war that had already insured victory over the Axis Powers in Europe and in which the tide in the Pacific was shifting rapidly in favor of the Allied Powers. Harry Truman described the environment in which his succession took place.

The presidency of the United States in recent times, even in the prewar period, had become a highly complicated and exacting job. But to this already heavy burden the war had added new and crushing responsibilities. Not only did the President now have to function as Commander in Chief of the armed forces of the United States, but he also had to assume the major share of the leadership of a far-flung coalition of allied nations. As I took the oath of office I was conscious of how vast in scope the presidency had become.[10]

Any unscheduled succession to the Presidency is a crisis; Truman's was a crisis in times of gravest crises. There is much American experience to demonstrate that a crisis government, particularly in wartime, is executive government, and FDR's Presidency had responded to crises characteristically. The majority of the American electorate had been willing to accept Roosevelt's forthright leadership. FDR's firmness in his policy convictions and capacity to lead and his support by his fellow Americans prompted his decision to fly in the face of custom and risk a third and then a fourth term. Roosevelt was always very much the Commander; no one around him had any doubt that he was completely in charge. For thirteen years, Roosevelt *was* the Presidency—and a crisis Presidency throughout. In responding to the exigencies of war, however, Roosevelt had dealt a serious blow to his successor.

Roosevelt's participation in Big Three conversations pertaining to the postwar world had been conducted in the same close-mouthed manner that had been the hallmark of his Presidency. He continued to drive himself, and he persisted in doing things singlehandedly, failing to share the leadership that would inevitably have to be passed on.

When Harry Truman took over the Presidency, he did not know what decisions Roosevelt, Churchill, and Stalin had reached. The first President in the Atomic Age had but three months' incumbency as a member of the fourth-term Roosevelt Administration before he had to take the reins of government. It is doubtful whether he would have been any better prepared if he had served longer. FDR had never done very much for Vice-Presidents. Indeed, the peculiarly uncertain position of the Vice-President, partially in the executive branch, partially in the Senate, but enjoying authority in neither, has set the scene for all incumbents of the office, although the Truman experience itself focuses on the need to rectify the level of vice-presidential preparation.

In the period beginning with the presidential campaign of 1944 and ending with his three months as Vice-President, Truman had seen the President only eight times. On these occasions, little of substance had been transmitted to the future President. Although Truman was not without access to the President, being able to contact Roosevelt, for example, if absolutely necessary, during his secret briefings in the Map Room, Truman was not present for these briefings; he knew that Roosevelt preferred to go to the Map Room alone. The deterioration of the President's health and his fragile condition make it understandable that he doubtless felt more comfortable when he was by himself. These same circumstances in retrospect make it seem the more lamentable that the Vice-President was to remain so ignorant of what was occurring in the prosecution of the war as well as in other public policies. Truman had to play "catch-up" on the piles of paper to which he had not been privy. He spent the early days and months of his Presidency conferring with the powerful who had surrounded Roosevelt, slowly piecing together a picture of the Roosevelt policies. One of the first pieces of business was presented by Secretary of State Edward R. Stettinius, Jr., who briefed Truman on diplomatic matters and the upcoming United Nations Conference at San Francisco. Stettinius informed Truman of the daily briefing papers Roosevelt had had prepared, and Truman received reports from that point. These reports, recalled Truman, were "immensely helpful in filling gaps in my information. In fact, they were indispenable as aids in dealing with many issues, and from the first I studied them with the greatest care."[11]

Only when he became President was information vital to the conduct of the war revealed to Truman, information to which he should have been granted access not only throughout his brief Vice-Presidency but also from the moment he received the 1944 Democratic vice-presidential nomination. The danger in neglecting the Vice-President and failing to share information was so obvious, and remedial measures were gravely needed.

The most astonishing piece of information transmitted to Truman was given to him following a special meeting of the Roosevelt Cabinet which Truman convened immediately after he took the oath of office as President. Following this meeting, Secretary of War Stimson lingered; he told the new President that a new explosive was in the works. Recalled Truman, "It was the first bit of information that had come to me about the atomic bomb, but he gave me no details."[12] Not until the next day did Truman learn of the immensity of the new weapon. Only a handful of men had known about the project; the Vice-President of the United States was clearly not one of those men. In fact, Truman, as chairman of the Senate Committee to Investigate the National Defense Program (more popularly known as the Truman Committee), had been asked by Stimson not to investigate plants in Tennessee and Washington since a very critical project was being undertaken. To this, Truman had agreed.[13] Later, as President, Truman was the individual to render the final decision of where and when to use the atomic bomb that was the product of the secret project.

Truman's preparation for the Presidency was, in a word, deplorable. Although he had attended Cabinet and Big Four meetings (consisting of the Vice-President, the Speaker of the House, the Majority Leader of the House, and the Majority Leader of the Senate), few of these meetings were held during his brief Vice-Presidency.[14] Besides, Roosevelt had been notorious for accomplishing little in larger meetings, which more closely resembled social gatherings than meetings to deal with substantive matters; the President had preferred dealing on a one-to-one basis, especially with Cabinet members.

While Truman's own background had fortunately provided him with some preparation, especially his tenure as chairman of the Truman Committee, he had little of the information he would need to win and conclude the war in an Atomic Age. In addition, he knew virtually nothing of what had happened at the Yalta Conference; nor did he have any information on FDR's personal agreements with Churchill and Stalin.[15] Once again, despite the fact that crisis government demands central decision-making, secrecy, and continuity—a demand amply met by Roosevelt—the four-term President performed a disservice not simply to the man who was to take up the burdens of the Presidency but to the nation as a whole. In his memoirs, Truman very graciously sought to rationalize what Roosevelt had failed to do.

No Vice-President is ever properly prepared to take over the presidency because of the nature of our presidential, or executive, office. The President is the man who decides every major domestic policy, and he is the man who makes foreign policy and negotiates treaties. In doing these things it would be very difficult for him to take the second man in the government . . . completely into his confidence. The President, by necessity, builds his own staff, and the Vice-President remains an outsider.

The Vice-President, Truman continues, is a politician, and "the President cannot afford to have his confidential matters discussed in Senate cloakrooms" where the Vice-President has a presence.[16]

While this is true, it would appear far from ideal with respect to the stability of government. The situation suggests *a fortiori* that a remedy be found to shorten the distance between the offices of President and Vice-President and to foster greater confidentiality between them. In the long run, it would seem far less detrimental to risk possible information leaks from the Vice-President than to have a repetition of the Truman transition. Moreover, the alleged notion that a Vice-President, in mingling with senators as he or she presides over that body, may make slips or betray presidential or executive department confidences is a very lame excuse for not keeping him or her informed. The argument is further weakened because of the far greater opportunities for and likelihood of leaks from within the burgeoning White House staff, privy as it is to so much classified information. In this regard, Truman spoke of the constitutional inadequacies in the preparation of a Vice-President.

I was beginning to realize how little the Founding Fathers had been able to anticipate the preparations necessary for a man to become President so suddenly. . . .

Under the present system a Vice-President cannot equip himself to become President merely by virtue of being second in rank. Ideally, he should be equipped for the presidency at the time he is elected as Vice-President. The voters, instead of considering a vice-presidential candidate as a sort of appendage to the presidency, should select him as a spare Chief Executive. As such he should be kept fully informed of all the major business transacted by the President.[17]

Truman stated two basic principles of enduring validity: the Vice-President must be presidential timber and be recognized as a likely substitute for the President; once he is elected as Vice-President, unless he is kept fully informed, whatever assets he brings with him will not suffice.

The history of presidential succession reveals that the passage of power is marked by uncertainties great and small. When the circumstances involve the death of a popular leader, the accession of the Vice-President is accompanied by a public sense of inadequate substitution, the Truman experience. In due course, Harry Truman was able to rise above the handicaps of his elevation to the Presidency. His painful experience contributed markedly to the evolution of the Vice-Presidency, which has witnessed the development of safeguards to insure that Vice-Presidents need not rely so heavily on God and good fortune.

Truman was also hampered because he followed the charming and charismatic FDR, and comparisons could not help but be made. While FDR had been "aristocratic," Truman was considered "side street American stock." Whereas "Roosevelt talked and people listened, [p]eople talk and Mr. Truman listens."[18]

Truman realized the difficult task lying ahead of him but was persistent in being himself. A humble man thrust into the shoes of a man who even on leg braces loomed tall, Truman felt and often expressed his awe at his sudden inheritance.

While his total lack of preparation for the job weighed heavily on Harry

Truman's mind as he assumed the office of the Presidency, he saw the necessities before him. He would have to retain and rely on many of the Roosevelt people in order to forge a sense of continuity across a grief-stricken, distraught nation; besides this, the information these men could provide was invaluable.

For some of the Roosevelt staff, as would be true of a greater number of the Kennedy people during the Johnson succession eighteen years later, it was impossible to transfer or even attempt to transfer loyalties that had been born years previously and nurtured through time. This is a critical problem that stems from the very nature of the Presidency. It is indeed a personal office, and any President succeeding to that office discovers how difficult a task awaits him in the delicate balance that must be struck between assuring stability and continuity by retaining the former President's staff to ease this process and putting together a working staff of his own.

On Truman's immediate agenda appeared the San Francisco Conference on Post-War Organization and the establishment of the United Nations, the surrender of Germany after years of bloody fighting, the Potsdam Conference, the birth of the Atomic Age, the surrender of Japan, and the restoration of a disheveled Europe. The short shrift he was obliged to give to domestic affairs plagued him.

Besides the necessity of keeping Roosevelt's staff on to assure the nation of continuity and stability, Truman needed the benefit of their information and experience to help see him through those first few overwhelming months during which he not only *served* as President but also *prepared* himself to serve as President. And so, to Samuel Rosenman, long-time counsel to Roosevelt and his personal representative in London, Truman turned for information regarding the late President's agreements on war criminals, about which Truman knew little.[19] He turned to Harry Hopkins, probably one of the most loyal of the Roosevelt aides, for insights into the working relationships among Roosevelt, Churchill, and Stalin.[20] Truman asked Hopkins to journey to Moscow, and he was an invaluable source of information and support to the new President. Truman recalled that as a "close [aide] to Roosevelt throughout his administration, [Hopkins] had performed many confidential tasks, and, as the President's personal representative, had carried out a number of secret missions."[21] Hopkins had been in a position occupied by few Vice-Presidents or vice-presidential candidates; he had information and insights from close contact and involvement with the President. That information and insight again proved beneficial once Truman succeeded to the Presidency.[22]

To James Byrnes, Roosevelt's former director of War Mobilization and the man who had desperately attempted to gain the 1944 vice-presidential nomination, Truman turned for a report on the events at Yalta, since Byrnes "had personally made shorthand notes of all the secret meetings he had attended."[23]

The former President's advisers served, on the one hand, as the strongest link in the chain of continuity. On the other hand, because of the personal loyalty which advisers feel to a President, they may also be the weakest links, for it becomes extremely difficult for these men and women to abruptly transfer personal loyalties. Harry Hopkins summed up the dilemma Truman was in. "Truman," he said, "has got to have his own people around him, not Roosevelt's. If we were around, we'd always be looking at him and he'd know we were thinking, 'The *President* wouldn't do it that way.' "[24] Hopkins expressed not only Truman's dilemma, but also the very nature of the Vice-Presidency when its incumbent is summoned to the Presidency. While continuity and stability warrant the temporary retention of former presidential staff, that staff is a personal staff, and all new Presidents eventually and as expeditiously as possible develop one of their own. Fortunately, Harry Truman was able to strike a balance between these two disparate needs. Perhaps the most natural thing for him to have done would have been to have relied so heavily on FDR's aides' advice as to become dependent, but Truman maintained his independence by managing to sift through the advice he received and reacting with his own judgment.[25] That another Vice-President *cum* President might have acted otherwise underlines the dangers of the lack of preparation behind Truman's succession to the Presidency. Truman's understanding of the Presidency and Vice-Presidency as well as of the demands of succession contributed to a successful transfer of power.

Beginning his Presidency during the turbulent war years and at the beginning of the Atomic Age and painfully aware that he was following a leader who had captured the hearts and minds of the American public and electorate for the past four presidential elections, Truman emphasized the importance not only of continuity but of openness as well. The Roosevelt Administration had not been a particularly open one, as Truman knew from first-hand experience, and the new President desperately felt the need to establish open relationships in order to assume full occupancy of his new office. Truman, who had spoken to members of the press with awe on the day after he assumed Roosevelt's place, pleased them at his first official press conference and again later on by the appointment of Charles G. Ross as his new press secretary. On May 17, 1945, Truman struck a theme that was to resound almost thirty years later in the words uttered by Gerald Ford upon his ascension to the Presidency. The Truman policy was open relations with both the press and the Congress.

All three Vice-Presidents who succeeded to the Presidency during the time period under study behaved in similar fashion in relationship to their constitutionally coequal branch of government, the Congress. Certainly, the circumstances under which each succession took place—all three different—contributed significantly to the tone of press and public reaction to each.

All three were met by a rush of emotionalism and sympathy, especially Truman and Johnson, for the poignant circumstances of their successions to the Presidency were quite different from those of Gerald Ford. All three new Presidents, in varying degree, nonetheless experienced the customary legislative honeymoon attaching to any new President. And Harry Truman struck the note of continuity necessary to the abrupt transition as he addressed a joint session of Congress shortly after assuming the Presidency.

Truman began his Presidency, as would Gerald Ford, by redefining the lines between the White House and the Congress. He asserted his desire for a cooperative relationship with the legislature and his intention to consult with Congress before reaching major decisions.[26] This was in stark contrast to the Roosevelt days of personal government.

Truman was fully aware from the start that he would have to deal with international affairs unfamiliar to him; he would have to have a cooperative Congress. From the first day onward, he met informally with congressional leaders, allotting considerable time and attention to the legislature with which he would have to work. Truman's down-to-earth, common-man approach, his willingness to go to *them*, even for a casual chat, pleased the congressmen. He talked with employees, page boys, anyone in sight. Everything Truman did during those early days was geared toward cementing a working relationship with the Congress.[27]

The need and desire for congressional cooperation was linked to the theme of continuity which Truman had enunciated in his first address to the Congress as President. Reflecting on his preparation for the address, the new President admitted his realization that it was "imperative to let the nation know through Congress that I proposed to continue the policies of the late President. I felt that it was important, too, to ask for continued bipartisan support for the conduct of the war."[28] The speech was well received.

A problem faced by any Vice-President called on to complete the term of his predecessor is the extent to which he is bound by the policies and programs of that predecessor. Truman appreciated this problem; he realized that both the nation and the world would be concerned about the directions, both domestic and foreign, which FDR's successor would take. For Truman, continuing Roosevelt's policies was not a problem, as he assured the nation and the world. He had always supported the late President's program and had easily run on the 1944 Democratic platform. In his reaffirmation of support for the United Nations, in his message to the Armed Forces, and in his determination to gain support from congressional leaders, Truman built a structure of continuity.[29]

Truman followed the precedent established by his six predecessors who unexpectedly became President: dealing with problems according to the late President's designs, commitments, and policies while slowly moving to make the Presidency entirely his own. It is theoretically possible for an incumbent of the Vice-Presidency who succeeds to the Presidency to abruptly alter policies and programs, as some of the Founding Fathers had feared. In practice, the policy of midterm Presidents has been to stress equilibrium and continuity. This is doubtless due to several factors: the Constitution seeks to insure that there be no hiatus in the exercise of governmental power; the government and the nation are proud of America's history of orderly transition; and vice-presidential candidates increasingly have been chosen who have been in basic agreement with the presidential candidate. Such factors, written and unwritten, make up the parameters within which a new leader may react in accordance with or diverge from the policies and programs of the leadership he has just replaced. Collectively, those parameters have developed in the direction of continuity. Thus, the American presidential type of government has evolved its own alternative to the solemn proclamation of continuity and longevity of its parent hereditary monarchy: "the King is dead; long live the King!"

The 1956 Committee for Economic Development (CED) study on "Presidential Succession and Inability" advised that

The Presidential successor should be basically sympathetic to the plans and aspirations of the incumbent President. Continuity and consistency require that he should not undertake abrupt shifts in governmental policy. To do so might disrupt public confidence in the aftermath of a succession crisis. . . .

Elsewhere, the CED report stated: "There must always be a full-time Vice President intimately associated with the President. . . . In line with this view, there has been an increasing tendency for Presidents to use their Vice Presidents for a variety of important assignments."[30]

The next Vice-President to succeed to the first office would come to that task as the most thoroughly prepared Vice-President to that date. But his succession would nonetheless have much in common with the 1945 Truman succession.

THE JOHNSON SUCCESSION: ESTABLISHING THE RIGHT TO GOVERN

Lyndon Baines Johnson, following his sudden ascension to the Presidency in Dallas immediately following the tragedy of November 22, 1963, echoed the thoughts and deep emotion reminiscent of the Truman experience. Understandably, like Truman eighteen years earlier, he invoked the Deity to help sustain him.

"All that I have I would gladly give not to be standing before you here today,"[31] Johnson said in an earnest voice in 1963. The emptiness of holding the highest office in the land had poignantly robbed both Truman and Johnson of the moment of glory that makes worthwhile all the hard years of work for presidential aspirants. Johnson, in marked contrast to Truman, however, became President as the best-prepared midterm Vice-President in history. Despite this wide difference in the preparation of the two men, the Truman and Johnson successions have much in common. Although John Tyler's succession to the Presidency in 1841 established the undisputed precedent of succession to the office as well as to its duties in the fullest sense and no Vice-President's right to do so has been questioned, the problems of transition remain.[32]

Regarding his own succession to the Presidency, Truman had written,

It is astonishing how much was crowded into those first few days. I felt as if I had lived several lifetimes. Among the burdensome duties and responsibilities of a President, I soon experienced the constant pressure and necessity of making immediate decisions.[33]

This same sentiment was expressed by Lyndon Johnson as he stepped into the shoes of the assassinated John F. Kennedy. The new President reflected: "I feel like I've been here a year already."[34]

The history of the Vice-Presidency reveals that all six Vice-Presidents prior to Harry Truman who succeeded to the Presidency had "mediocre administrations."[35] For Harry Truman, following the popular, overbearing FDR, the question had been whether he would follow in that "tradition" set by his predecessors. By all estimations, he had met the test; now it was Lyndon Johnson's turn.

Much as Truman had found himself with the seemingly insurmountable task of measuring up not only to the office but also to the *image* of the man who had been its previous incumbent, Johnson's problem was poignantly similar. The charismatic, attractive Kennedy in death became a larger-than-life myth. Johnson found himself haunted by that myth throughout his White House years. As with the Truman succession, Lyndon Johnson could lay claim to no national mandate. Vice-Presidents are the also-rans, the product of a national convention and its presidential candidate. Such Presidents by succession must therefore face the major burden of gaining the authority of the Presidency in their own right.

The first days of the Johnson Presidency were filled with the confusion, the sense of urgency and crisis that had filled those days of the Truman succession eighteen years previously. Once again the American governmental structure and political system were tested by the unscheduled passage of power and responsibility from one leader to another.

Unlike Truman, however, Johnson was prepared for the test; he always maintained that there was nothing more President Kennedy could have done to have kept his Vice-President better informed and thereby prepared. Moreover, the events in Dallas dictated the first and immediate acts of the new President. He had first to preside over the chaos; he had to be sworn in forthwith; he knew he had to act immediately in all respects as the Chief of State.

The jolt that had struck the nation would linger for months, probably years, to come, and Johnson knew it. Immediately following the Kennedy assassination, the conspiracy theories began to circulate; the doubts, fears, and anxieties of the shaken nation were suddenly thrust upon Lyndon Johnson's shoulders. He thought his first and most immediate task was to quell those fears and to reinstate a sense of trust and confidence in government; aware of a "need for a renewed sense of national unity," he set about "building a consensus."[36] Johnson knew, too, that these tasks must begin immediately, even before Kennedy's burial. And so mourning and meetings alternated.

Confronted by the nation's tears and sorrow, Johnson believed above all else that the prime need was for consensus. In emphasizing this from the start, Johnson struck a major theme that would prevail throughout his Presidency. He also emphasized continuity—continuity in thought, in substance, in purpose, in personnel. One of his first acts was to ask, and, in some cases, to plead, for the Kennedy team to stay on, at least for a while. He did not need them to fill an information gap, as Harry Truman had needed the Roosevelt men, but in order to retain "the experience they had gained in nearly three years at the seat of power"[37] and to bridge the emotional gap from the Kennedy Administration under John F. Kennedy to the Kennedy Administration under Lyndon B. Johnson.

The personal nature of the American Presidency emerges strikingly when a Vice-President succeeds to that high office. While the machinery of that institutionalized office continues to operate in the usual manner, the personal nature of the office echoes the abrupt passage from one leader to another. Indeed, immediately following the death of a President, even the late President's files are sealed and emptied; until recently, presidential papers have been personal, not state, property. In 1963, this process began within one short hour after the world learned of the Kennedy assassination.[38]

An inherent and critical aspect of the American Presidency as an institution is that the personnel who surround the President exercise power and are powerful only at the pleasure of one person—their President. No one elected these people; only the President can guarantee their length or type of service. Understandably, there is a jealousy between those who surround the President and those who sit in the shadows waiting to take over with a change of Presidents. Should change come by way of succession, animosity of the same sort prevails, although it is more difficult to perceive the full extent of it. Former Vice-President Hubert Humphrey has provided some interesting and fresh material on this subject, derived from his experience in the Johnson Administration.

If one became too popular or too effective, whoever the Vice President, the President says "What's he up to?" Not so much the President—his staff. One of the things that happens to a President and a Vice President is that the presidential staff looks upon a Vice President as an extra wheel that ought not to be on the vehicle of government—it's a fifth wheel, so to speak. And as far as that staff is concerned, it never needs a spare, you know. To them, a spare is extraneous; it's surplus baggage. And that staff will cut you out time after time—almost without malice. It's just sort of subconscious. They just say, "Well, he isn't really needed." I remember Johnson, from time to time, exploding to his staff, saying, "Why didn't you have Hubert over here?" "Oh, I didn't know you wanted him, Mr. President." "Well, I want him around here," he'd say. And I used to wonder, is he doing that as an act or what? In fact I found out that sometimes they'd just plain forget.[39]

As Vice-President, Johnson, too, had experienced either neglect or malevolence at the hands of the Kennedy staff, and Gerald Ford, when serving as Vice-President, admitted to this writer that staff can be a problem. He added that the staffs of a President and his Vice-President seem to be more concerned with their respective bosses' prestige and power than are the officeholders themselves.[40]

While tension is common and pervades the staffs of both the President and Vice-President, it reaches a fever-pitch at the moment the Vice-President assumes the Presidency. Staff tension was relatively nonexistent during the Truman succession inasmuch as the Vice-President had little staff. It was not until the second Nixon term as Vice-President that the office of the Vice-Presidency began to acquire any sizable staff of its own. As vice-presidential assignments and activities increased, the Vice-President's staff was increased accordingly, accompanied by growing animosities. By the time Lyndon Johnson succeeded to the Presidency, tensions between presidential and vice-presidential staff members had reached an all-time high.

Lyndon Johnson had never enjoyed a congenial relationship with the Kennedy staff. As discussed earlier, much of this animosity was a holdover from the 1960 presidential nomination race; many Kennedy staffers had never forgiven Johnson for some negative remarks made by the Texas senator. But despite this deep-seated dislike, Johnson deemed the retention of the Kennedy staff necessary to promote a smoother transition and stability when confusion and mistrust in government were widespread. In addition to the peculiar circumstances of his succession, the new President had to contend with the general problems resulting from the doubt and suspicion surrounding the Kennedy assassination. Johnson described the special problems attending his succession:

In spite of more than three decades of public service, I knew I was an unknown quantity to many of my countrymen and to much of the world when I assumed office. I suffered another handicap, since I had come to the Presidency not through the collective will of the people but in the wake of tragedy. I had no mandate from the voters.[41]

Toward this end, the Kennedy staff played a critical part in achieving a sense of continuity, which President Johnson realized was so vital. While many of the Kennedy people stayed on, others could not. That very *personal* nature of staff, unlike the Cabinet, made the transfer of loyalties virtually impossible. President by accident, Johnson was as acutely aware of the Kennedy people's negative feelings toward him as he was of their intense loyalty to the deceased President. He knew, too, that he would have to earn their respect as well as that of the nation.

Johnson's first order of business was rapprochement with Congress, to which Johnson extended his efforts at consensus and continuity. As the former Majority Leader of the Senate, Johnson had been on intimate terms with most of the men who now sat before him as he delivered his first address as President to a joint session of Congress the day following John Kennedy's funeral. Millions, who in the preceding four days had watched on nationwide television a President and later his alleged assassin shot to death, and who had watched Lyndon Baines Johnson take the oath of office to become the nation's thirty-sixth President, now watched the new President address their elected representatives in the Congress. Johnson, his voice saddened but firm, began his determined course of action. He was aware of his legislative ability, as well as of the sentiment pervading the country. Thus, he set about establishing a national sense of legitimacy with the ringing statement, ''Let us continue.''

Johnson, as had Truman years before him, knew that he would enjoy a honeymoon period with the sympathetic Congress. But he knew, too, that that period would be brief; if he were to make the most of it, he would have to act quickly. Without hesitation, he made a major effort during those early days of transition, stressing the need for legislation in the critical area of civil rights—legislation, he added, which had been dear to the late President's heart and which would be a fitting tribute to the slain President. Seizing the opportunity of the moment, Johnson spelled out his request for legislation which he hoped would forge that sense of continuity and consensus that the nation, and he, so urgently needed. Not only did the stability of the system make consensus an imperative; Lyndon Johnson also needed to demonstrate an ability to achieve consensus to overcome his image as both a Southerner and a nonelected President.[42]

In his congressional address, Johnson called for quick legislative action on much of the Kennedy program: medical care for the elderly, youth employment, and education. He also stressed the administration's continued commitments to its allies abroad and to the maintenance of a strong—indeed, the strongest—defense system. As Johnson recalled, "The people were ready for action. And when I looked inside myself, I believed I could provide the disposition to lead."[43]

Thus, Lyndon Johnson linked himself to the Kennedy men, policies, and programs, meeting almost immediately after the assassination with the Kennedy Cabinet, civil rights groups, and other interest group leaders as well as congressional leaders, assuring the continuation of the Kennedy policy in both domestic and foreign affairs. With "Let us continue" as the keynote of his advent to the Presidency, Johnson was in reality expressing a plea to allow him to begin.

Johnson had not only inherited Kennedy's policies; he gladly embraced them. As had Truman before him, as well as the six other Vice-Presidents who had succeeded to the Presidency, Johnson wanted to avoid any abrupt change. "I never lost sight of the fact," reflected Johnson, "that I was the trustee and custodian of the Kennedy administration."[44] He had spent three years in the shadow of the young man from Massachusetts whose death had given him the office he probably could never have obtained on his own. He was acutely aware of that as well as of the contrast that would frequently be made between himself and the deceased President. Throughout the course of his Vice-Presidency, he had been the target of the Kennedy people's jokes and abuse; in his Presidency, he received more of the same from a wider source. As he sadly reflected in his memoirs, there were numerous "derisive articles about my style, my clothes, my manner, my accent, and my family. . . . I received enough of that kind of treatment in my first months as President to last a lifetime."[45]

Much as Truman had, Johnson faced the seemingly insurmountable task of filling another man's shoes. Once again, a nation would make comparisons. Johnson, suggested Tom Wicker of the *New York Times*, was "something of a throwback to another time,"[46] and the new President knew it. His task, in succeeding to the Presidency, was to create the "right to govern." In stressing consensus, Johnson had begun the arduous task of solidly building that legitimacy.

THE FORD SUCCESSION: PRESIDENTIAL RESIGNATION

As had Truman and Johnson, Gerald Ford needed to assure the nation that the Presidency and government do indeed go on under stable conditions following the exit of a particular President. Unlike his predecessors, however, Ford had to strike resounding chords of change rather than promote continuity with the preceding administration, for it can be aptly said that Gerald Ford's succession to the Presidency began the day Richard Nixon nominated him for the Vice-Presidency.

In early November 1973, as the Senate Rules Committee began to hold hearings on the confirmation of Congressman Ford of Michigan as the fortieth Vice-President of the United States, a grave drama was unfolding within the other branch of the national legislature. This drama, which was to extend throughout months of agonizing investigation, opened when the House Judiciary Committee's meetings explored the possible impeachment of President Richard M. Nixon. Not for over 100 years had this question been addressed. Its movement to the fore coincided with the Ford confirmation hearings and set the stage for those momentous vice-presidential hearings.

Two constitutional provisions were being tested simultaneously—one for the second time and the other for the first. Each was theoretically and constitutionally distinct from the other, but in this case they were bound inextricably together, that is, the power of the Congress to impeach a President for misconduct in office and the exercise of the recently adopted Twenty-fifth Amendment providing for the filling of a vacancy in the Vice-Presidency. The seriousness of each underscored the urgency of the other. As the impeachment of Richard Nixon became an increasing possibility, it became all the more critical to have a ready standby in the Vice-Presidency. A delay in the Ford confirmation might either hinder the willingness of impeachment forces to carry forth vigorously or would make likely the succession of House Speaker Carl Albert, a Democrat, thereby raising the possible outcry of political motivations behind the Nixon ouster.[47] Many feared that impeachment under these circumstances would appear to have been forced by the Democrats in order to take the White House from the Republicans. (It was considered likely, however, that the mild-mannered Speaker, with no presidential aspirations, would have resigned the office of the Presidency once Ford had been confirmed, handing the White House over to the newly selected Vice-President.[48]) Clearly, the Ford hearings and confirmation needed to be conducted with all deliberate speed if presidential continuity and stability were to be maintained. Throughout the lengthy confirmation hearings, the inevitable linkup was made between the question of confirmation for the office of the Vice-Presidency and succession to the office of the Presidency.

The Ford nomination, coming just two days after the first resignation of a Vice-President, Spiro Agnew, for criminal charges, was accompanied by a promise from President Nixon that the nomination was "a new beginning for America."[49] This promise held prophetic irony for the President: it was made on the very day the U.S. Court of Appeals for the District of Columbia upheld a lower court decision requiring Nixon to release taped Watergate conversations.[50]

The Agnew scandal and resignation was just one more element in the growing Watergate-related climate of lost confidence and questioned legitimacy in government. The resignation of the Vice-President provided an unforeseen opportunity for the President to offer a conciliatory gesture to the Congress and nation. In considering a vice-presidential replacement, Nixon toyed with controversial Republican figures such as John Connally, his former Treasury secretary; Governor Nelson Rockefeller; and Governor Ronald Reagan. All of these men, however, were regarded as potential presidential candidates for the 1976 election and would, therefore, evoke hostile reactions from both the Democratically controlled Congress and the Republican aspirants to the 1976 nomination. Among other candidates who seemed to be acceptable were several senators: Barry Goldwater of Arizona; Hugh Scott of Pennsylvania; and Robert Griffin of Michigan, as well as White House counselor Melvin Laird. The President finally settled on the House Minority Leader, Gerald Ford, who was not widely known nationally but was very well liked across the board in Congress. Moreover, the Minority Leader had been recommended by House Speaker Carl Albert himself.[51]

As the machinery for the Ford hearings moved into gear, it became more and more evident that the man under scrutiny could conceivably spend very little time in the Vice-Presidency. Ford would not only be "one heartbeat away" from the Presidency, but also one impeachment away. The hearings produced some novel experiences in the history of American government and politics. For the first time, a President had been able to handpick his successor; for the first time, a Vice-President, unelected by the people, was instead confirmed by their elected representatives, filling an existing vacancy; and most importantly, for the first time a vice-presidential "candidate" received most careful and deliberated public scrutiny.

Gerald Ford by most accounts lacked charisma and was not particularly inspiring or qualified to be Vice-President or, if fate so chose, President. Nonetheless, as the hearings demonstrated, he had no serious flaws in his political or personal background.

The Ford Vice-Presidency, more so than all others throughout the Republic's history, was marked by a steady questioning as to what Ford would be like as President. The Vice-President was therefore placed in an extremely difficult position and was forced to walk a political tightrope much of the time. He could not ignore the political environment in which he was moving as Vice-President, but as Richard Nixon's choice he could not appear to be eager to grab power by engaging in public criticism of or commentary on the floundering Nixon Presidency. Thus, Gerald Ford seemed to be constantly hedging two positions: one critical of the anti-Nixon forces and the other semicritical of the course the Nixon people themselves were following. The Ford Vice-Presidency fluctuated between assertions of loyalty to Nixon and innuendoes against the President.

Following his Atlantic City speech only a month after he stepped into the

Vice-Presidency, in which he criticized the partisan effort to hurt Nixon via "massive propaganda," Ford himself was accused of being nothing more than a White House puppet, another Spiro Agnew.[52] In response to this criticism, Ford snapped back that he was running his own show. His actions, however, were far more indicative of his new position. As the President's future became more and more doubtful, Ford increasingly became the rallying point for an embarrassed and jeopardized party. As Ford jetted about the country campaigning for Republican candidates in an effort to overcome the damage wrought by Watergate, his emphasis moved from a defense of Nixon to a salvaging of the Republican party. Above all else, Gerry Ford had been a staunch party man; initially, that meant his solid support of the President. But as conditions worsened, solid support of the President became antithetical to solid support of the party. Something had to give, even if within the confines of his delicate position as the likely beneficiary of a Nixon impeachment or resignation. Thus, in early March, it was Vice-President Gerald Ford who was the first top official within the administration to state publicly that the secret report of the federal grand jury should and must be handed over to the House Judiciary Committee.[53] But still the Vice-President felt obliged to hedge. During mid-March, Ford criticized the Judiciary Committee in its attempt to gain access to forty-two tapes, saying that the committee had allowed its staff to "dictate proceedings," a charge that was then being made by the White House itself.[54]

As Ford's short term as Vice-President progressed, he increasingly assumed party leadership, a position Nixon could not command. This made it imperative that Ford take a more independent and detached stand. While insisting that he fully expected to be Vice-President for the duration of Nixon's full term,[55] Ford well understood that he might momentarily succeed to the Presidency. John Osborne, in a piece for the *New Republic* on April 13, 1974, indicated that Ford had actually gone as far as to speculate what his policies and personnel would be like as President—which members of the Nixon Cabinet and staff would remain. Osborne also indicated that Ford had expressed his impressions of the Richard Nixon then in office, especially in terms of Nixon's newly developed penchant for "small talk."

As he struggled to remain detached within his peculiarly sensitive position, Ford began to speak subtly against the Nixon Administration. For example, he admitted that he found portions of the edited White House transcripts "disappointing and disturbing."[56]

During the Ford vice-presidential confirmation hearings, a House Democrat had been quoted as saying,

The Agnew thing has stirred up some feeling that we ought to get to the central question of Presidential succession. Gerry Ford won't have any trouble getting confirmed, but we're going to do it carefully. It's possible we could be picking a man who will be President nine months from now.[57]

This prediction proved to be very accurate, for nine months to the day which marked his assumption of the Vice-Presidency, Gerald Rudolph Ford became the nation's thirty-eighth President. Thereafter it was revealed that a special Transition Committee had been operating on the Ford staff since April, in anticipation of a Nixon removal or resignation.

The Ford succession followed a week of political and personal turmoil for Richard Nixon during which a court ruling had forced his hand by ordering him to deliver a tape that indicated that he had, indeed, been lying about his part in Watergate. Following Nixon's public statement on the contents of the tapes, the President's support plummeted to an all-time low. Even his staunchest supporters on the House Judiciary Committee which was handling the impeachment hearings could no longer lend him support. Even more indicative of the approaching climax was his rapid loss of support in the Senate, which could anticipate the need to sit in judgment should the House vote for impeachment, which seemed likely. On August 8, 1974, Richard Nixon, after much deliberation and wavering, resigned. For the fifth time in this century and for the third time since World War II, an unscheduled transfer of power had taken place but under circumstances that were in sharp contrast to the two previous occasions. The Presidency on this occasion came to a man who had run for neither the Presidency nor the Vice-Presidency.

Following his succession to the Presidency, Harry Truman repeatedly said he had achieved the Presidency by accident, that he had not sought the Presidency. In his initial speech to the nation as President, Gerald Ford repeated this theme, but for very different reasons. While Truman had not sought the office of the Presidency, he had run for and been *elected* to the office of the Vice-Presidency. In contrast, Ford was elevated to the Vice-Presidency by one man, the discredited President Nixon who was forced to resign. Before he could establish his "right to govern," Ford's initial task both as the first "appointed" Vice-President in history and the first "appointed" Vice-President to succeed to the Presidency was to legitimize his right to succession. He tackled the problem squarely as he spoke immediately following his taking of the oath of office as President.

I am acutely aware that you have not elected me as your President by your ballots. So I ask you to confirm me as your President with your prayers. . . . I believe that truth is the glue that holds government together. . . . That bond, though stained, is unbroken.[58]

Ford's actions during those first days of transition were framed, as had been those of Truman and Johnson, by time and circumstances. The nation, most observers agreed, was being slowly torn apart by political scandal; cynicism was rampant. As in all successions, the maintenance of stability was essential. Because of the unique events surrounding the Nixon resignation, however, the new Ford regime grasped the need for a sense of stability combined with restoration. "A national nightmare is over," Ford said in his first speech as President. His actions during those first days were calculated both to demonstrate the workability of the system in the transfer of power and to separate the Nixon Administration under Ford from the ills of the Nixon Administration under Nixon. The President went on to say: "Our Constitution works; our great Republic is a Government of laws and not of men. Here the people rule." In short, the aim was to establish a new beginning for a tired nation, a new beginning that Richard Nixon had promised months before but had failed to deliver.

The Ford transition points to some interesting contrasts and parallels to the Truman and Johnson successions. Never before had a President resigned from office or been removed under the heavy weight of wrongdoing. Never before had an unelected Vice-President assumed the Presidency. And both firsts had occurred simultaneously.

From the moment he uttered the words "So help me God," Ford had to represent the continuity implicit in the very existence of a Vice-Presidency. He also had to strike a critical chord of separateness, of independence, from the bankrupt Nixon Administration[59] while avoiding any radical policy changes. Neither Truman nor Johnson had had to confront such problems.

One by one, in marked contrast to the paths followed by Truman and Johnson, most of the former President's men, tainted by Watergate, had to go. General Alexander Haig, Nixon's Chief of Staff, lingered awhile but was soon assigned abroad. Ford constructed a new administration that was entirely his own; the tattered remains of the old had to be discarded.

Continuity in foreign affairs would be the keynote; Secretary of State Henry Kissinger would stay, as would much of the Nixon Cabinet. Ford himself admitted his rather paltry knowledge of foreign affairs. Like Truman in 1945, Ford would have to rely on the advice and expertise of others, and in this respect the presence of Secretary of State Henry Kissinger was critical. As one commentator noted, Ford "ha[d] a great advantage over Truman who had to scrounge around for some time before he found the secretary of state he needed in George Marshall."[60] The Cabinet, unlike the Nixon staff, could remain for a while. Those of the Nixon Cabinet who had been sullied by Watergate had already exited. In his first full meeting with his inherited Cabinet, held on his first full day in office, Ford underscored the need for "continuity and stability," adding, however, that there would be a very different tone at the White House than that which had existed under Nixon.[61]

The Nixon staff was in a very different position, for it bore its own very negative identity. Unlike past successions, Ford could not ask the Nixon staff to stay on, even for a relatively short period of time as he planned a new beginning and a "clean" administration. Among the very first to go was one who had been very negatively associated with the Nixon debacle, Press Secretary Ronald Ziegler. He was replaced immediately by a well-like Ford man, Jerry TerHorst.

Ford noted that his administration would be an open one: "In all my public and private acts as your President, I expect to follow my instincts of openness and candor." As he worked through those first difficult days, openness, candor, and honesty became the keynotes. For this task the Ford personality and background were well suited; he seemed to embody personally the wholesomeness and decent aspects of American society, which a disillusioned nation most needed.

The advent of President Ford ushered in a new open relationship with the public media for which the press had long thirsted. This in turn was productive of a new presidential image which the public as well as the media had long sought. As Truman had done, Ford promised a new, free flow of information with the press. Cabinet members were encouraged to be "affirmative in their press relations."[62] This was in sharp contrast to the Nixon Administration during which an Office of Communication had been in charge of all press releases.[63] Press conferences were to become more frequent and more candid, and the press was elated. The love affair with the press that followed had been absent from presidential politics since the early part of the Johnson Administration. Gerald Ford seemingly could do no wrong. His folksiness, his common-man demeanor, his down-to-earth approach—all became part of the material used by the press to reestablish the idealized image that has come to belong to the American Presidency. For an allegedly noncharismatic (some said quite colorless) individual, the press attempted to establish some distinct personality. What it developed was a glorification of the Ford "style"—everything from carrying his own briefcase to making his own breakfast. For a short period, at least, the benevolent leader, the father figure, had returned.

As with past successions, part of the sense of continuity and stability involved a "renewal" of relationships with the Congress, and here Ford again seemed to do no wrong. In the midst of his inaugural speech, he casually asked the congressional leaders to remain for a few minutes following the speech to confer with him. In a subsequent address to the Congress, Ford's demeanor was in sharp contrast to that of his predecessor. At every juncture, he seemed humble. For example, he referred to his "privilege of appearing before Congress."[64] Among his fellow Republicans, he was viewed as the possible savior of what had appeared to be an inevitable debacle; among the Democrats, he was viewed as the likable former House leader, even though his succession to the Presidency had altered the prospects of a Democratic victory in 1976.

For a Congress that had spent the past several years in confrontation with the Presidency—the impoundment of funds, the secret bombings of Cambodia, the Watergate tapes, and ultimately the impeachment process were among the largest issues—the Ford Presidency appeared to mark a positive reconciliation between the two branches of government. Leaders on both sides of the fence applauded the new President, predicting a honeymoon period of two to three months and a Presidency far more willing to engage in consultation and cooperation with Congress than the preceding one had been. Within the framework of a renewed spirit of cooperation, Ford solicited suggestions from both parties regarding possible vice-presidential nominees to fill the newly existing vacancy.[65] Ford, whose entire political life had been spent in the lower house of the legislature, "understands Congress in a way that Nixon didn't," noted Republican Senator Charles Percy of Illinois. "He knows the workings of the Congress, he'll work with the Congress, and more importantly he listens and will take political advice from the political sources he respects,'' echoed Massachusetts Republican Senator Edward Brooke in 1974. Gerald Ford had adroitly established his right to govern.

PROBLEMS OF THE HEIR APPARENT: DISABILITY, SUCCESSION, AND THE NEED FOR PREPARATION

The growth of the power, primacy, and prestige of the Presidency during the modern era has focused considerable attention on a two-sided coin: the questions of disability and succession. One result has been the swift enactment and ratification of the Twenty-fifth Amendment, providing remedies for instances of presidential disability as well as for potential vacancies in the Vice-Presidency. This section offers a critique of this amendment as well as a commentary on the preparation of the heir apparent.

The Twenty-fifth Amendment was a response to a long-overdue gap in the Constitution. Unfortunately, in attempting to fill that gap, it also created a Pandora's box of additional gaps and dangers, only one of which came to fruition in the Ford-Rockefeller Administration commencing in 1974—that of the first entirely unelected administration in the history of the Republic. Two hundred years of democracy culminated in moving that democracy one giant step backward—and away from the people. But this is only one of the problems.

The history of the amendment is a long one.[66] If the Constitution, as is evident from even the most cursory reading of it, is relatively mute on the parameters of the Presidency, it is a veritable deaf and dumb stone on the question of the ramifications of the dual problems of succession and disability.

The Founding Fathers, for all their foresight and wisdom, frequently omitted clarifications precisely because they could reach little agreement. The Presidency as a whole was one area of nonagreement, as is evidenced by the ambiguity of Article II.

The Twenty-fifth Amendment's object of clarification (ironically, filling a vacancy in the Vice-Presidency was only a secondary function of the amendment) was the role of the Vice-President during presidential disability. The clause reading "In case of the Removal of the President from Office, or at his Death, Resignation, or Inability to discharge the Powers and Duties of the said Office, the same shall devolve on the Vice President. . . . '' is one of several muddled inclusions by the Framers. In this clause, they have managed to include a variety of states of being that are both temporary and permanent, and therefore have provided the basis for confusion.

Death, removal, and resignation are all one-time events, but not so disability. Yet the Constitution assigns the Vice-President the task of discharging the powers and duties of the office under all of these conditions. From a reading of the records of the Constitutional Convention, it would seem that the Founding Fathers had *intended* the Vice-President merely to *act* as President, but they did not clearly say so. Of even greater importance is the Tyler precedent which interpreted the role of the Vice-President otherwise. (See Chapter 1 for a discussion of this precedent.)[67]

Because of the resulting uncertainty over whether a temporarily disabled President could return to office once recovered,[68] no Vice-President seemed willing to test the question, and during periods of presidential disability the problem lingered. Vice-President Thomas Marshall refused to pick up the constitutionally ambiguous gauntlet of the gap in the Presidency; as a result, the nation endured an absence of leadership while President Woodrow Wilson lay incapacitated.

President Eisenhower himself was well aware of the ambiguities of the Constitution regarding disability, but despite a brief flurry of attention to the question following his three disabilities, it was not until the shock of the Kennedy assassination that the dangers of constitutional ambiguities were again underscored.[69] While Kennedy and Johnson had entered into an informal agreement (as had Eisenhower and Nixon, and later Johnson and Speaker of the House John McCormack) providing that Johnson would *temporarily* assume the Presidency upon presidential disability, that agreement was not a legal or a constitutional document, carrying the legitimizing weight of neither.

Within four years following the Kennedy assassination, the Twenty-fifth Amendment had been formulated and ratified, and the question hanging over the head of the executive branch had been answered. The Vice-President, says the amendment, temporarily assumes the powers and duties of the office during periods of presidential disability. Furthermore, it provides a solution for those potential instances in which a President is unable to, or won't, declare himself temporarily disabled, and here is another area in which the Pandora's box has been opened.

Wanting to keep the determination of presidential disability within the executive branch of government (to keep, for as long as possible, within the basic tenet of the system of separation of powers which guides the Constitution),[70] the authors of the amendment empowered the Vice-President and a majority of the Cabinet to declare a President temporarily disabled, upon which declaration, of course, the Vice-President acts as President, and herein lies the absurdity of this part of the amendment. Is it likely that the beneficiary of a presidential disability would be willing to put himself in the position of being criticized for acting out of self-interest? In addition, would the members of the Cabinet, whose very jobs are tied to the President, be likely to risk inquiring into the President's capability of running the Presidency? A President disabled by a gunshot wound and unable to speak is a clearcut candidate for a determination of disability by the Vice-President and the Cabinet; a President who is suspected of being insane presents an entirely more ambiguous and politically more cautious case. And there are numerous grey areas of disability. One might argue, for example, that Richard Nixon, in losing his "right to govern," as seemed to be indicated by the public opinion polls, was, in a very important way, disabled. Yet there was never any indication that Vice-President Ford or any Nixon Cabinet member was moving to utilize the Twenty-fifth Amendment. In short, under less than glaringly blatant circumstances of presidential (physical) disability, it is unlikely that this part of the amendment will be utilized. Could it not be argued that, in fact, having such a provision is in itself far worse in that the very disuse of it seems to imply a stamp of approval on the state of physical and, more importantly (because less clearcut), mental well-being of a President?

And if a Vice-President and the Cabinet should be willing to explore the question of presidential well-being, what of the potential disagreements a President may have with their findings? What recourse does a recovered President have if his examiners disagree that he is ready to assume his office? The Twenty-fifth Amendment has an answer for this as well. It is at this point, says the amendment, that separation of powers takes a secondary role to a determination. The dispute is sent to Congress, which must decide, by a two-thirds vote, for or against the President and within a period of three weeks. Once again the unknowns of the Pandora's box are set loose, particularly in the form of the overriding questions: What is the state of the nation during the controversy? What is the level of national confidence in a "recovered" President who has barely received his two-thirds vote in Congress? What is the level of national confidence in a Vice-President acting as President because a President has failed by just one vote to be restored to office? Certainly, these are hypothetical situations, but recent American politics has taught us that the hypothetical does occasionally come to pass, and we should be ready for it.

The Ford-Rockefeller Administration was clearly an aberration that departed widely from a basic principle of American government, that is, that the President is elected by and represents all of the people. This is a deviation not to be repeated. If the Twenty-fifth Amendment is to remain an operative part of the Constitution, it should be qualified by a further amendment that will provide for a special national election in the event an *unelected* Vice-President succeeds to the Presidency for a remainder of a presidential term exceeding two years. This would help assure the stability of succession via the Vice-Presidency and minimize the length of time a President by succession (who had not been elected to the Vice-Presidency) would be apt to serve as the only national leader of the United States.

The Twenty-fifth Amendment has little merit; its flaws are obvious in every clause. While it requires immediate reexamination, its defects should not work against the Vice-Presidency.

Arthur Schlesinger, Jr., maintains that the only function of the Vice-Presidency is to provide its incumbents with a jumping ground to the Presidency, or at least presidential nominations. While this is obviously true, what Schlesinger perceives negatively may be viewed alternatively as a slowly evolving solution to the challenging problem of the position of the Vice-Presidency: how to find individuals capable enough to be President who are willing to spend several years in the second office, virtually at the mercy of the President's whim. Precisely because the Vice-Presidency provides a built-in advantage, the office has appealed to individuals of the stature of Hubert Humphrey, Nelson Rockefeller, Walter Mondale, and, most recently, George Bush. What appears superficially to be a negative result, with gains from exposure accruing only to the incumbent, is, in reality, a positive gain from which the national community may benefit. Moreover, politicians who show interest in the Vice-Presidency today are aware that the office has far more public interest and potential than it had a generation ago. Those who come to occupy the second highest office, even though they may never succeed to the Presidency, are much less likely to remain remote political figures than was often characteristic in the past.

Whatever formal changes may be made by constitutional amendment, statutory elaboration, or presidential order, the evolution of the Vice-Presidency will be conditioned by the history of that office and by the actions of its past occupants as well as by the opportunities and challenges which the unfolding of future events will provide. It may be said that such developments as do occur in the foreseeable future will continue to depend in large measure on the person who occupies the Presidency and on what that President is willing to share with and assign to the Vice-President.

THE GROOMING OF THE VICE-PRESIDENT

The dual question of presidential disability and succession implies an even deeper problem in the Vice-Presidency: the events of the past thirty years have emphasized that the Vice-President must be fully prepared to assume the Presidency. The extent of such preparation is vital in considering presidential succession.[71]

The highly inadequate preparation of Vice-President Harry S Truman dramatized the need to insure that no future Vice-President would find himself so ill equipped to assume the highest office in the land. Truman as President was mindful of the important potentialities of being in line of succession and of the need to possess information relative to those potentialities. He and each of his successors have been aware of vice-presidential needs, regardless of the varying roles assigned to them. While preparation in an informational sense is distinct from policymaking and administrative activity, each subsequent Vice-President has been provided with considerable basic knowledge of affairs of state from the start.

Truman began this process of information sharing by having the Vice-President listed as a statutory member of the National Security Council. He also invited his Vice-President, Alben Barkley, to participate in Cabinet meetings.[72] The next Vice-President, Richard M. Nixon, in addition to serving on the National Security Council (NSC), had the opportunity to preside over its meetings during the Eisenhower illnesses.[73] Nixon had been a very active Vice-President, and his incumbency marked a significant turning point in the office. Benefiting from Eisenhower's staff system and his disdain for politics, Nixon soon developed a national and international forum. Nixon similarly was involved in NSC meetings and developed a keen training in foreign affairs, a training that would greatly enhance his political future.

Even in those instances in which the Vice-President had no actual participation in decision-making, he was kept informed of proceedings and developments at home and abroad.[74] Subsequently, Nixon would stress the wealth of information made available to him, along with his intense knowledge of issues and policies, as a precis for his own presidential campaign during which he emphasized that "experience counts."[75]

Eisenhower's illnesses gave Nixon the opportunity to assume greater executive duties. They pointed up the need for a Vice-President who would be ready, if necessary, to take over in an emergency. They also drew attention to the continuing need to resolve the question of what action should be followed in the event of sudden and lingering presidential disability. (The last question was not dealt with until the Kennedy assassination revived it so dramatically.)

During the Constitutional Convention, John Dickinson, a delegate from Delaware, had asked the question, "What is the extent of the term 'disability' and who is to be the judge of it?"[76] The question went unanswered for nearly two centuries. Eisenhower's three illnesses called attention more than ever to the confusing state of the term "disability" and the question of what was to be done in the face of it.

President Eisenhower's views on the office of the Presidency, as well as his application of these views to his own administration, provided the framework for special administration arrangements and applied during the three periods of disability that occurred while he was President. A hallmark of the Eisenhower Administration was its emphasis on staff organization, responsibility, and co-ordination. Eisenhower brought to the White House his years of experience in military life and the chain of command organization. In true military fashion, the White House Chief of Staff became the most important link in the communications chain of the administration, with the top man, the President, communicating all decisions and orders via his Chief of Staff. In this respect, even the nationally elected Vice-President was subordinate to the Chief of Staff.

In the course of the Eisenhower Administration, it became increasingly apparent that the President preferred to delegate authority to a select group of top assistants, in particular Sherman Adams, his Chief of Staff, on the domestic side, and Secretary of State John Foster Dulles on the foreign. Adams and Dulles soon took the two critical centers of responsibility under the President. The "Eisenhower Team" was thus ready to keep the machinery of the Presidency running without its general, if the necessity arose.

When Eisenhower experienced his first heart attack on September 23, 1955, he was quite aware of the dangers inherent in the situation. The President, determined to avoid a repetition of the secrecy that surrounded Wilson's disability, ordered total honesty in reporting his condition.[77] In addition, upon Dulles's suggestion, he agreed to have Sherman Adams reside at Fitzsimmons General Hospital in Denver and directed him to serve as a conduit for crucial matters.[78]

Again, to avoid a repetition of the confusion surrounding the Wilson disability, Eisenhower made it clear that he wanted the Vice-President to chair all meetings of the NSC and the Cabinet and that all heads of departments be kept regularly and fully informed of world affairs.[79] Eisenhower's most important and frequent visitor, aside from family members, was Adams.[80] Adams, remembering those frequent meetings, said that the President

had never given me directions for such an emergency, but then he had never given me many directions of any kind and we had gotten along all right. By that time, after working with Eisenhower for three years, I was able to rely upon a good deal more than instinct in deciding what he wanted done.[81]

Attorney General Herbert Brownell, after consultation with Eisenhower's doctors, had already ruled that the President's illness was not severe enough to warrant a constitutional claim of disability.[82] Moreover, the relative political calm of the moment did not seem to warrant such action.[83] This calm allowed a relatively trouble-free presidential disability. This additional reprieve, while fortunate in assuring the nation, was unfortunate in that it destroyed the momentum for seeking a satisfactory solution to the grave issue of presidential disability.[84] As Adams remarked, "It was only good fortune that carried the government without crisis through that last week of September of 1955,"[85] and the Eisenhower team was well aware of this. Government by "committee" prevailed—a committee consisting of Vice-President Nixon, Dulles, Brownell, George Humphrey, Jerry Persons, and Adams. As Adams himself has noted, however, this group was "well aware that a national or international emergency could have arisen during the President's illness to make this unofficial government by 'community of understanding' entirely inadequate."[86]

Without doubt, the Eisenhower team was in charge. During a period of presidential disabililty, as throughout his incumbency, the President's men are aware of their unique relationship to one man. Their power stems from his power, and it is highly unlikely that they would easily hand over the reins of government to another. As one observer remarked during the Eisenhower disability, "All of the men around Eisenhower did not wish to take any step that could result in giving Mr. Nixon greater authority or even in giving Mr. Nixon the impression that greater authority was soon to be his."[87] Nixon's own reflections in his book *Six Crises* indicate his understanding of the necessities of the moment. "My own position as Vice President," said Nixon, "called for maintaining a balance of the utmost delicacy. . . . Any move on my part which could be interpreted, even incorrectly, as an attempt to usurp powers of the presidency would disrupt the Eisenhower team, cause dissension in the nation, and disturb the President and his family." Such a Vice-President is caught in a dilemma, as Nixon indicated. "My problem was to provide leadership without appearing to lead."[88] Nixon also realized that his position was further affected by the timing of the Eisenhower illness. The Republican National Convention was almost a year away, and speculation already had it that the President would not be a candidate, leaving Nixon as the heir apparent. To be perceived as attempting to seize power during the Eisenhower disability would have cast Nixon in a particularly negative light.

The business of government went on relatively smoothly. Meanwhile, Adams, stationed by the President's side in the Denver hospital where he was recuperating from the attack, served as the "sole official channel of information between Eisenhower and the world outside of his hospital room."[89]

Eisenhower suffered two additional disabilities during his incumbency. However, neither his ileitis operation during June 1956 nor his cerebral occlusion of November 1957, which impaired his speech temporarily, was as severe as the 1955 heart attack.[90]

Following his initial heart attack, Eisenhower worked out an agreement with the Vice-President whereby Nixon, if necessary, could assume the Presidency on a temporary basis until Eisenhower's disability was over. The second and third disabilities were not severe enough to warrant use of the agreement, and again Adams served as "captain of the team resum[ing] his 'caretaker' role" since Attorney General William Rogers had ruled out the necessity for Nixon's temporary succession to the Presidency, inasmuch as the President remained "capable of making emergency decisions."[91] It would seem that Sherman Adams was "the central figure in blocking the rise of Nixon to a position of greater power."[92]

Nixon's active Vice-Presidency, coupled with the President's poor health, continued to emphasize the need to prepare the Vice-President in order never to repeat the Truman experience. And apparently a lesson was learned, for both Lyndon Johnson and Gerald Ford were very well informed Vice-Presidents.

President Ronald Reagan's designation of Vice-President Bush as the head of a special "crisis management" team—prophetically just prior to the assassination attempt on the President in 1981—underscored the President's appreciation of the Vice-President's position. Bush's comportment during the crisis—calm, assured, part of the Reagan "team"—gained him the respect of the White House staff. Although the Twenty-fifth Amendment was not invoked and there was no official declaration of presidential inability, Bush's good working relationship with the President allowed him at least to unofficially assume the reins of government and to serve as the President's stand-in during the crisis. This instance further underlined the importance of the Vice-Presidency, to which this administration, with the oldest elected President in history, had pointed from its outset.

Beginning with the Nixon incumbency, Vice-Presidents have received intensive briefings on vital issues and policies; presidential and vice-presidential *candidates* of both political parties receive similar briefings during the course of the campaign. Both Franklin Roosevelt and Harry Truman had seen the necessity of providing some link and communications with the opposition candidate, and by 1952 Truman, probably remembering his own untimely and unprepared elevation to the Presidency, set a precedent that all future outgoing administrations would follow: an extensive briefing period during the interregnum between election and inauguration.

In conclusion, while the Twenty-fifth Amendment evolved from a gnawing need to bridge a constitutional gap and insures that the United States has a Vice-President to take up the executive reins if the need arises, only the incumbent President can insure that the Vice-President will be ready. While all Vice-Presidents since Truman have been briefed and marked progress has taken place in this area, consideration should be given to the rather casual and flexible method for vice-presidential preparation. A more formal standardization of the critical process of vice-presidential grooming as the heir apparent would be desirable.

NOTES

1. Hubert H. Humphrey, Interview held at the U.S. Senate, Washington, D.C., March 1974.
2. Harry S Truman, *Years of Decisions* (New York: Doubleday, 1955), p. 5.

Frank McNaughton, commenting on Roosevelt's appearance before Congress on March 2, 1945, described at length the marked changes that had taken place in the President.

The President was jovial enough, but one impression struck forcibly on those who chatted with him in the Speaker's office: He wasn't the Roosevelt of two years ago.

When he was wheeled into the chamber, there was a shocked hush for an instant before Congress and the galleries applauded. It seemed unreal, almost fantastic to see Franklin D. Roosevelt rolled into the chamber on a wheel chair. Never before had he uncloaked his infirmity so openly, so frankly, before so many people. . . .

Everybody knew that Roosevelt couldn't walk without steel braces; it was something else to see him wheeled in a chair, admitting his physical disabilities.

The President was dressed in a blue suit that hung slackly on his shoulders. It accentuated a marked loss of weight, and his wrists seemed to have lost their beefy, rugged marks of strength. They were slender, markedly slender. . . . The skin of his face was a good color, but it had one greatly distinguished quality: it seemed to droop in folds along the neck, at the collar line, and from the point of the chin to the Adam's apple it was stretched in a loose thin line that is the mark of advanced age.

The body did not have the buoyancy of yesteryears. When he sat in the chair, his shoulders and body seemed slightly hunched—not markedly but perceptibly. There was a good deal of evidence of strain in the face. . . .

The tremble in the hands—always noticeable over the past years—was plainly accentuated. . . .

His voice was weak; it did not have the pitch and timber of Roosevelt's voice. . . .

The President spoke immediately of the wild rumors concerning his health that had swept Washington. . . . He sought to scotch those rumors, and did a good, witty job by remarking that he had been ill only when he got back to Washington and heard rumors about his health.

But the impression stuck, even as he spoke—this was more than a public appearance on Yalta; it was also to convince Congress that Franklin D. Roosevelt is still a well man, full of faculties and reason, albeit deathly tired and worn.

He was talking through Congress and over it to the millions at fireside radios . . . and he was demonstrating that Roosevelt is still at the throttle in domestic and world affairs.

Frank McNaughton to Don Permingham, March 2, 1945, The Papers of Frank McNaughton, Harry S Truman Library, Independence, Missouri; see also Frank Mc-Naughton, *This Man Truman* (New York: McGraw-Hill, 1945), p. 200.

John Gunther, *Roosevelt in Retrospect* (New York: Harper, 1950) p. 345, wrote:

Age clamped down on him. If one looks at photographs taken month by month it seems that he became white-haired almost overnight. But in some respects nobody could accuse him of losing grip; in fact as he grew older he held the reins of power even more tightly, as if to compensate for fatigue and growing weakness. Nothing was going to budge him from the driver's seat except death. Soon, death did.

Roosevelt's press secretary, Jonathan Daniels, in an oral history interview for the Truman Library, p. 26, has admitted being part of the "protective mechanism" in portraying Roosevelt as healthy and able to carry on his work.

I remember that when the pictures came back from Yalta, the only photographs there were made by the Signals Corps, and all the pictures from Yalta came back to my desk. And I had to select the pictures to be released. Some of them were appalling. I must admit that I picked only those pictures which seemed to me to be the best ones of Franklin Roosevelt. Now I am subject to criticism for that, but I figured that was my duty at the time.

3. Gunther, *Roosevelt in Retrospect*, p. 352.
4. The Papers of Harry Hopkins, Box 95, Unpublished Gallup Poll, July 5, 1944, Franklin D. Roosevelt Library, Hyde Park, New York.
5. Truman, *Years of Decisions*, p. 193.
6. Ibid.
7. Ibid., p. 194.
8. *Time*, April 23, 1945, p. 23.
9. Truman, *Years of Decisions*, p. 19; see also Alben Barkley, *That Reminds Me* (New York: Doubleday, 1954), p. 196ff.
10. Truman, *Years of Decisions*, p. 199.
11. Ibid., p. 14.
12. Ibid., pp. 10–11.
13. Ibid.
14. Ibid., p. 56.
15. Harry H. Vaughan, Oral History Interview, Harry S Truman Library, Independence, Missouri, p. 36.

Roosevelt's negligence of his Vice-President has been recalled by General Vaughan:

Mr. Roosevelt, even though he must have known that his health was not good, probably took the same attitude that Mr. Truman did, just didn't want to think of it—if you don't think about it it won't happen. He had never talked to Mr. Truman a minute on what happened at Teheran, and what happened at Yalta, and what happened at Casablanca, so Truman was not prepared at all. He didn't know of any of the commitments we had made to Russia or to France or to Great Britain, and so . . . all of a sudden he had to do a terrific lot of reading and research.

As Vaughan points out, Truman did precisely that:

He talked to everybody that had been to Yalta; everybody that had been to Teheran and everybody that had been to Casablanca, to any of these conferences; he talked to Mrs. Roosevelt and even talked to Anna Roosevelt, the President's daughter, becuse she had accompanied the President. I'm sure she wasn't in on any of the conferences but he thought that might give him some pointers. It was a terrific job to try to prepare himself because the Potsdam Conference was scheduled. . . . I can recall meetings at the Potsdam Conference when some item would come up and Mr. Churchill said, "Now, Mr. Roosevelt promised me he would do so-and-so." Well, you don't want to doubt Mr. Churchill's word, but Mr. Churchill is a man who is dedicated to do everything possible [sic] in the interests of the British Empire. I'm sure he demonstrated that sufficiently. Mr. Joe Stalin would say, "Now the President Roosevelt [sic] promised that he would. . . . " Everybody within the sound of his voice suspected that it was a lie from start to finish but how could you prove it?

16. Truman, *Years of Decisions*, pp. 54–55.
17. Ibid., p. 53; see also Herman Finer, *The Presidency: Crisis and Regeneration* (Chicago: University of Chicago Press, 1960), p. 210; *New York Times Magazine*, June 24, 1973.
18. *Newsweek*, April 23, 1945, p. 23.
19. Truman, *Years of Decisions*, p. 283.
20. Ibid., p. 257ff.
21. Ibid., pp. 367–68.
22. Ibid., p. 31.
23. Ibid., p. 22.

Truman, intent on forging the sense of tranquility and unity which the country so desperately needed, advanced this effort in another direction and was even willing to soothe the ruffled feathers of Byrnes, who had expected to receive the 1944 vice-presidential nomination. Byrnes was a bitter man; now it was painfully apparent to him that he might have been President of the United States. Truman decided to make a conciliatory gesture, inviting Byrnes back to Washington to help ease the transition as well as to offer him the position of Secretary of State, which Byrnes eagerly accepted.

Jonathan Daniels, *The Man of Independence* (Philadelphia: Lippincott, 1950), pp. 264–65; see also Sidney Shalett, Interviews with Alben Barkley, reel 7, side 2, page 1, Harry S Truman Library, Independence, Missouri; Franklin D. Roosevelt Library, Hyde Park, New York.

24. Daniels, *The Man of Independence*, p. 266.
25. Vaughan, Oral History Interview, p. 40.
26. *New York Times*, April 23, 1945; April 17, 1945.
27. Ibid., May 2, 1945.
28. Truman, *Years of Decisions*, p. 19.

Truman reflected,

I pledged myself to carry out the war and peace policies of Franklin Roosevelt, and I made it clear that I would work for the peace and security of the world. I asked for public support for a strong and lasting United Nations organization. I called upon all Americans to help me keep our nation united in defense of those ideals which had been so eloquently proclaimed by Roosevelt.

I reaffirmed our demand for unconditional surrender and expressed my full confidence in the grand strategy of the United States and our allies. I expressed, as well, my confidence in the ability of Admirals Leahy, King, and Nimitz, and Generals Marshall, Arnold, Eisenhower, and MacArthur to carry out the task assigned to them, and left no doubt that this direction would remain unchanged and unhampered. (Truman, *Years of Decisions*, p. 42.)

Truman appealed to the Congress for its support in this way:

You, the members of Congress, surely know how I feel. Only with your help can I hope to complete one of the greatest tasks ever assigned to a public servant. With divine guidance, and your help, we will find the new passage to a far better world, a kindly and friendly place, with just and lasting peace. (*Public Papers of the Presidents of the United States: Harry S Truman*, April 12 to December 3, 1945, pp. 5–6.)

29. Truman, *Years of Decisions*, pp. 17, 272, 291.

30. Committee for Economic Development, ''Presidential Succession and Inability,'' A Statement on National Policy by the Research and Policy Committee of the CED, January 1965, p. 13; hereafter cited as CED, ''Presidential Succession and Inability.''

31. Speech before a Joint Session of Congress, November 26, 1963.

32. See Marcus Cunliffe, *American Presidents and the Presidency* (New York: McGraw-Hill, 1968, 1972), p. 68, for more on Tyler's succession; Louis Clinton Hatch, *History of the Vice-Presidency of the United States*, revised by Earl L. Shoup (Westport, Conn.: Greenwood Press, 1934, 1970), p. 57ff.

33. Truman, *Years of Decisions*, p. 111.

34. Lyndon B. Johnson, *The Vantage Point* (New York: Holt, Rinehart & Winston, 1971), chap. 2.

35. Hatch, *History of the Vice-Presidency*, p. 413.

36. Johnson, *The Vantage Point*, p. 27.

37. Ibid., p. 15.

38. Louis Heren, *No Hail, No Farewell* (New York: Harper & Row, 1970), p. 16. Truman noted in his memoirs, *Years of Decisions*, p. 87:

From the moment I first sat down in the President's chair I found myself part of an immense administrative operation. There had been a change of executives, but the machinery kept going on in its customary routine manner and properly so. It would have been sheer nonsense to expect anything else.

39. Hubert H. Humphrey, Interview held at a U.S. Senate reception room, March 1974.

40. Gerald R. Ford, Interview conducted at his U.S. Senate office, March 1974.

41. Johnson, *The Vantage Point*, p. 18.

42. Ibid.

43. Ibid., p. 73.

44. Ibid., p. 19.

45. Ibid., p. 95.

46. Tom Wicker, *JFK and LBJ* (New York: Morrow, 1968), p. 195.

47. *Time*, November 12, 1973, p. 37.

48. Ibid.

49. *New York Times*, October 14, 1973, p. 1.

50. Ibid., pp. 1, 4.

51. Ibid., p. 1.

52. *New York Times*, March 10, 1974, p. 51.

53. Ibid.

54. *New York Times*, March 17, 1974, p. 14.

55. Ibid.; Ford, Interview, March 1974.

56. *New York Times*, May 12, 1974, p. 2.

57. As quoted by the *New York Times*, October 14, 1973, p. 1.

58. *Public Papers of the Presidents of the United States*: Gerald R. Ford, August 9, 1974, p. 1.

59. See *Christian Science Monitor*, August 9, 1974, for more on this point.

60. *Boston Globe*, August 9, 1974, p. 49.

61. Boston Globe., August 11, 1974, p. 1ff.

62. *New York Times*, August 11, 1974, p. 1; *Boston Globe*, August 11, 1974.

63. *Boston Globe*, August 11, 1974, p. 16.

64. *Newsweek*, August 19, 1974, p. 25.

65. *New York Times*, August 11, 1974, p. 1; *Boston Globe*, August 11, 1974, p. 17.

66. Birch Bayh, *One Heartbeat Away* (New York: Bobbs-Merrill, 1968) provides a useful discussion of the formulation of the Twenty-fifth Amendment, as does the Report of the Subcommittee on Constitutional Amendments to the Committee on the Judiciary. "Selected Materials on the Twenty-Fifth Amendment." 93d Congress, 1st Session (Washington, D.C.: U.S. Government Printing Office, 1973), hereafter referred to as "Subcommittee Report."

67. "Subcommittee Report," p. 49ff. See also CED, "Presidential Succession and Inability."

68. "Subcommittee Report," p. 51.

69. Dwight D. Eisenhower, *Mandate for Change* (New York: Doubleday, 1963), pp. 545–46. See John C. Kirby, Jr., "A Breakthrough on Presidential Inability: The ABA Conference Consensus," *The Vanderbilt Law Review*, 18, No. 12 (March 1964) p. 47ff. for a discussion of the renewed attention on the issue of disability.

70. See American Bar Association, "Supplemental Report of the Standing Committee on Jurisprudence and Law Reform: Presidential Inability and Succession," 1964, pp. 4ff., 201ff., for a review of presidential–vice-presidential agreements on disability.

71. CED, "Presidential Succession and Inability," p. 13.

72. See also George Reedy's memo to LBJ, March 21, 1963, Re: ABC Program. Vice-Presidential Statements, Box 43, Papers of Lyndon B. Johnson, Lyndon B. Johnson Library, Austin, Texas. See OF 339. 99B, CBS Broadcast, pp. 16–21; Papers of Harry S Truman, Harry S Truman Library, Independence, Missouri. See also "The Vice Presidency," Speech File 63M143, Box XXII, Papers of Alben W. Barkley, University of Kentucky Library, Lexington, Kentucky.

73. CED, "Presidential Succession and Inability," p. 13.

74. "Nixon's Own Story," *U.S. News* 48 (May 16, 1960): 98–106.

75. On this point, see Howard K. Smith, Oral History Interview, Eisenhower Administration Oral History Collection, Columbia University, New York, New York, p. 45, who suggests Eisenhower's possible annoyance that Nixon had been building up what he was doing as Vice-President in order to enhance his position in the presidential campaign. Nevertheless, noted Smith, Nixon did grow in the Vice-Presidency, and "he became a very good travelling ambassador. I followed him through Africa, and I think he did a good job in many respects" (p. 28ff). See also Ralph DeToledano, *One Man Alone: Richard Nixon* (New York: Funk & Wagnalls, 1969), p. 170ff., for material on Nixon's Asian trip as Vice-President.

76. Max Farrand, ed., *The Records of the Federal Convention,* vol. 2 (New Haven: Yale University Press, 1937, 1966), p. 427.

77. See Hansen to Merriman Smith, September 5, 1961, Richard Hansen Microfilms, Harry S Truman Library, Independence, Missouri. Smith apparently noted that Eisenhower's openness with the press was in pointed contrast to the handling of John F. Kennedy's not very serious illness in early 1961. Hansen, in an August 10, 1961, letter to Richard Nixon noted: "Disability is not . . . a series of isolated illnesses or instances,

but actually concerns the whole problem of the president's general health. . . . Legislation should be adopted to insure public disclosure of the president's physical condition during serious illnesses."

78. Eisenhower, *Mandate for Change*, p. 540.

79. Ibid., p. 538.

Regarding the first Cabinet meeting decisions under Vice-President Nixon, Eisenhower (*Mandate for Change*, p. 540) noted:

(1) On actions which Cabinet members would normally take without consulting either the Cabinet or the President, there would be no change in procedure from the normal.

(2) Questions which would normally be brought before the Cabinet for discussion before decision should continue to be discussed there.

(3) *Decisions* which would require consultation with me should go first to the Cabinet or the National Security Council for thorough discussion and possible recommendation and then go to Denver for my consideration.

(4) The proper channel for submission to me of matters requiring presidential decisions should go to General Persons in the White House and then through Governor Adams to me in Denver.

The Vice President had emphasized that any important new administration policies should be set only by me.

See also Roscoe Drummond, Oral History Interview, Eisenhower Administration Oral History Collection, Columbia University, New York, New York, p. 19.

80. Eisenhower, *Mandate for Change*, p. 542.

81. Sherman Adams, *Firsthand Report* (New York: Harper, 1961), p. 181.

82. Herbert Brownell, Oral History Interview, Eisenhower Administration Oral History Collection, Columbia University, New York, New York, p. 241; see also Adams, *Firsthand Report*, p. 181.

83. Eisenhower, *Mandate for Change*, p. 545.

Eisenhower further reflected:

I could not have selected a better time . . . to have a heart attack. . . . The economy was booming, Congress was not in session. I had been able to handle with Foster the major foreign-policy problems, and at the moment there was no new crisis pending in the world. Thus it was not necessary to consult daily with members of the Council of Economic Advisers, or to approve or veto bills passed by the Congress, or to send messages recommending courses to that body. Probably most important was the fact that I was not required to make any immediate operation decisions involving the use of the armed forces of the United States. . . . *However, had a situation arisen such as occurred in 1958 in which I eventually sent troops ashore in Lebanon, the concentration, the weighing of pros and cons, and the final determination would have represented a burden,* during the first week of my illness, which the doctors would likely have found unacceptable for a new cardiac patient to bear. [Italics added]

84. "Presidential Inability Study Raises Problems," *Washington Evening Star*, February 10, 1956.

85. Adams, *Firsthand Report*, p. 192.

86. Ibid., pp. 185–86. See also "A Reminder from Mr. Adams," *St. Louis Post-Dispatch*, May 29–June 24, 1961, Hansen Microfilms, Harry S Truman Library, Independence, Missouri.

87. Richard Rovere, *The Eisenhower Years* (New York: Farrar, Straus & Cudahy, 1956), p. 322.

88. Richard M. Nixon, *Six Crises* (New York: Doubleday, 1962), p. 144.
89. Adams, *Firsthand Report*, p. 186ff.
90. Ibid.
91. Ibid., p. 193.
92. Herbert S. Parmet, *Eisenhower and the American Crusades* (New York: Macmillan, 1972), p. 516.

4

The Vice-President as Heir Apparent

Once there were two brothers. One ran away to sea, the other became Vice President, and nothing was heard of either of them again.

The Vice-Presidency has come a long way since Thomas Marshall, Woodrow Wilson's Vice-President, told that story. A backward glance over the period of the modern Vice-Presidency is testimony to the new position of that office: three Vice-Presidents succeeded to the Presidency, Harry Truman, Lyndon Johnson, and Gerald Ford. Richard Nixon defeated another Vice-President, Hubert Humphrey, for the Presidency. Spiro Agnew and subsequently Gerald Ford were seriously discussed from the outset of their taking office as Vice-President as the potential nominee of the Republican party in the next presidential election. And once it became abundantly clear that the aging Ronald Reagan would be the 1980 Republican presidential nominee, great attention was focused on his choice of a running mate. Indeed, the only Vice-President during the modern Vice-Presidency not to have been a potential presidential candidate was Alben Barkley, and that was only because of his advanced age. Clearly, the modern Vice-President has come to be the heir apparent and the party standard-bearer.

Constitutional change has contributed to this trend. The Twenty-second Amendment, limiting presidential eligibility to two terms, guarantees speculation regarding who will take over.

In addition, as the source of potential occupants of the Presidency has shifted from the governors' mansions to the U.S. Senate, so too, the Senate has become a primary source for the office of the Vice-President. Both U.S. senators and the Vice-President are better versed than incumbents of other offices in what has become the dominant issue since World War II, foreign affairs. Following the unprepared succession of Harry Truman, incumbent Vice-Presidents have been better informed and prepared to assume the Presidency as a result of daily and extensive briefings.

Another force at work has been the expansion of the Presidency itself. As

Presidents since Franklin Roosevelt have experienced increasingly complex problems and relations, there has been a need to delegate responsibilities. Certainly, the greatest manifestation of this change has been the expansion and institutionalization of the presidential staff. The Vice-President, too, has been given additional duties and assignments, notwithstanding the tendency of the President's burgeoning staff to overshadow the Vice-President and shunt him aside from the political mainstream. The image of the Vice-Presidency, together with the political potential accruing to it, has also been enhanced.

Clearly, then, the Vice-Presidency, despite the political pundits' jokes, has become a stepping stone (some have gone to far as to call it a "springboard")[1] to the Presidency. But it can be a stumbling block as well. For while the incumbent Vice-President has advantages over other aspiring presidential candidates, he has great handicaps as well. He may have a maxiumum of four to eight years of an administration's record to defend, a record he might have had very little hand in shaping. If the administration has done exceedingly well, he can, of course, ride on that record. At the same time, he is saddled with explaining the blunders and setbacks that may have occurred. He must simultaneously strike an independent note and not alienate the President under whom he has served. That President still wields power that can help or hurt the heir apparent.

A large part of the incumbent's problems stems from the nominating process itself. Since the vice-presidential candidate is selected with one end in mind— winning the White House—he or she must help unite an extremely heterogeneous party as well as round out the ticket's appeal to a very diversified and complex electorate. The person who manages to do both will be sought after by the presidential nominee. Usually, even if the views of a vice-presidential candidate are within range of those of the presidential candidate, their policy preferences will differ. President Ronald Reagan and Vice-President George Bush represent the most recent example.

In many cases, the "second man" has been seen as a necessary evil, someone to be utilized for the election but later to be ignored or subjugated to the whim of the President and his staff. With the Vice-Presidency becoming more prominent and with individuals of greater reknown occupying the office, many a Vice-President will have been a competitor for the presidential nomination, as indeed was the case with the 1980 Republican vice-presidential nominee, George Bush.

In accepting the vice-presidential nomination, a candidate actually engages in a trade-off: a place in the national arena in exchange for little or no power within that arena. As the Vice-Presidency has steadily become a source from which presidential candidates are nominated, the trade-off has become more appealing to individuals of prominence, and the office has increasingly been sought-after. For some, it involves a diminution of power and prestige, and for others, it is a step upward. Johnson's acceptance of the nomination was a demotion of sorts. On the other hand, for a relatively obscure governor like Spiro Agnew, it was quite a promotion. Other nominees probably fall somewhere in between these two extremes. To speak only of the winners of the vice-presidential office,

Truman's willingness to give up, even if reluctantly, his Senate seat, Barkley's desire for the office at the expense of his position as Majority Leader, Humphrey's quest for it, and Nixon's rapid rise to it, all indicate the increasing desirability of the office.[2] Others have sought the nomination and lost, such as James Byrnes, John Kennedy, Eugene McCarthy, Robert Kennedy, and Endicott Peabody. Clearly, then, there has been a higher regard for the office since World War II, especially its ability to place its incumbents within an arm's length of the presidential nomination.

Truman, having succeeded to the Presidency upon the death of FDR, was renominated despite his unpopularity. His Vice-President, Barkley, although handicapped and "disqualified" by age, was the subject of serious speculation for the 1952 presidential nomination once Truman had taken himself out of the running. Barkley had hardly received more than a lukewarm nod from the White House, but the speculation regarding his status as successor was present nonetheless.[3] Since Barkley was not a presidential candidate, it is justifiable to limit this discussion of his short-lived attempt at the nomination. Because the primary concern here is with the Vice-President's liabilities and assets as party standard-bearer, the focus will be on Nixon's 1960 and Humphrey's 1968 presidential bids, as well as on two of the more recent Vice-Presidents, Gerald Ford and Spiro Agnew, who were early labeled "heirs apparent."

RICHARD M. NIXON: PARTY STANDARD-BEARER, 1960

As a result of the Twenty-second Amendment, Dwight Eisenhower was ineligible to serve a third term. With a "lame duck" President in office, there was speculation regarding a successor throughout his entire second term, and Eisenhower's young, energetic, and politically minded Vice-President was an obvious possibility.

The President plays an important part in the incumbent Vice-President's nomination quest. On the one hand, the President, whether he is ineligible to run or has taken himself out of the running, is party leader; on the other, his Vice-President is the party standard-bearer. The President has all the resources of the office at his disposal; his Vice-President has none. An incumbent President can be, and usually is, influential in the election of his successor.

Recent developments, however, have given the Vice-President an edge toward the nomination, with or without the President's help. As early as March 1958, poll results indicated that Nixon was the Republicans' favored nominee for 1960,[4] and soon he became the "obvious nominee."[5] Thus, while Eisenhower did not overwhelmingly endorse Nixon for the 1960 presidential nomination, the Vice-President, as a result of his performance in a party capacity, had built up a considerable cache of political IOUs. For example, as early as the New Year of 1960, Nelson Rockefeller had indicated his feeling that Nixon would undoubtedly be nominated as the 1960 Republican presidential candidate.[6] And Barry Goldwater, in March and April 1959, had come out in support of Nixon as a "legitimate conservative," worthy of Southern support for the Presidency.[7]

Eisenhower, however, was not convinced that Nixon was presidential timber. He would have much preferred someone like Treasury Secretary Robert Anderson as his successor.[8] The President circumvented the Nixon candidacy by stating in a press conference during the spring of 1960 that the selection of a successor was the business of the Republican party and that he himself had "no responsibility for trying to groom my successor."[9]

Following Nixon's early January statement in which he threw his hat in the ring for the presidential nomination and indicated his intention of participating in all of the primaries, Eisenhower still said almost nothing. As a matter of fact, what he did say was more embarrassing to Nixon than if he had said nothing at all, especially when the President indicated, in a January 24 press conference, that there were "half a dozen, or ten, or maybe a dozen fine, virile men in the Republican Party that I would gladly support." It was not until March that Eisenhower gave Nixon a lukewarm endorsement.[10]

The more duties assigned to Nixon and the more public attention he received, the greater the enhancement of his claim to be heir to the throne, especially because of his extensive preparation in national affairs. To a large extent, it might be said that ultimately there was little else that Eisenhower could do. Ironically, it was the President himself who had done the most to bolster Nixon's position, which slowly but steadily gained in prestige.

Eisenhower's delegation of political chores[11] held another irony—and this one with negative effects on Nixon's fate. Because Eisenhower was so apolitical, because he had so little interest in or real knowledge of politics, Nixon had been able to build an "empire" of sorts for himself. He had been able to go out and play party politics to its utmost. He was "the Republican Party's most energetic campaigner during the previous eight years,"[12] thereby slowly building his strength. The irony is that Eisenhower's apolitical nature also led him to give only minimal support to the Republican party and thus to fail to transfer his own popularity to it. There has been considerable conjecture that Nixon might have won the 1960 presidential election had he had a strong party behind him.[13]

While Eisenhower did not particularly want Nixon for the 1960 nomination, he did not openly oppose him either. Nonetheless, the President was troubled by the question of political succession in the Republican party. He regretted his inability to convince Nixon to leave the Vice-Presidency after his first term, and apparently he tried to deny the inevitability of Nixon's nomination as the party standard-bearer.[14] The President's early reluctance regarding a potential Nixon nomination became the Vice-President's principal handicap, and it appears that Eisenhower eventually threw his support to Nixon only when no alternative emerged. Eisenhower took no particular role in the convention and was merely advised of the "master plan" which Nixon and his aides laid out for the campaign.[15]

If Nixon had a central approach in his attempt to capture the Presidency in

1960, it was his emphasis on experience.[16] He had enjoyed a rapid rise in his political life, with only four years of experience in the House of Representatives and two years in the Senate before achieving the Vice-Presidency, a period shorter than his two-term tenure as Vice-President. Despite his relatively young age, he could present an image of experience and stress his superior knowledge over his opponent. John Kennedy had come to the national legislature in the very same year Nixon had, 1946; their length of governmental service was equivalent. But Nixon could and did boast of executive experience, which Kennedy could not.

Nixon had headed two intergovernmental bodies: the President's Committee on Government Contracts and the Cabinet Committee on Price Stability for Economic Growth. He stressed both appointments during the campaign to strengthen his position on the civil rights issue.[17] He had also built up an impressive record in foreign affairs: he was Eisenhower's good-will ambassador to some fifty-five countries, including South America in 1958, a trip that brought him far-reaching publicity and sympathy, especially since his life had been endangered there.[18]

As one Eisenhower Administration official put it, Nixon was as Vice-President "mentally grooming himself for the Presidency."[19] His campaign against Kennedy highlighted an "Experience Counts" slogan, on the basis of his own record and that of his vice-presidential running mate, Ambassador Henry Cabot Lodge.

Given Nixon's record, it would seem that a single event or unwanted remark would not likely damage his position. But in the strange game of presidential campaigning, such an event did occur. President Eisenhower, the man who had allowed Nixon to build his record, was the cause of it. A simple off-the-cuff remark by the President at a press conference on August 24, 1960, served challenger Kennedy well. In response to the request "to give us an example of a major idea of his (Nixon's) that you adopted. . . . "the President answered "If you give me a week, I might think of one."[20]

The Nixon camp "damn near fainted, at the thought of such cavalier treatment."[21] Understandably, the opposition immediately seized on the comment. Most observers claim that the statement was not made with any malice on Eisenhower's part, but that it was his way of bringing the press conference to a close.[22] Eisenhower's comment was, one observer noted, "blown all out of proportion, and almost looked as though the President was demeaning any contribution Nixon had made in foreign policy."[23] Nonetheless, the idea that Eisenhower was striking at Nixon endured. One interpretation suggests that the President was irked that Nixon was giving the impression that the President could not make decisions without his Vice-President's assistance; the press conference statement was thus a way of striking back and humiliating Nixon.[24]

With or without the "give me a week" statement, Nixon was in a precarious position. On the one hand, he could point to his experience and knowledgeability, especially in foreign affairs. On the other, he had to prove he was not constantly in the shadow of the popular Eisenhower; that he had not been, and was not now, planning to ride on the President's lengthy coattails. He had to prove he was his own man.

While Nixon entered the presidential debates "because he was convinced he could win" and apparently never considered declining to participate, Kennedy managed to use the debates to counteract Nixon's major resource of experience.[25] Perhaps Nixon's previous year's "success" in the "Kitchen Debate" with Khrushchev had reinforced his belief that he could deal similarly with Kennedy. Eisenhower presidential adviser Emmet John Hughes has maintained that Nixon was undone primarily by his readiness to debate on television, for the debates erased the notion of the Vice-President's superiority and maturity.[26] Before millions of television viewers, Kennedy was placed on an equal footing. Nixon himself admitted understanding that "the incumbent or whoever represents an incumbent Administration—will generally be at a disadvantage in debate because his opponent can attack while he must defend."[27]

Although the Vice-President's position was not the volatile one that would plague Hubert Humphrey eight years later, he nonetheless had to deal with a number of events that reflected poorly on the Eisenhower Administration. The U-2 spying incident,[28] the debacle of the Paris summit and Eisenhower's subsequent embarrassment at the hands of Nikita Khrushchev,[29] the advent of a recession as the campaign approached,[30] and an apparent missile gap in relation to the Russians[31]—all had damaging effects on Nixon's campaign.

Nixon soon found himself in the unenviable defensive position.[32] Saddled with the mistakes of the Eisenhower Administration as well as its merits, he had to proceed cautiously, unable to assume the accusing stance of past campaigns. Kennedy could attack all he wanted and Nixon had to respond.[33] The Democrats, aware of the unfavorable position Nixon was in, took every opportunity to refer pointedly to the mistakes not of the Eisenhower Administration but of the *Eisenhower-Nixon* Administration.[34]

While Kennedy could run on a "Let's get the country moving again" theme,[35] Nixon had to protest that it *had* been moving under Eisenhower, whether or not he had entirely agreed with the President's policies. The Vice-President attempted to defend the administration, in part, by transferring the blame to Congress. "Putting it bluntly," Nixon said, "there has been a political stalemate between the Administration and Congress over the past five years."[36] As one observer noted, "Kennedy was the challenger, the aggressor—everything to win and nothing to lose, really. Nixon had to fight a sort of *status quo* battle."[37] Nixon, as would Hubert Humphrey years later, struggled with the dilemma imposed by his split identity, for the quest for the Presidency required the demonstration of a forceful single identity.

A more subtle complication for the incumbent Vice-President seeking election to the Presidency is that he is usually privy to more information than his opponent. This distinction has been steadily fading, as more recent Presidents have provided comprehensive briefings for all serious contenders for the nomination and then for the two presidential candidates themselves. But this was a very real problem for Nixon in 1960, especially within one area.

One of Kennedy's prime targets concerned the administration's policy toward Cuba. Kennedy, in taking the offensive, had begun with a general criticism of the Eisenhower-Nixon Administration for its seemingly lax stand on Castro. He ultimately became more specific and focused his criticism on the administration's lack of fortification for Cuban counterrevolutionaries.[38]

What Kennedy did not know was that a covert operation was under way. Nixon, aware of what was taking place, could do nothing lest he endanger the administration's efforts.[39]

Nixon's attempt to maintain his positive identity with Eisenhower while establishing his independence was complicated by the President himself,[40] who was very sensitive to criticism of his record.[41] Eisenhower expected, therefore, that the campaign would be run as a defense of that record. As early as March 1958, he had indicated he would refuse to support any candidates in 1960 "who failed to share his own views on the 'big issues.' "[42] As the presidential campaign got under way, the President's concern, as well as that of his staff, was to safeguard the Eisenhower record.[43]

Eisenhower did virtually nothing on Nixon's behalf throughout the major part of the campaign,[44] and when his help was requested, and came, during those last days of the campaign, it was too late.

With regard to Eisenhower's direct involvement, or lack of it, in the campaign, the picture is blurred. Only when the polls indicated that Nixon was losing did he turn to Eisenhower for help. He had probably not sought that help earlier because he felt it necessary to demonstrate an independent identity.[45] Nixon's purpose, noted Donald Paarlberg, a member of the Eisenhower Administration, was "to carry his own banner, to prove he could do it on his own."[46] Nixon wanted to make it on his own, with everyone else in supporting roles, noted another.[47] As Robert Finch observed:

I think it's fair to say that was quite a natural desire for Nixon to prove that he could do it on his own. He's been constantly subjected to the criticism that he had been sort of carried in by Eisenhower, in both the '52 and '56 elections.[48]

Nixon's solution to the dilemma—to establish his own identity—ultimately contributed to his defeat. He neglected the President as a potent political figure in his own right, and so the critical element in the development of the Nixon Vice-Presidency, Eisenhower's apolitical nature, worked against Nixon in the 1960 campaign.

HUBERT H. HUMPHREY: PARTY STANDARD-BEARER, 1968

The incumbent Vice-President not only cannot take the offensive, but is also handicapped by an inability to rally the resources available to an incumbent

President seeking reelection—the powers and prestige of the Presidency itself. Such a person is in the same position he has often been in during his Vice-Presidency: he continues to be subject to the President's whims.

Few Vice-Presidents have been in as awkward a position as was Vice-President Humphrey during the campaign of 1968. He had been involved in decision-making concerning the issue that was tearing the administration apart, the war in Southeast Asia, and had agreed with the administration. But both his involvement and agreement had been limited. Although he had served as the administration's spokesman, he had many moments of private disagreement.[49] In the mind of the electorate, these varying degrees of involvement and agreement blurred, and Humphrey seemed to be nothing more than a stand-in, a puppet, for the dominating figure of Lyndon Johnson. In this regard, Humphrey's personality played a critical role. He was, as former Secretary of State Dean Rusk once remarked, "a loyal fellow";[50] "an extremely loyal man," said former Johnson aide Walter Jenkins;[51] "loyal to a fault," observed former Kennedy aide Kenneth O'Donnell.[52]

Hubert Humphrey understood the uniqueness of the vice-presidential office. He also understood what Lyndon Johnson wanted in a Vice-President, and Johnson knew he could count on Humphrey to serve him loyally. In offering the nomination to Humphrey in 1964, the President had stressed the importance of loyalty, and Humphrey kept his promise. Despite some private disagreement, in public he was a solid Johnson man. Under normal conditions, this association might have proven immeasurably beneficial; under the conditions of 1968 America, it was a disaster. One of Humphrey's major functions as vice-president, the defense and explanation of administration policy in Vietnam, contributed to his downfall in the 1968 presidential campaign.

Humphrey had bound up his fate with that of Lyndon Johnson; he was aware of the potential disaster of Vietnam, but he had had to make a choice. Johnson, he had decided, would make him or break him. Everything Humphrey had accomplished in his years of national service was somehow linked to Johnson. "Humphrey is always aware of the political umbilical cord linking his fortunes with those of Lyndon Johnson," remarked one observer.[53] Humphrey himself noted his indebtedness to Johnson.

I became Vice President because he made me Vice President. . . . I became Whip because he made me Whip. As a matter of fact, I've had a helping hand from Lyndon Johnson from the beginning. I remember him saying to me, "Hubert, you should get better acquainted with more Senators," and we'd have lunch with Walter George or Dick Russell, or someone like that, in the private dining room.[54]

It was Senator Johnson who had placed Humphrey on the very important Foreign Relations Committee, as well as on the Agriculture Committee,[55] two assignments Humphrey had coveted. When the possibility of the vice-presidential nomination was presented to him, Humphrey yearned and vowed to serve Johnson loyally.[56] As he became increasingly involved in the Johnson Administration, Humphrey, formerly the darling of the liberal community, became identified as the one who had "sold out" all he believed in to become Johnson's "hatchet man."[57]

Humphrey, knowing that his greatest chance of being President rested in his relationship with LBJ, had compromised himself so that he could remain on Johnson's 1968 ticket. Ironically, when Johnson chose not to run in 1968, Humphrey's chance at the Presidency came even sooner than he had anticipated, but his past compromises, particularly his backing of Johnson on Vietnam, hurt his campaign.

In 1968, Humphrey had to defend an unpopular administration's record; he also suffered from an identity problem. His association and identification with Lyndon Johnson had become so fused that for all intents and purposes he *was* Lyndon Johnson.[58] His presidential campaign was a futile effort to sever that identification, to forge his own identity.

Humphrey himself, in a meeting with newsmen during the campaign, stated his basic problems: "My most serious dilemma, the thing that is at the core of our whole campaign is how on the one hand do you chart an independent course and yet at the same time not repudiate the course of which you've been a part." And then he stated the essence of the dilemma confronting any Vice-President:

I don't think any vice president is going to be able to fundamentally alter the policy of this country between now and January 20. Our advice and counsel may be sought, but *we are not in charge, any of us*. Comes January 20, high noon, 12:00 a.m. in the afternoon, then I will be in charge. And I will set the policy. And I will determine what we are going to do about our foreign relations and our national security, including Vietnam. And I have some rather strong ideas about it.[59]

As Richard Scammon and Ben Wattenberg have pointed out, the "I'm displeased" feeling prevalent in 1968 America became an anti-Johnson and ultimately an anti-Humphrey feeling.[60] An "era of bad feeling" had set in, and Johnson and all those associated with him personified it.

Humphrey's problem was similar to Nixon's in 1960, but with a different twist. Whereas Nixon had to maintain his identification with the popular Eisenhower while showing that he was ready to win and take over the Presidency on his own, Humphrey had to avoid identification with Johnson.

During the campaign, Humphrey attempted to play down his association with the President. For example, he emphasized his independent choice of Maine Senator Edmund Muskie as a running mate. In focusing attention as a contrast to Nixon's choice of Spiro Agnew, the strategy was to play up the Humphrey-Muskie team and to divert attention from the negatively perceived Johnson-Humphrey team. So, for example, Muskie was given wide coverage in a television program that associated him with famous fellow Democrats, with Lyndon Johnson conspicuous by exclusion.[61] Indeed, it sometimes appeared that focusing attention away from the Johnson Administration and on Muskie was the only way out for Humphrey.

Muskie, then, emerged as one of Humphrey's strongest assets. He handled himself well with demonstrators and hecklers; he was liked by the press; above all, Muskie had no opposition.[62] He was an even more potent asset because he represented a stark contrast to Nixon's running mate. Spiro Agnew rapidly emerged as a political incompetent. Among some of his numerous faux pas of the campaign were his references to "Polacks," his calling one Japanese-American newsman a "fat Jap," and his claim that "if you've seen one slum, you've seen them all."[63]

Humphrey was stifled in his endeavor to establish his own identity, limited by his own view of the Vice-Presidency and its relationship to the Presidency, boxed in by his own determination to keep his word. The result was a sort of "hedginess"—a flirting with—an independent posture. Humphrey defended Lyndon Johnson's domestic policies but ignored Vietnam.[64] He announced Muskie as his running mate, despite Johnson's preference for a candidate further to the right, such as Governor John Connally of Texas, and he made it clear that President Johnson was "informed of his choice of Muskie."[65] Humphrey's hedginess was characteristic of his remarks in the wake of the wreck of the Democratic National Convention in Chicago. "The policies of tomorrow need not be limited by the policies of yesterday,"[66] said Humphrey. At the same time, he was obliged to support and run on the strong Vietnam plank adopted by the convention.[67] This was the only course possible for a man who had gone along with administration policy in that area and had to operate in the ominous shadow of Lyndon Johnson. Johnson was a master at cajoling, persuading, convincing, and intimidating. He had had years of practice at getting what he wanted. And in 1968, as he had during his entire incumbency, he wanted loyalty from Hubert Humphrey. Johnson seemed to be calling the shots; the nomination had been literally dangled before Humphrey, even though Johnson had seemingly kept his neutrality.[68] If Humphrey was to gain the nomination, it would be with Johnson's help, if not entirely Johnson's doing.[69]

Despite the fact that he was the front runner for the nomination and the incumbent Vice-President, Humphrey reportedly had little control over convention decisions. For example, although he had wanted the convention held in Miami, the President insisted on and got Chicago. When Humphrey asked Chicago Mayor Richard Daley for a special hall for demonstrators, it was to no avail; he did not even receive a reply. Reportedly, Humphrey even had difficulty getting tickets for the convention.[70] Johnson might not have been running for the Presidency, but he certainly planned to control who would. In fact, he had insisted that the 1968 Democratic presidential nominee be, above all, someone who had followed and would continue to follow the White House line on the sensitive issue of Vietnam.[71]

Incumbent Presidents have a vested interest in the continued support of their policies, and it is understandable that they will use the powers of their office to insure that end. Eisenhower had insisted on that in 1960; now it was Johnson's turn. But Johnson's position and his ability to command obedience were far different from what Eisenhower's had been. Both men had the perquisites of the office at their disposal; both had records about which they were sensitive. In sharp contrast, however, as President, Johnson had enjoyed both the heights and the depths of public opinion. A candidate running on a strong White House line in 1968 would not repudiate the Johnson Administration. Once Humphrey won the nomination, the Cabinet and White House staff began to join the campaign, further defending the Johnson record. Johnson was determined to control to the end.

Humphrey was in a peculiar position. He was the heir apparent to a President who could conceivably change his mind and seek reelection. Humphrey's only alternative, if he was to win the nomination, was to ride with Johnson, and it was the Johnson delegates who gave Humphrey the nomination.[72]

Having won the nomination, Humphrey began to engage in a battle that would bring many moments of doubt and hesitation. Johnson had helped him win the nomination, but would he lose the Presidency out of loyalty to Johnson? Was there any balance that could be struck that would establish Humphrey as an independent candidate and at the same time not alienate the man who was responsible for his being there and who still commanded vast resources?

Some of Humphrey's advisers, fearing the disastrous effects of overidentification with and defense of Lyndon Johnson, had recommended the most clearcut method of severing ties: Humphrey would have to resign from the Vice-Presidency.[73] Although he knew he had to extricate himself from the unpopular administration, resignation was not the answer for Humphrey; he had a contract with the American people, he said, and it would not do to break that contract.[74] Besides, doing so might have cost him more in the long run.[75] The President still wielded tremendous power.

And so he struggled through the campaign, attempting to concentrate on the administration's domestic achievements and to play down the debacle of Vietnam. His opponent was the benefactor of the dilemma. It has often been said that the Democratic party's most effective unifying device is Richard Nixon; in 1968, the Democratic party was Richard Nixon's strongest resource. Unlike his position in 1960, Nixon could return to the campaign position with which he was most comfortable—the offensive—and Humphrey was the disadvantaged opponent.

Aware of the sentiment of disgust throughout the country and a general sense of dissatisfaction, Nixon employed his strategy. His strength, wrote Scammon and Wattenberg, was that "he was *not* Humphrey, and didn't have anything to do with anything that people were angry about."[76]

Nixon had little to say about Vietnam. The adoption of a strong Democratic party Vietnam plank (Hubert Humphrey would have preferred a more dovish one which would have enabled him to engage in a smoother break from Johnson) forced the Vice-President into a position of defending the record. Moreover,

Humphrey avoided bringing the issue into the campaign; he knew it could only hurt him. Nixon was able to get a free ride on the most volatile issue of the year and perhaps the generation.

Nixon, with a united Republican party behind him, attacked the Democratic record on all its vulnerable points. Vietnam, law and order, big spending, and the "security gap," an issue through which John Kennedy, at the turn of the decade, had put Nixon on the defensive.[77]

As the challenger, especially of an unpopular administration, Nixon had a flexibility Humphrey would have relished. As one Nixon aide put it, "Nixon was locked in in 1960. He was a member of Ike's team and Ike was a popular President, so he had to go along. Now he's freer."[78] Moreover, Nixon was the beneficiary of the "Social Issues" that pervaded the environment, as Scammon and Wattenberg explain.

On the Social Issues that disturbed the nation—crime, race, student disorders, among others—the Republicans were perceived as somewhat "tougher" than the Democrats, somewhat more in tune with the attitudes of the electorate. . . . The feelings that Nixon capitalized upon were not part of a Southern strategy or a Border strategy—they were part of a national strategy that was attuned to the national malaise.[79]

Circumstances were working against Humphrey. Not only did he have to defend the record; he was also a Democrat at a time when Democrats were identified as being out of harmony with the issues outraging the electorate.

Humphrey's position, especially on law and order, had been worsened as a result of the turmoil at the Chicago Convention, the assassinations of Robert Kennedy and of Martin Luther King, Jr., and the resulting riots. The year 1968 was a violent year in American politics, and America was weary of violence— violence 6,000 miles away and violence around the corner.

As Humphrey's position in the polls grew increasingly worse, it became obvious that he had to break or seem to break with Lyndon Johnson.[80]

Humphrey's September 30 speech in Salt Lake City represented the sharpest break from the Johnson Vietnam policy in the campaign and a marked deviation from his past policy of not disagreeing with the President in public.[81] It was an ambiguous speech at best, as had been all his attempts to establish an independent posture. Although Humphrey claims the speech "liberated him internally,"[82] it failed to extricate him from his association with the administration's record or position on Vietnam.

Symbolically, Humphrey spoke from a lectern that bore no vice-presidential seal; he was not even introduced as the Vice-President, and he began his speech by declaring, "Tonight I want to share with you my thoughts as a citizen and a candidate for President of the United States."[83] Throughout his speech, he remained not Hubert H. Humphrey, Vice-President of the United States under Lyndon B. Johnson, but Hubert H. Humphrey, presidential candidate.

Humphrey's Salt Lake City speech is remarkable for its indication of the dilemma he was in. Although his advisers wanted him to openly declare his independence from the President, he realized he could not say anything that would jeopardize the President in the peace negotiations. He could, however, say what he would do as President. At the outset of the speech, he stated his pledge on the Vietnam War. There followed an assertion of his involvement in decision-making, but the indication was that Johnson, and not Humphrey, made the decisions. To avoid alienating Johnson, however, Humphrey added that "the choices have not been simple or easy." Then he reemphasized that Johnson's Vietnam policy belonged to Johnson and that the "President . . . will continue—until January 20, 1969—to make the decisions in Vietnam." The implication was that if Humphrey were President, things would be different; a Humphrey Administration would not be the Johnson Administration revisited. "The policies of tomorrow need not be limited by the policies of yesterday," voiced Humphrey. And then Humphrey returned to an appeasement of Johnson. "Neither vindication nor repudiation of our role in Vietnam will bring peace or be worthy of our country." Then he made another attempt to extricate the entire administration from bearing the full brunt of the war, and he cited the role played by the Eisenhower and Kennedy administrations in the development of the conflict. Having made clear, even if apologetically, that the policies of Johnson, Kennedy, and Eisenhower were *their* policies, Humphrey noted his opponent's link with past Vietnam decisions; he then set out to draw an identity of his own on Vietnam. This identity was designed to solicit support from the hawks as well as the doves and all those falling somewhere in between.[84]

Johnson was livid. Humphrey, who had consulted with the President on several occasions during the preparation of the speech, had "waited until the last minute, when the text of the speech was already in the hands of the reporters."[85] Johnson apparently had been reassured that there was nothing detrimental in the speech; nonetheless, the President reportedly warned his Vice-President: "Hubert, you give that speech and you'll be screwed."[86]

Humphrey, who had defended the Johnson policy almost to the death, had wavered. He had tried to hedge his bets, but he suffered the consequences of playing both ends against the middle; in the end, he satisfied neither.

Johnson's involvement in the campaign itself was rather mixed. On the one hand, he had considerable powers at his disposal. The entire thrust of the campaign could change in a moment depending on what Johnson decided to do, especially regarding the Vietnam bombing. For a "lame duck" President, he wielded tremendous potential authority. It was Johnson who had the power to halt the bombing of North Vietnam; it was he who had the power to enliven the Paris peace talks.[87] Humphrey's political fate was irrefutably linked to a man who was intransigent on Vietnam and who demanded loyalty. The combination was both compelling and frustrating.

Johnson was committed to do something about Vietnam and to vindicate himself. It is not possible to separate domestic from foreign politics, especially in an election year. What Hubert Humphrey was trying to achieve as a candidate in 1968 was not always compatible with what Lyndon Johnson was trying to achieve as President.[88]

Following Humphrey's Salt Lake City speech, Nixon, who had been quietly riding out the issue of Vietnam on the Vice-President's dilemma, snapped into position. Nixon denounced Humphrey for "undercutting the United States position in Paris." Referring to the proposed bombing halt, Nixon hoped "Vice President Humphrey would clarify his position and not pull the rug out from under the negotiators and take away the trump card the negotiators have."[89]

Later in the campaign, when Nixon suspected that President Johnson might just pull a bombing halt out of his hat to aid Humphrey, he made a clever effort to head it off. Nixon offered his support to Johnson, should the President decide on a bombing halt to save American lives and bring peace. "The one man who makes the determination," said Nixon, "is the President of the United States. Let's let him make that determination, and if he makes it, we will support him because we want peace, and we do not want to play politics with peace."[90] Nixon killed two birds with one stone. He both anticipated Johnson's potential move, and he set up the conditions under which he would approve the bombing halt.

To further undercut the possibility of a bombing halt, Nixon rose to the President's defense in refutation of the rumor of a bombing halt, using it to his best advantage to stab at Humphrey as well.

I am . . . told that this spurt of activity (meetings in the White House) is a cynical, last-minute attempt by President Johnson to salvage the candidacy of Mr. Humphrey. This I do not believe. . . . At no time in the campaign have I found the President anything but impartial and candid in his dealings with the major Presidential contenders about Vietnam. I know this has not been easy for him. Beginning long before the Republican Convention in early August, influential elements within and outside his party have subjected him to intense pressure to contrive what he has aptly described as a "fake peace." It is to his credit that he has withstood these pressures. . . .

In foreign affairs the President must be our nation's only spokesman. The Paris negotiations are critically important and exceedingly delicate. At such a time I believe every presidential candidate should mind his tongue to avoid weakening our diplomatic hand by irresponsible comments on the matters at issue. This has been my position throughout the campaign.[91]

Nixon both struck at Humphrey, whose reputation for not knowing when to keep silent was proverbial, and justified his own lack of a Vietnam position. Nixon used this same stance on CBS's *Face the Nation*: "I think we ought to be consistent on this and I think President Johnson has been consistent. I've been consistent. Mr. Humphrey ought to get in line, agree with his President for a change."[92]

Humphrey had been damned for agreeing, and now he was damned for disagreeing. It seemed impossible for him to win. He was locked in by even more confining circumstances than Nixon had been in 1960. The year 1968 was an unparalleled year in American politics, and Humphrey was its prime victim. Vietnam, ghetto riots, assassinations, all created a tense atmosphere fraught with impending eruption; all this was well before Humphrey went to Mayor Daley's Chicago, the city Johnson had thought would be safe for the Democratic Convention.

Vice-President, heir to the presidential throne following Robert Kennedy's death and the short-lived Jesse Unruh-Richard Daley movement to draft Senator Edward M. Kennedy,[93] Humphrey came out of the Chicago Convention at about the same level at which he went in, which is a calamitous situation for any presidential candidate. Kennedy's death, while it virtually assured Humphrey the nomination, implicitly held other consequences for the Vice-President. The assassination of the second Kennedy brother, just sixty days after that of civil rights leader Martin Luther King, Jr., was in large measure "a mental breakdown for the American political community."[94] A nation stunned by the events of a year only half over wondered what would come next. Humphrey's problem was to make certain that the nomination he got by default was worth having.

The traumatic events of the Chicago Convention further diminished Humphrey's possibilities of winning the election. Millions of Americans watched on nationwide television as police, national guardsmen, and demonstrators clashed on the Chicago streets, while divided Democrats clashed on the convention floor. As a candidate associated with an administration immutably tied to the violence of Vietnam, Humphrey's nomination was a hollow victory. While "law and order" was emerging as the principal issue of the campaign and the third-party candidacy of Governor George Wallace served to alter the strategy and positions of both major party candidates,[95] law and order broke down for the Democratic party on the streets of Chicago.

The war and the bitter dissent and violence hurt Humphrey in a double way. Because of the turmoil during and following the Chicago Convention, the Democratic party, which had been identified as soft on the social issues, was further identified as contributing to the crisis ravaging America. This did irreparable damage to the Humphrey candidacy.[96] Not only was Humphrey's liberalism compromised by his identification with President Johnson and his administration; the law and order issues also made him fearful of being branded a racist. Of all the candidates in 1968, Nixon appeared to be most closely identified with the center in his enormous appeal to "Middle America."[97] Forced to take a stand but wanting to avoid the racist overtones associated with "law and order," the Democratic party chose to use the phrase "justice and law" in its plank, which declared, "In fighting crime we must not foster injustice. Lawlessness cannot be ended by curtailing the hard-won liberties of all Americans."[98]

Humphrey was plagued by dissension within his party. The President's withdrawal from the race was symptomatic of the deep division within the party. Although Johnson claimed to have made his decision a year before, it is more likely that the challenge by Eugene McCarthy contributed in no small measure to the President's announcement on March 31 that he would not run for reelection.[99]

On March 12, the man who had not been taken very seriously almost won the New Hampshire primary, jeopardizing the President's renomination. Eugene McCarthy's strong showing prompted a heretofore reluctant and cautious Robert Kennedy to throw his hat into the presidential ring as well,[100] and the stage was set for a confrontation between the challengers. In a wider sense, the confrontation was between the Old Politics (represented by the administration and Hubert Humphrey) and the New Politics (represented by McCarthy and Kennedy).[101] Humphrey, as Johnson's political heir, had the unpleasant and disadvantageous task of defending an unpopular administration in not just one forum, but two— one within his own party and one with the "out party." If Lyndon Johnson's nomination had been in doubt, this feeling was transferred to his Vice-President. If Johnson was, as one observer referred to him, the "Anti-Christ of the New Politics,"[102] Humphrey's problem was that he was guilty by association. It is small wonder that Humphrey did not believe he could win the election.

Following his victory in the nomination battle, Humphrey was left with the tattered remains of a party. Only four years earlier, following the debacle of the Goldwater defeat at the hands of the Johnson-Humphrey ticket, it was wondered whether the Republican party could ever pull itself together again. Now, the Republican party was united behind its candidate, Richard Milhous Nixon, who was eager to enter combat with the shreds of its opposition. Robert Kennedy was dead; Eugene McCarthy was embittered; Hubert Humphrey was the nominee. In a society with little in the way of ideological politics, 1968 was the year of the flood. The additional burden placed on Humphrey as he waged an uphill battle against the opposition was to woo and win the disillusioned and disdainful supporters of Kennedy and McCarthy.[103]

While many of the Kennedy people eventually fell into line behind the Vice-President, McCarthy and many of his ardent supporters sulked and thereby widely advertised the dissension within the party. McCarthy was a tough man. If Humphrey was to win back the dissidents, something dramatic had to be done on the question of the Vietnam bombing.

The resulting Salt Lake City speech, however, had done little to change McCarthy's position; McCarthy felt the speech was too much the product of semantics and too little of substance.[104] McCarthy's support, coming only at the very end of October, on October 29, was too weak and, above all, too late. McCarthy merely said that Humphrey, even if unsatisfactory, was better than Nixon. The "establishment" had miscalculated, or possibly had not taken the time to calculate, the temper of the country,[105] and Hubert Humphrey suffered as a result. As one Johnson Administration official said, "Maybe Hubert Humphrey's situation is simply impossible. Maybe his dilemma on the war is just insoluble. Maybe he is bound to be nominated, but he can't be elected."[106]

In order to fully understand what happened to Hubert Humphrey in 1968, it is necessary to recall the traumatic mood of 1968 America. The war, the violence, the bitterness, the change engulfed those who were seemingly responsible for it, and Hubert Humphrey was no exception. The year was a year of losers:

Lyndon Johnson "lost" the right to seek reelection; Robert Kennedy and Martin Luther King, Jr., lost their lives; the Democratic Convention lost control; youth lost its faith in the system; the system lost faith in itself. It is no wonder that in the midst of such events Hubert Humphrey lost what he had been striving for all his political life, the Presidency of the United States.[107]

THE HEIRS APPARENT: THE AGNEW AND FORD CASES

Spiro Agnew's Vice-Presidency was a very mixed one. On the one hand, he enjoyed national exposure which few Vice-Presidents have experienced; on the other, the controversial nature of that exposure made him the subject of severe criticism as well as adulation. Agnew became progressively a master at rhetoric and used it effectively. His promise, made at the 1968 Republican National Convention, to become a household word was overwhelmingly fulfilled. He had gone from a seemingly clumsy, inept campaigner to an adroit vocalizer of much of the nation's grievances. Agnew had almost singlehandedly taken on the networks, radicals, liberals, Democrats, opponents to the war—whatever "enemy" plagued the administration. While alienating many segments within the electorate, he skillfully realigned others. At the same time that it was "political suicide to tackle the networks,"[108] for example, Agnew's attack on the media forged a critical link in his appeal to the more conservative element in America. Since Agnew was simultaneously a most idolized and most despised political figure, any attempt to reach for the Presidency in 1976 would meet mixed reactions.

During his Vice-Presidency, Agnew utilized every opportunity to obtain nationwide exposure. He had successfully transformed himself into a star, however controversial. As he began to look to the next presidential election, other considerations confronted him. As one confidential source explained, "What the White House wanted and what Spiro Agnew wanted were the same thing, but for two different purposes. Agnew wanted to be in a good position for the '76 election. He wanted to be low keyed and to be a party person and the White House wanted someone to speak for the party, which is exactly what Agnew wanted."

Following the 1972 election, with Richard Nixon as the incumbent President ineligible for reelection and unable to remove his running mate, Agnew's attentions began to move in new directions. He began a more purposeful courtship of the party professionals and the press.[109] At the same time, however, the President was grooming his own successor, namely, John Connally, and began to reduce Agnew's staff, ominous signs that were not too propitious for his presidential ambitions.[110]

At this juncture, Agnew found himself the benefactor of events. The Watergate scandals, while tarnishing most of the administration, including the President himself, not only left Agnew unscathed but also made him appear more favorable. Agnew was emerging as the "Mr. Clean" of the administration, one who had

had nothing to do with Watergate, at any stage.[111] In addition, John Connally left the White House.

Agnew's position was singular. He had managed to achieve national prominence and to be the object of serious speculation for the 1976 Republican presidential nomination. Meanwhile, he avoided any commitment regarding his plans or goals for 1976 by maintaining that "Vice Presidents aren't automatically accepted as the logical successors of Presidents."[112]

In order to emphasize that he was presidential timber, Agnew had to show that he had an active role in the administration. But Watergate forced him to strike a peculiar sort of balance: he had to stay "above the Watergate battle"[113] while at the same time making the most of his experience in office. In this instance, *not* having participated in decision-making was decidedly more beneficial to Agnew's political fate. Regarding Agnew's role, Senator Barry Goldwater sarcastically remarked, "If there is one thing the Vice President can back up it's that he doesn't know what the hell is going on at the White House."[114] Agnew also had to keep the immaculate image bestowed on him by Watergate without displaying disloyalty to the President. The result was a very cautious posture. For example, while he expressed approval of Nixon's foreign policy, he said he would approach domestic problems differently.[115] In assuming this ambivalent stance, Agnew sought to avoid alienating the President by adding, "That dosen't mean my ideas are superior to those of the President."[116]

When questioned specifically about Watergate, Agnew, in a *Time* magazine interview of July 1973, strove to find a path that would do him the least damage, from whatever side. While asserting his confidence in the President, he cautiously based this sentiment on faith rather than fact.[117] Agnew was equally cautious in his statements concerning the President himself:

I would assume that if he's human and fallible like the rest of us, he's made mistakes. But I think they have been very minimal. . . .

Watergate does show one thing. In a job as big as the presidency, you can't watch everything. You're at the mercy of the people carrying out your instructions. I don't think there's any foolproof way in which a person who heads a large enterprise can protect himself against people who work for him. You want people with initiative. You don't want people who check with you before doing anything, because that's of no value to you. . . . There isn't any other way. We're all locked into the people we work for.

In laying out a suggested course of action for the President to follow, Agnew maintained that

it is important to get the President before the people. I think a freewheeling press conference would be a mistake. I don't think the President can be put in a position where there's an inquisition with people screaming and yelling the way they've been known to. Out of that volatile atmosphere comes an impression that's highly misleading sometimes.

But Agnew was cautious enough to add,

If you could get some of the giants of your profession, you could figure out a proper kind of interview. You could screen out the matters that are highly improper... and concentrate strictly on information concerning the President's position.

And with respect to the specific issue of "bugging," Agnew said, "The entire idea of bugging I find personally repulsive. . . . I would never sanction listening in on somebody else's personal conversations."

Moving away from specific Watergate issues, Agnew built on his immaculate image by striking a sanctimonious note on campaign spending. "No matter how good your reforms are and how ideal the method of financing campaigns, there will always be those who break the law. . . . [E]very serious candidate [should have] enough money to run a decent, respectable campaign without raising funds through private sources."[118] This response was in sharp contrast to President Nixon's policy in vetoing related legislation.

In short, Agnew, by avoiding overidentification with the administration, was attempting to spare himself the fate of past Vice-Presidents who had been the innocent victims of presidential problems. The head of steam Agnew's political future gained throughout his incumbency and especially during the Watergate scandal was suddenly and completely exhausted in 1973 by his *nolo contendere* plea in a criminal charge and his prompt resignation.

Following his appointment as Agnew's vice-presidential successor, Gerald R. Ford was confronted by a similar mixed blessing. Thrown into the position of being one heartbeat, one resignation, or one impeachment away from the Presidency in the midst of the most devastating political scandal since Teapot Dome, Ford reacted similarly to past Vice-Presidents: he was obliged to hedge his position. There was one important difference, however: Ford was confirmed after congressional hearings that pointedly and in advance sought out his credentials to be President. Unlike Spiro Agnew who had *emerged* as the "Mr. Clean" of the administration, Ford assumed his duties with a clean slate. Thus, Ford began his Vice-Presidency amid speculation of a Ford presidential bid in 1976, if not a succession before that.

As the President's problems grew more complex, Ford's position became more uncomfortable and frequently more flexible. In the awkward position of being the beneficiary of President Nixon's spiraling problems, Ford probably had little choice but to maintain a low-keyed, balanced line of support and defense of the President, with an occasional criticism of the Watergate state of affairs. He was at once linked to the President but free of him.

While he still relied on the President for his duties, Ford was also able to sound an independent chord. More importantly, he was expected to. However often he disavowed any interest in achieving the highest office in the land, he was in line for the Presidency, if not as a replacement for a denounced Richard Nixon, then on his own in 1976.[119]

With the events of the week of August 5, 1974, especially Nixon's announcement that he had lied to the American public and had halted the Watergate investigation, his impeachment or resignation grew more inevitable. As the President's remaining strength in Congress evaporated rapidly, the succession of the much-respected Ford became more and more imminent.[120]

Finally, on August 8, following several days of conferences with his staff and legal advisers, Richard Nixon, perhaps the most "imperial" President in American history, made his decision to resign from the Presidency. Gerald Ford thus became the first man not elected to office to serve as President.[121]

As Ford's short tenure in the Vice-Presidency had made him the likely 1976 Republican presidential nominee, now his succession to the Presidency seemed virtually to assure him of that nomination.

CONCLUDING NOTE

The Vice-President is elected by all the people and is intended to represent them. Nearly all of his assignments, however, come as "gifts" from the President whom he must serve loyally if he is to be more than a titleholder. If he is to build a record of service and experience to hold up as a resource toward his own election to the Presidency, he must be willing to strap himself to someone else's policies.

Thus, while the office provides visibility, it provides vulnerability as well, a vulnerability that may ultimately prove so costly as to outweigh whatever advantages the office may offer. It is a stepping stone; it is a stumbling block. It provides opportunity; it produces frustration. This is a dilemma inherent in the second office.

NOTES

1. *America* 113 (October 2, 1965): 363.
2. Robert Finch, who had been with Nixon when Nixon served as Vice-President, said:

I came aboard with the clear understanding that he was going to be a Presidential candidate, so that the major thrust of my activity was along that line. That is, first of all, assessing his time in terms of what needed to be done, what had to be done to strengthen, prepare us right away for the nomination; the places he had to go, the people he had to see.

Robert Finch, Oral History Interview, Eisenhower Administration Oral History Collection, Columbia University, New York, New York, p. 28.
3. For additional material on Alben Barkley's 1952 availability, see Alben Barkley, *That Reminds Me* (Garden City, N.Y.: Doubleday, 1954), chap. 17; Cabell Phillips, *The Truman Presidency* (New York: Macmillan, 1966), p. 420ff.; The Papers of Alben Barkley, University of Kentucky, Lexington, Kentucky; Sidney Shalett, *Interviews with Alben Barkley*, Harry S Truman Library, Independence, Missouri, and Franklin D. Roosevelt Library, Hyde Park, New York, passim; *New York Times*, July 19, 1952; Michael Dorman, *The Second Man* (New York: Delacorte Press, 1968), p. 196ff.; Harry S Truman, *Years of Trial and Hope* (New York: Doubleday, 1956); The Papers of Harry S Truman, Harry

S Truman Library, Independence, Missouri; the oral history interviews of Joseph G. Feeney and Donald Hansen, Harry S Truman Library, Independence, Missouri.

4. Earl Mazo and Stephen Hess, *Nixon: A Political Portrait* (New York: Harper & Row, 1968), p. 220ff.

5. Leverett Saltonstall, Oral History Interview, Eisenhower Administration Oral History Collection, Columbia University, New York, New York, p. 146.

6. Emmet John Hughes, *The Ordeal of Power* (New York: Atheneum, 1963), p. 297.

7. Herbert S. Parmet, *Eisenhower and the American Crusades* (New York: Macmillan, 1972), p. 527ff.

8. Ibid., p. 350.

9. *New York Times*, May 4, 1960. Herman Finer, *The Presidency: Crisis and Regeneration* (Chicago: University of Chicago Press, 1960), p. 295, points out that, while the Vice-President is the potential successor, it is more likely that an incumbent President would avoid naming him publicly.

10. Sidney Warren, *The Battle for the Presidency* (Philadelphia: Lippincott, 1968), p. 301.

11. For more on the delegation of political duties to the Vice-President, see Richard Rovere, Oral History Interview, Eisenhower Administration Oral History Collection, Columbia University, New York, New York, pp. 35–36.

12. Dorman, *The Second Man*, p. 240.

13. Kenneth Keating, Oral History Interview, Eisenhower Administration Oral History Collection, Columbia University, New York, New York, p. 13ff.

14. Hughes, *The Ordeal of Power*, pp. 323; 200.

15. Several observers have pointed out Nixon's views on the party platform. The presidential candidate, he felt, should have the strongest say. Accordingly, Nixon had "insisted upon some revisions," noted Prescott Bush in an Oral History Interview for the Eisenhower Administration Oral History Collection, Columbia University, New York, New York, pp. 13–14.

16. Ibid.

17. In a memo from Max Rabb to James Hagerty, dated June 20, 1965, the message was transmitted: "Nixon wants publicity for work of Committee on Government Contracts" (Official File 101–I–2 Box 441, Dwight D. Eisenhower Papers, Dwight D. Eisenhower Library, Abilene, Kansas).

18. Finch, in his Oral History Interview for the Eisenhower Administration Oral History Collection, noted the importance of civil rights legislation to the impending 1960 campaign. Thus, he and William P. Rogers worked on civil rights legislation. See p. 34ff. for more on this point. See pp. 35–36 for Nixon's work with the National Urban League/NAACP.

Finch also discusses the usefulness of Nixon's foreign travel to the 1960 campaign strategy, p. 65ff.

Milton S. Eisenhower points out that, although Nixon suffered indignity during his Latin American trip, it gained him sympathy. Oral History Interview, Eisenhower Administration Oral History Collection, Columbia University, New York, New York, p. 94.

19. Donald Paarlberg, Interview held at his Washington, D.C., office, March 1974.

20. Mazo and Hess, *Nixon*, p. 238.

21. Howard K. Smith, Oral History Interview, Eisenhower Administration Oral History Collection, Columbia University, New York, New York, p. 44.

22. Mazo and Hess, *Nixon*, p. 238. "It was just a mistake," according to Roscoe

Drummond, although it was, he continued, "a bumbling answer," "awkward," and "embarrassing . . . unfair to Nixon." Oral History Interview, Eisenhower Administration Oral History Collection, Columbia University, New York, New York, p. 20.

Prescott Bush suggests the possibility that the President viewed the question as demeaning to his own decision-making abilities, about which he was sensitive. Oral History Interview, p. 20.

Richard Rovere suggests that it was because Eisenhower was "a rather fuzzy-minded man. Also, he didn't have the facts at his disposal a good part of the time, unlike Truman, and Kennedy and Johnson." Rovere also observes, "He probably didn't know really what Nixon had been doing. Whereas Johnson knows from minute to minute what Humphrey's doing." Oral History Interview, p. 28.

Regarding the remark, Nixon said:

It was to plague me the rest of the campaign. . . . Eisenhower had called me on the phone and expressed chagrin at the way this exchange had been handled by the press. He pointed out that he was simply being facetious and yet they played it straight and wrote it seriously. . . . I am sure that to millions of unsophisticated televiewers, this question had been most effective in raising a doubt in their minds with regard to one of my strongest campaign themes and assets—my experience as Vice President. (Richard M. Nixon, *Six Crises* [New York: Doubleday, 1962], p. 339.)

23. William F. Knowland, Oral History Interview, Eisenhower Administration Oral History Collection, Columbia University, New York, New York, pp. 83–84.

24. Howard K. Smith, Oral History Interview, p. 44.

25. Mazo and Hess, *Nixon*, p. 234ff. See also Parmet, *Eisenhower and the American Crusades*, Edward McCabe in his oral history interview for the Dwight D. Eisenhower Library, pointed out that during the debates Nixon

had to watch his Ps and Qs every step, and Kennedy . . . was in a position to take a gamble, if he could look good, or take the chance of looking good. . . . That's the difference between the fellow in office and the fellow seeking office. It'll always be that way, I suspect (p. 76).

Regarding the debates, Nixon himself wrote (*Six Crises*, p. 323):

I felt it was absolutely essential that I not only agree to debate but enthusiastically welcomed the opportunity. Had I refused the challenge, I would have opened myself to the charge that I was afraid to defend the Administration's and my own record.

26. Hughes, *The Ordeal of Power*, p. 323.

The "couple of telephone calls" referred to relate to the incident of the arrest of civil rights leader Martin Luther King, Jr., in Atlanta. John Kennedy telephoned a Georgia judge to intercede on King's behalf. See Arthur M. Schlesinger, Jr., *A Thousand Days* (Boston: Houghton Mifflin, 1965), p. 74.

King himself remarked of the action: "I am deeply indebted to Senator Kennedy, who served as a great force in making my release possible. It took a lot of courage for Senator Kennedy to do this, especially in Georgia."

Kennedy received a huge percentage of the Negro vote in the election; see Schlesinger, *A Thousand Days*, pp. 929–30.

Nixon, meanwhile, was trying to work via the resources he thought were at his disposal, and, as Finch observes, "Dick tried to reach Bill Rogers, or tried to reach someone at the White House to intercede, on King's behalf. But some hangup occurred someplace. In the meantime, Kennedy had made the call and the damage was done." Oral History Interview, p. 54. See also Harris Wofford, Oral History Interview, John F. Kennedy Library, Columbia Point, Massachusetts, p. 23.

Nixon's greater accessibility to power and influence had backfired.

27. Nixon, *Six Crises*, p. 357.

28. Edward McCabe remarked that the timing of the unfortunate incident did

a great deal of damage to the Nixon candidacy. It set the stage . . . for a downgrading of the administration, its handling of foreign affairs. It set in motion . . . a feeling of great public annoyance, irritation, dissatisfaction . . . an undefinable kind of reaction that things weren't going well. (Oral History Interview, p. 74.)

Nixon found himself with no alternative but to defend the administration, as he did on a May 1960 television show with David Susskind; see McCabe, Oral History Interview, p. 103. See also Hughes, *The Ordeal of Power*, p. 314.

29. *Minneapolis Sunday Tribune*, December 22, 1957.

30. Apparently, Nixon and several others in the administration had wanted a tax cut in order to give the economy a lift, but it was turned down. Agnes Waldron, Interview at her Washington, D.C., office, March 1974.

This is a clear indication of the bottleneck the incumbent Vice-President is in. His candidacy is often jeopardized by circumstances, yet he has little or no decision-making power to ameliorate those circumstances. See Mazo and Hess, *Nixon*, p. 243.

31. Finch, Oral History Interview, pp. 43–44, 50. Finch also reports that by 1959 a great deal of Nixon's time was spent in anticipation that Rockefeller would be his most critical opponent within the party; p. 50ff.

32. "Nixon's Way to the Top," *The New Republic* (June 9, 1973): 15ff.

33. Mazo and Hess, *Nixon*, p. 232ff.

34. Waldron, Interview, March 1974.

35. William Lawrence, Oral History Interview, John F. Kennedy Library, Columbia Point, Massachusetts, p. 13.

36. Vice-President's remarks re: farm policy June 21, 1960, Box No. 9, The Papers of Donald Paarlberg, Dwight D. Eisenhower Library, Abilene, Kansas.

37. Lawrence, Oral History Interview, p. 13.

Finch, in his Oral History Interview, pp. 59–60, comments:

The ultimate problem . . . was that he was essentially defending an administration; an eight-year administration. So he was on the defensive, to that extent, and Kennedy could bring the attack to him, and did.

I recall he [Nixon] kept referring to the Eisenhower years as "the best years of our lives," and he was sensitive about his role in it. . . . I think on balance, he felt that it had been a good administration and he was doing his best to defend it. But obviously there had accumulated ills that build up against any incumbent administration that's been in for eight years, and those were the things that Kennedy played on very well.

Hughes (*The Ordeal of Power*, p. 316), commenting on Nixon's "oddly mixed retorts" to Kennedy's accusations, concluded:

There was a tone to many of these . . . that strongly suggested the extravagance of a man angrily defying his own private doubts as much as those of the public. And the fact was that, for many months in Washington, there had been—not for the first time, his critics would have insisted—two Richard Nixons occupying the office of the vice presidency. The first, the public Nixon, acclaimed Eisenhower as a savior of world peace, a statesman of rare acumen, and a national hero whom a thankful electorate would not dare to slight by a vote for the Democratic party. The second, the private Nixon, patiently explained to visitors and journalists, in off-the-record conversations or over intimate dinners, his dismay with White House leadership, his dissent from decisions in the field of national defense and foreign policy, and his anxiety to offer the nation a more youthful, more vigorous, and more coherent presidency—in the person of himself.

38. Parmet, *Eisenhower and the American Crusades*, p. 562; James David Barber, *The Presidential Character* (Englewood Cliffs, N.J.: Prentice-Hall, 1972), pp. 364ff.; 322. See also George Smathers, Oral History Interview, John F. Kennedy Library, Columbia Point, Massachusetts, p. 4.

39. Barber, *The Presidential Character*, p. 322.

40. Mazo and Hess point out that a Republican candidate has the added burden of dissociating himself from his party in order to capture Democratic votes. See *Nixon*, p. 321.

41. Hauge, Oral History Interview, p. 118.

42. Parmet, *Eisenhower and the American Crusades*, p. 517.

43. Hughes, *The Ordeal of Power*, pp. 320; 315ff.

44. Several observers noted Eisenhower's regret at not having participated in the campaign at an earlier stage. See Milton S. Eisenhower, Oral History Interview, p. 45; Howard K. Smith, Oral History Interview, p. 30.

Howard K. Smith maintains that the President was annoyed by the decision that he would not be needed in the 1960 campaign, a decision he felt was a mistake.

Sherman Adams claims Eisenhower was disappointed that the party had not been able to convert the younger independent vote. See *Firsthand Report* (New York: Harper, 1961), pp. 48–49.

45. Sigmund Larmon, an adviser from the business community, maintains that Eisenhower called Nixon and volunteered his help, which the Vice-President accepted.

Eisenhower reportedly kept saying, "Mr. Nixon has never asked me. He's never asked me. I've always been available." Following the bad results in the polls, Larmon and two other advisers, A. Alton Jones and Len Hall, decided that Eisenhower should make a television appearance for Nixon.

Oral History Interview, Eisenhower Administration Oral History Collection, Columbia University, New York, New York, pp. 82; 31.

Milton S. Eisenhower contends the Nixon people had not sought President Eisenhower's help earlier because they felt it would create the impression that Dick Nixon was "riding on the coattails of President Eisenhower." The President's brother also notes that Eisenhower thought the President of the United States should "represent all the people and not be partisan." However, he adds, the President did participate when the tides turned against Nixon, and although he was disappointed by Nixon's defeat, he did not regard that defeat as a rejection of the administration. Oral History Interview, pp. 40; 44. See also Chalmers Roberts, Oral History Interview, Eisenhower Administration Oral History Collection, Columbia University, New York, New York, pp. 26–28 and 38, for more on the President's role in the 1960 campaign.

Larmon responds to one theory that Nixon had rejected large-scale politicking by Eisenhower because of concern over the President's health; see, for examle, Mazo and

Hess, *Nixon*, pp. 26–27. Larmon does not believe that this was a primary consideration in Nixon's decision not to enlist the President's aid. Oral History Interview, pp. 33–34.

46. Paarlberg, Interview, March 1974. Paarlberg also noted that this was "a misguided effort and may have cost Nixon the election."

47. McCabe, Oral History Interview, p. 73. See also Drummond, Oral History Interview, pp. 26–27; James R. Shepley, Oral History Interview, Eisenhower Administration Oral History Collection, Columbia University, New York, New York, p. 31; and Charles Halleck, Oral History Interview, John F. Kennedy Library, Columbia Point, Massachusetts, p. 34.

McCabe also noted that Nixon had been labeled "the hand-picked candidate who was going to continue the Eisenhower Administration."

48. Finch, Oral History Interview, p. 50.

49. George Christian, *The President Steps Down* (New York: Macmillan, 1970), pp. 148–49. Christian further notes:

On war policy Humphrey was left pretty much to his own devices. He sat on the National Security Council, but this body dealt mostly with broad policies other than Vietnam. The critical decisions on the war were made at the "Tuesday lunch" and supplemental meetings, especially in the last two years of the Johnson Administration. Humphrey was only rarely a participant in these sessions. Most of his insight into the President's deeper feelings about Vietnam came from private conversations with Johnson and from the routine flow of war information. As Vice President he participated in a few Vietnam decisions—such as the decision to bomb the North Vietnamese depots in 1966—but only a few.

50. Dean Rusk, Interview held at his Athens, Georgia, office, May 1973.

51. Walter Jenkins, Interview held at his Austin, Texas, office, April 1973.

52. Kenneth P. O'Connell, Telephone Interview, Boston, Massachusetts, February 1974.

During the 1968 campaign, Humphrey was vulnerable on the very issue of loyalty, regarding which vice-presidential candidate Spiro Agnew said,

The Vice President must become convinced of the logic of the President's position. If it does such violence with his theory and his philosophy, I guess he has nothing left to do but to resign if he was really seriously concerned about his disagreement with the President.

Agnew's opponent for the Vice-Presidency, Humphrey's running mate, Ed Muskie, agreed, saying, "I don't believe I could in any public office endorse a policy that violated my conscience." See "If a President and 'Veep' Disagree," *U.S. News* 65 (September 16, 1968): 14.

53. Allan H. Ryskind, *Hubert* (New York: Arlington House, 1968), p. 319. See also Jules Witcover, *The Resurrection of Richard Nixon* (New York: Putnam, 1970), p. 323.

54. Ryskind, *Hubert*, p. 319; see also pp. 174–75.

55. Ibid., p. 176.

56. *Saturday Review* 48 (May 8, 1965): 16–17.

57. "The Bright Spirit," *Time* 87 (April 1, 1966): 21–25. Ryskind (*Hubert*, pp. 321–22) observed:

Humphrey has received some sharp criticism for his loyalty to the Johnson Administration, particularly from his old left-wing friends who cannot understand why their long-time ally is supporting

128   American Prince, American Pauper

the war effort. Yet his friends ignore the practical realities of politics. Assuming Humphrey desperately wishes to succeed to the Presidency—which, of course, no one doubts—he must be at least loyal to the crown.

His extravagant eulogizing of the President may be entirely in earnest, yet it is also the surest road to the White House. If Johnson were unhappy with the Vice President's performance, one can be certain that Lyndon would be making plans to unload Humphrey in 1968. Furthermore, Humphrey is well aware that his popular appeal is less than over-whelming, and that his most likely chance of succeeding to the Presidency is either through Lyndon Johnson's death, or by becoming LBJ's handpicked successor after the Texan retires. Whatever Humphrey actually believes, his future welfare rests with what voters think about the Johnson Administration. Thus, it is clearly to his advantage to be the Saint Paul of the Great Society, the total defender of the faith.

58. David W. Abbott and Edward R. Rogowsky, *Political Parties: Leadership, Organization, Linkage* (New York: Rand McNally, 1971), p. 254ff.; see also *"Politics Without Joy—On the Road with Humphrey" U.S. News* 65 (August 12, 1968): 30–31; Senator Herman Talmadge, Interview held at his Washington, D.C., Senate office, March 1974.

"His basic problem," wrote Albert Eisele, " . . . was that too many Americans regarded him as Lyndon Johnson without the Texas accent." *Almost to the Presidency* (Minnesota: Piper Co., 1972), p. 334.

Said another observer, "He had won the nomination because he had accepted the loss of his own identity. . . . He had availed himself of the President's piggy-back to the nomination." Lewis Chester et al., *An American Melodrama: The Presidential Campaign of 1968* (New York: Viking Press, 1968), p. 577.

59. As cited by Eisele, *Almost to the Presidency*, p. 372.

60. Richard M. Scammon and Ben J. Wattenberg, *The Real Majority* (New York: Coward, McCann & Geoghegan, 1970), p. 119.

61. Christian, *The President Steps Down*, p. 157.

62. Chester, et al., *An American Melodrama*, p. 718.

63. Ibid.

64. "Chicago: The Assumptions About Nixon and Humphrey," *New York Times*, September 1, 1968.

65. *Wall Street Journal*, August 30, 1968.

66. *New York Times*, September 1, 1968.

67. See Eisele, *Almost to the Presidency*, p. 344ff., for a discussion of Humphrey's difficult position on the plank. The plank read: "We strongly support the Paris talks and applaud the initiative of President Johnson which brought North Vietnam to the peace table."

"Promises the Democrats Make: Promises for 1968," U.S. News 65 (September 9, 1968): 50–52. See *New York Times*, September 1, 1968, "Planks to Run On—Or Away From" for a comparison of the Democratic and Republican 1968 platforms, both very similar in content.

68. Lyndon B. Johnson, *The Vantage Point: Perspectives of the Presidency* (New York: Holt, Rinehart & Winston, 1971), p. 432.

Johnson claims to have informed Humphrey of his decision the previous year and to have suggested that the Vice-President begin to ready himself for a campaign. See pp. 541ff. regarding Johnson's account of his conversation with Robert F. Kennedy.

69. See "Candidates Sure That Johnson Is Calling Signals on Convention," *New York Times*, August 15, 1968.

70. Eisele, *Almost to the Presidency*, pp. 347–48.

71. *"L. B. J., Nixon and the Campaign,"* *U.S. News* 65 (September 9, 1968): 17–18.

72. Gerald R. Ford, Interview held at his Washington, D.C., office, March 1974; Dean Rusk, Interview, May 1973.

Ford, in response to a question asking him to comment on the suspicion that arises between the President and his Vice-President, pointed out that, in the Johnson-Humphrey case, even though Johnson had said he would not run, there was always the expectation that he might. Vice-President Ford went on to say that that certainly was not the case in his relationship with President Nixon, since Nixon was ineligible for reelection and he (Ford) had "no intention of running . . . so the competition isn't there."

73. Bill Welch, Interview held at his Washington, D.C., office, March 1974; Christian, *The President Steps Down*, p. 157.

74. Hubert H. Humphrey, Interview held in a U.S. Senate reception room, Washington, D.C., March 1974.

75. Jenkins, Interview, March 1973.

76. Scammon and Wattenberg, *The Real Majority*, p. 170.

77. "Humphrey vs. Nixon vs. Wallace," *U.S. News* 65 (September 9, 1968): 31–33. For more on the Republican party's seeming unity, see Chester et al., *An American Melodrama*, p. 451ff.

78. As cited *"Nixon Looks to November: Here's His Strategy,"* in *U.S. News* 65 (July 29, 1968): 28.

79. Scammon and Wattenberg, *The Real Majority*, pp. 206–209. The authors add, "Perhaps the clearest indication Nixon gave that he understood these factors . . . was his choice of Spiro Agnew as Vice President. It may be said, in fact, that Agnewism as a social thought won the election for Nixon, while Agnew, the individual, almost lost it for him."

80. See Eisele, *Almost to the Presidency*, p. 333ff.; Rusk, Interview, May 1973; *New York Times*, September 1, 1968; *Chicago Daily News*, August 14, 1968.

81. Johnson, *The Vantage Point*, p. 517.

82. Eisele, *Almost to the Presidency*, pp. 378–79.

83. *Vital Speeches* 35 (1968/9): 8–11.

84. Ibid.

85. Eisele, *Almost to the Presidency*, p. 377.

86. Ibid., pp. 377–78.

87. For more on Johnson's role, see Christian, *The President Steps Down*, pp. 153–54; 165ff.; 381ff.

Stephen A. Mitchell noted in a September 4, 1968, "Memo to Political File" that in a conversation with Humphrey

we talked about the possibility of helping his ticket in Texas; that I had some standing among the liberal elements here and we would need all the help we could get, and he said "I know that very well and I realize that the leaders there have been making it very hard for me." (The reference was clearly to L. B. J.) He also said, "Yes, and the governor, too, had made it very hard for me." (Papers of Stephen A. Mitchell, Harry S. Truman Library, Independence, Missouri.)

88. Johnson, *The Vantage Point*, pp. 513, 517. Johnson noted in his memoirs: "An election is a difficult time to try to carry out an objective foreign policy—or a domestic

policy. . . . I had deliberately taken myself out of political contention in order to devote all my energy to the urgent tasks that remained.'' See Johnson, pp. 513, 548–50, for his views regarding Vice-President Humphrey's Salt Lake City speech and its potential impact on the ongoing peace talks with Hanoi.

89. Witcover, *The Resurrection of Richard Nixon*, p. 407.

90. As cited by ibid., p. 420.

91. Ibid., pp. 429–30.

92. Ibid., p. 432.

93. Eisele, *Almost to the Presidency*, p. 350.

94. Ibid., p. 332.

95. Scammon and Wattenberg, *The Real Majority*, p. 175ff.

96. Eisele, *Almost to the Presidency*, p. 357.

97. Scammon and Wattenberg, *The Real Majority*, pp. 144, 201.

Regarding the relative ability to perform effectively on law and order, the September Gallup poll indicated the following breakdown, as cited by Scammon and Wattenberg.

Nixon	36%
Wallace	26%
Humphrey	23%
Not sure	15%

98. "*Promises the Democrats Make: Platform for 1968*," *U.S. News* 65 (September 9, 1968): 50–52.

99. Johnson, *The Vantage Point*, p. 424; David Halberstam, *The Unfinished Odyssey of Robert Kennedy* (New York: Random House, 1968), p. 113ff.; Chester et al., *An American Melodrama*, pp. 6–7.

100. Jack Newfield, *Robert Kennedy: A Memoir* (New York: E. P. Dutton, 1969), p. 218.

Newfield reports of Kennedy's hesitation that Kennedy had said,

My own brother suggested Lyndon Johnson to be the Vice President of the United States. All that is involved inside me. To break with the party that made my brother the President isn't a simple thing for me to do. . . . I keep thinking that I represent something more than just myself, or my own ambition (Ibid., p. 224).

101. Eisele, *Almost to the Presidency*, p. 331. See also "Hubert Recycled," *Economist* 235: (June 13, 1970): 54 + ; Newfield, *Robert Kennedy*, p. 274ff., for Kennedy's attacks on Humphrey; "McCarthy's Win Strategy—Act II—Confrontation with Robert Kennedy," *New Republic* (April 23, 1968); and Chester et al., *An American Melodrama*, p. 310.

Chester, et al., *An American Melodrama*, p. 738, also cite a summary of the situation by one of McCarthy's aides: "I thought the United States could only get out of the war if we cleared out everybody who had been locked into Johnson's policies. And that meant getting rid of Humphrey."

102. Newfield, *Robert Kennedy*, 169ff.

103. See "Era of Democrats Ending? A Shattered Strategy," *U.S. News* 65 (September 16, 1968): 29ff.; "Politics Without Joy—On the Road with Humphrey," *U.S. News* 65 (August 12, 1968): 30–31; *Los Angeles Times*, August 28, 1968, for Joseph Kraft's views in "The Democrats in Transition"; *New York Times*, Part II-5, March 5, 1968, for James Reston's expansion of this point in "Washington: The Decline of Party Politics."

104. See Chester et al., *An American Ordeal*, p. 343; p. 742, for more on McCarthy's reaction to the speech, as well as Eisele, *Almost to the Presidency*, p. 382ff.

105. Halberstam, *The Unfinished Odyssey of Robert Kennedy*, p. 48.

106. As quoted by Chester, et al., *An American Ordeal*, p. 424.

107. See Johnson, pp. 548ff., for his insightful analysis on the growing resentment toward the Democratic party on domestic issues and the war in Vietnam, and its effect on Humphrey's bid for the Presidency.

108. Robert Curran, *Spiro Agnew: Spokesman for America* (New York: Lancer Books, 1970), p. 143ff.

109. *New York Times*, June 24, 1973, p. 40.

110. Ibid.

111. According to a confidential source, Agnew's popularity in general, but especially his "Mr. Clean" image after the Watergate scandal broke, had resulted in a bitterness within the White House, a bitterness that reportedly turned to glee once Agnew's own problems were disclosed.

112. *New York Times Magazine*, pp. 38; 11.

113. Ibid., p. 10ff.

114. Ibid., p. 11.

115. This is just the reverse of what Humphrey had said in 1968, and for precisely the same reason. Johnson's foreign policy was in serious trouble, while his domestic policy was well received. For Nixon, the problems were the reverse. Each Vice-President, respectively, struck a note of independence only within the area of his President's troublespot.

116. *Time*, July 2, 1973, p. 17.

117. *New York Times Magazine*, June 24, 1973, p. 11.

118. *Time*, July 2, 1973, p. 17.

119. Gerald R. Ford, Interview held at his U.S. Senate office, March 1974.

120. For a fuller account of the Nixon resignation, see *New York Times*, August 5, 6, 7, 8, 9, 1974.

121. In addition, under the provisions of the Twenty-fifth Amendment, Ford would be called upon to name his own successor to the Vice-Presidency. The confirmation process through which he had been scrutinized just ten months earlier would begin anew, and Congress would find its impeachment proceedings against President Richard Nixon replaced by hearings on a new Vice-President. Nelson A. Rockefeller, confirmed as Vice-President in November 1974, was to be the second candidate within a matter of months to experience the close scrutiny of the Congress as a presidential appointee to the second highest office.

5

The Role of the Modern Vice-Presidency: Growth of the Alter-Ego

It's like being naked in the middle of a blizzard, with no one to even offer you a match to help you keep warm—that's the Vice Presidency. You are trapped, vulnerable and alone and it does not matter who happens to be President.[1]

Although the modern Vice-Presidency has developed significant roles and duties, it is nonetheless subject to the frustrations that Hubert Humphrey so aptly described. A Vice-President soon learns what he has to do to become a viable part of the administration. Thus, an introductory comment on incumbents' perspectives provides an invaluable backdrop against which to view the development of the office.

Harry S Truman once called the Vice-President "a cow's fifth teat,"[2] and his own Vice-President, Alben Barkley, recognized that the second office could be used to get rid of competitors. Barkley, however, seemed to adapt well to the uncertainties of the office and was considerably more optimistic that the office was much more than the "fifth wheel on the machinery of government" that John Adams had proclaimed it to be.[3] (Adams had also referred to the office as "Your Superfluous Excellency."[4])

John Nance Garner, who had served as Vice-President under FDR for two terms and had been ignored, advised Lyndon Johnson to decline the offer to be John Kennedy's running mate; the office, Garner said, "isn't worth a pitcher of warm spit."[5] Johnson himself, as senator and Majority Leader, had often said he would never accept the Vice-Presidency; the Vice-President, he said, does nothing in the legislature, and he was not about to trade a vote for a gavel.[6] But Johnson did accept it, and once he did he was more frustrated by the office than he had ever imagined possible.[7] Johnson had nonetheless astutely grasped the nature of the office: to be entirely at the disposal of the President.[8] A Vice-President, he would later emphasize, must above all be loyal to his President.[9] As he reflected in his memoirs, he had been the kind of Vice-President he would want—loyal and self-effacing.[10] Johnson clearly transmitted his expectations to his own Vice-President, and just several days prior to being selected as Johnson's running mate, Hubert Humphrey indicated how well he understood the necessities of the office: "he must have a quality of fidelity, a willingness literally to give himself, to be what the President wants him to be, a loyal, faithful friend and servant."[11] This understanding of the office was echoed in Spiro Agnew's statement, "Whatever the President wants is what I want. . . . I envisage this as the principal role of the Vice-Presidency—to implement the policies of the Chief Executive."[12]

President Dwight Eisenhower was undoubtedly responsible for the turning point in the Vice-Presidency. "I personally believe," he said, "the Vice President of the United States should never be a nonentity. I believe he should be used. I believe he should have a very useful job."[13] Eisenhower met with Nixon prior to the 1952 campaign to discuss what was promised to be a more active role for the Vice-President.

Nixon seemed to fluctuate in his view of the office. "A hollow shell," Nixon had once said of the second office,[14] although he reportedly preferred the Vice-Presidency to the legislature.[15] As Vice-President, Nixon felt the second office must be "given vast responsibility."[16] As President, he stated,

Because of the burden of the Presidency, particularly with foreign policy problems becoming more acute than they had been previously . . . the Vice President can and should be used more than he has been in either the Kennedy or the Eisenhower administration.[17]

Emphasizing the need for and anticipating that future Presidents would make greater use of their Vice-Presidents, Nixon noted the most critical duties of the office:

First, his participation in the deliberations of the National Security Council, his participation in the deliberations of the Cabinet; and then the increasingly greater use of the Vice-President as a trouble-shooter and as a representative of the President in the field of foreign policy.[18]

While Nixon's view did not fully coincide with the assignments he gave to his own Vice-Presidents other expressions of his views emphasized the trouble-shooter function. "The Vice President," he said, "should sustain Presidential policy";[19] he should "clearly represent views of the President and be [someone] the President could trust to carry out very important assignments."[20] As President, Nixon said of the Vice-President, "He is dealing with expressing established policy to opinion leaders throughout the country."[21]

Vice-President George Bush's two most recent predecessors, Nelson Rockefeller and Walter Mondale, both succinctly grasped the essence of the office. Despite the peculiar circumstances under which he had come to the Vice-Presidency, despite his own notoriety which went far beyond that of the President who had appointed him, Nelson Rockefeller knew what his future as Vice-President would be. Commenting that he had known every Vice-President since Henry Wallace, Rockefeller noted that "they were all frustrated, every one of them."[22] At another point, he said, "I don't expect anything. This, I think, is my greatest strength."[23]

Walter Mondale, who had prepared himself for the office by talking with Rockefeller and Humphrey, immediately saw his job as that of the President's "advisor on crucial, broad issues affecting government; to be the bearer of bad news. . . . My future in public life really depends upon the success of the Carter Presidency."[24] Just one month prior to this statement, the newly inaugurated Vice-President Mondale symbolically underscored another key understanding of his relationship to the President, and he talked about this in a February television interview. "When he walked in that parade . . . I told the President, 'I don't want to upstage you, I think I'll ride—I wouldn't want to take this away from you.' "[25] Mondale astutely knew that a low profile was crucial to the second office.

Vice-President George Bush rather quickly and adeptly discerned this principle and has behaved accordingly. He has consistently defended the President and has spoken forcefully in support of administration policies. Candidly referring to his role, Bush has stated, "I have a very low profile. Because I think that the way you become an effective vice-president—have something substantive to do—is to have the confidence of the President. And if you are always out there in the newspapers or in some news conference and talking about your close relationship with the President—well, it just won't work." Early on, Bush anticipated having the same potential room for activity as had Mondale, "if I don't blow it. Because the President is giving me every opportunity."[26]

THE GROWTH OF THE VICE-PRESIDENCY: AN OVERVIEW

The understanding expressed by Mondale that a Vice-President's success is inextricably linked to the President and his administration is at the heart of the office's growth. The growth of the Presidency itself has undoubtedly contributed to the increased role of the Vice-President. A succession of events has likewise continued to call attention to the likelihood that a Vice-President may be called on to lead the nation. Franklin Roosevelt's death left his new Vice-President with the seemingly inhuman task of filling the shoes of a President who had been larger than life, who had singlehandedly guided the Untied States through twelve incredible years of Depression and war, and who had done little to prepare his Vice-Presidents for the possibility of taking over. The Truman succession marked the beginning of a new Vice-Presidency; henceforth, all Vice-Presidents would be conscious of their responsibility to prepare for the smooth transfer of power and leadership should the need arise. Other events would continue to promote an increased awareness of the office.

The very active Nixon Vice-Presidency of the 1950s coincided with the three

Eisenhower disabilities, and the new image of the Vice-Presidency was well on its way. Increasingly, individuals of stature would be attracted to it as candidates.

No sensitive person old enough to recall the hours of anxiety following the assassination of President John F. Kennedy in Dallas on November 22, 1963, can fail to appreciate the reassurance of having a Vice-President available and ready to assume the reins of government. The Kennedy assassination definitively established the importance of the office; the death of the youngest elected President in the history of the Republic loudly proclaimed the mortality of all humankind. Lyndon Johnson, the man nobody had chosen for the Presidency, masterfully assumed the stewardship of the country he inherited. The Kennedy assassination also created renewed interest in providing a mechanism for filling vacancies in the Vice-Presidency, and thus the relatively swift drafting and ratification of the Twenty-fifth Amendment. Never again would the country be long without a crowned prince, as it had been for practically the duration of the first Truman Administration following FDR's death in office.

The events of the 1970s—first the hasty selection of Senator Thomas Eagleton in 1972 as presidential candidate George McGovern's running mate and then the resignation of Vice-President Spiro Agnew in 1973 following charges of misconduct during his tenure as Baltimore County executive several years earlier, followed by the floodgates of Watergate and, finally, the protracted congressional hearings over Gerald Ford's nominee for the Vice-Presidency, Nelson Rockefeller—would create unprecedented interest in the Vice-Presidency. Politicians and average citizens alike would be hard-pressed to forget that one in five Presidents have come to that office via the Vice-Presidency.

The development of the Vice-President's role as administration spokesman, first during Humphrey's incumbency and later during Spiro Agnew's tenure, established a new unofficial assignment that would have profound political reverberations. Serving as administration spokesman would have mixed blessings, as this work will explore.

That Vice-Presidents often find themselves ''naked in the middle of a blizzard'' despite their own expertise and constituencies was especially true of the Rockefeller Vice-Presidency. The office had come a long way, attracting the likes of Lyndon Johnson, Hubert Humphrey, and Nelson Rockefeller. The peculiar circumstances of the Rockefeller incumbency might have suggested that he would have had a freer hand in carving out a role for himself under the Ford Presidency. One of the most prestigious and influential men to serve in the second office, Rockefeller had an extensive interest and background in foreign affairs. He found himself serving under a President who admitted he had little expertise in that area. The figure of Secretary of State Henry Kissinger was dominant in foreign affairs, and personal relations between Kissinger and Rockefeller were friendly and harmonious. At the outset of his incumbency, Rockefeller did not seem apt to suffer the same fate of many of his predecessors, who spent a good deal of time making good-will tours and raising funds for the party. In his initial functioning as Vice-President, Rockefeller maintained a low profile, seemingly deferring to the higher office of the Presidency. This is essentially the position any Vice-President who hopes to survive must maintain, as Mondale has noted.

Unlike many of his predecessors, too, Rockefeller, a major political figure for years, did not need to waste time attracting public notice nor did he need to convince the President of his abilities or usefulness. Indeed, the President himself seemed awed by the Rockefeller power and talent. In short, the Rockefeller Vice-Presidency was in many ways unique. Ultimately, however, Rockefeller's promise never fully materialized. Essentially, he was the victim of political considerations for the 1976 campaign. The conservative wing of the Republican party took exception to Rockefeller, and the threat of a Reagan challenge for the presidential nomination forced Ford to award the running mate spot to a candidate acceptable to the right. Rockefeller, too, was expendable. In the end, the interests of the President always prevail. Hubert Humphrey's insights on the presidential-vice-presidential relationship were well stated.

In most instances you will find a President never remembered when he called on a Vice President. There is a love-hate relationship. There is a faith and doubt relationship. A comradeship and an adversary—if not an adversary, at least a competitor. It's just in the nature of it. It's a marriage, as Lyndon Johnson pointed out to me, but it's one in which both the husband and wife are constantly looking at each other, and saying, "What's he/ she up to?" And in this sense, male chauvinism is supreme.[27]

Walter Mondale, Humphrey's protege of many years, understood this relationship very well. He enjoyed the more active role Jimmy Carter had promised from the outset, but this increased role also reflected the basic fact of the Vice-Presidency: the Vice-President is entirely subject to the wishes of the President. Mondale was viable because he was not visible.

George Bush has also discovered that this is what the Vice-Presidency is all about. During his early incumbency at least the symbolic change brought by the Carter-Mondale White House continued. The Vice-President's office remains in the White House, exactly where Mondale's was. Bush's early assignments were to head a task force to investigate governmental regulations and later to deal with the growing tragedy of the serial murders of black children in Atlanta. Reagan thus continued the historical precedent that Presidents initially promise an active role for their Vice-Presidents and fulfill this promise by assignments early in the administration. What follows, of course, is subject to all of the traditional variables. One of Vice-President Bush's assignments—as head of the administration's "crisis management team"—might have been made to undercut what had been the growing power of then Secretary of State Alexander M. Haig, Jr. Nonetheless, Bush's roles are the product of what the President of the United States wants them to be. And this is probably what the future holds for all future Vice-Presidents.

THE IMPACT OF THE PRESIDENCY ON THE SECOND OFFICE

By the time Harry Truman became Vice-President, the office had experienced an enduring history of "Throttlebottomism."[28] As Vice-President under Franklin Roosevelt, who had never treated Vice-Presidents particularly well, Truman could expect little in the way of assignments. He realized that the office, especially under FDR, consisted of little more than ceremonial and social activities. His short tenure in office was not particularly busy, although there was the usual initial presidential promise of increased involvement.[29] The lack of prestige and importance attached to the Vice-Presidency during the FDR years is demonstrated by the public's lack of concern for a vacancy in the office of almost four years during Truman's first term. On a number of occasions in the past, the office had been left vacant and had caused little worry.

Truman's Vice-President in his second term, Alben Barkley, was a congenial, very popular legislator with a penchant for storytelling. Although he sought little power from the second office, he was not idle during his four years, and his devotion and wisdom, together with the public respect he commanded, served President Truman's needs very well. In addition to relieving the President of some of his social commitments and foreign travel,[30] Barkley participated in decision-making, notably in the President's decision to dismiss General Douglas MacArthur.[31] Through Truman's efforts, Barkley was better briefed than previous constitutional heirs to the Presidency. An astute and experienced legislator who for years had served as Senate Majority Leader, Barkley was able to assist the President's legislative program.[32] Truman's laudable intentions and efforts to elevate the Vice-Presidency did not produce spectacular results. Barkley's congeniality and lightheartedness during the 1948 presidential campaign and the Truman Presidency projected "Dear Alben" as primarily an attractive public relations man. His elevation to the second office was a tribute to an elder statesman who had served long and faithfully in the legislature and deserved the prestige of high executive office.[33]

Vice-President Barkley's failure to take greater advantage of the statutory changes that were intended to widen the Vice-Presidency is only partly to blame for the lack of spectacular developments. The main reason lies in the vast growth of presidential responsibilities, power, and influence which has necessitated the astonishing expansion of the White House staff. As a result, the Presidency has become "dispersed," with a hidden arm of presidential aides and advisers responsible to no one but the President and extremely difficult, if not impossible, for him to assess or control.[34]

The second highest office has likewise expanded, with added office and staff facilities. This change signals added prestige for the Vice-Presidency and is another indication of growth, diffusion, and increasing applicability of "Parkinson's Law" within the executive branch.

While the presidential staff has grown larger in both numbers and responsibilities and authority, the Presidency has become increasingly a singular job with increased constitutional obligations, powers, and responsibilities that cannot be shared. Because the President cannot delegate his office, he remains accountable for his staff. In *The President's Men*, Patrick Anderson discusses the problem of presidential staffing and the seeming paradox of vast increases in the number of presidential advisers in recent years paired with greater presidential duties. He states: "It is of the nature of Presidents to use many men, to need a few, and to love almost none."[35] The presidential aides perform the thankless tasks of the Presidency: "Credit flows upward and blame downward. . . . The President's good works are carved in marble; his aides' are writ on water."[36]

As noted earlier, Hubert Humphrey pointed out that a Vice-President suffers a similar treatment. "In most instances you will find a President seldom ever remembered when he called on a Vice President as spokesman." The Vice-President can be a spokesman, Humphrey continued, because the "President can always disavow you . . . if you get too far out."[37] Presidents, then, use the people around them, be they aides or Vice-Presidents.

In referring to President Roosevelt as an example, Anderson believes that "it is oversimple to say that Roosevelt 'used' his advisers as shields of criticism—the system used them whether or not the President liked it. But it is true that he rarely spoke out publicly in their defense; he expected them to fight their own battles, or to suffer in silence if that suited his interests."[38]

FDR was not unique in this behavior, for there have been recent applications of the "silent treatment." There were notable similarities between Eisenhower's handling of Nixon's slush fund problems during the campaign of 1952 and Nixon's handling of Agnew's scandal in 1973. In the first case, Eisenhower was a presidential candidate, while in the second Nixon was an incumbent President with the Watergate atmosphere pervading. Nevertheless, both presidential candidate Eisenhower and President Nixon behaved similarly with regard to their second man. Neither said anything, preferring to leave their heirs apparent on their own. Thus, both Eisenhower and Nixon maximized their options.

In sharp contrast was George McGovern's initial and premature statement of "1,000% support" for Senator Thomas Eagleton in the 1972 campaign when Eagleton's psychiatric record, previously unrevealed, became a public controversy. Despite his initial support, McGovern eventually came to a position similar to that taken by Eisenhower and Nixon. He began to be less committal in his support for Eagleton, until Eagleton found no other alternative but to remove himself from the Democratic ticket. In 1952, Eisenhower had played a waiting game, watching public reaction to Nixon's problems and his television address to the nation, before any decision was made regarding Nixon's place on the ticket.

A President may, of course, eliminate those staff members who become a hindrance to him. In a very important sense, this is his ultimate check on them. Anderson notes that "one of Roosevelt's political ploys was to whisk controversial aides out of view at election time. . . . Roosevelt's aides had to learn to accept such indignities; if they couldn't, their days were numbered."[39] The Vice-President, however, is not so easily disposed of; barring malfeasance, resignation, impeachment, or death, the Vice-President is there to stay.

The Vice-President, as an elected rather than an appointed official, brings greater status to the tasks a President may assign to him; similarly, he can more legitimately serve as a substitute for the President. For example, Kennedy dispatched Vice-President Johnson to Berlin in 1961 in order to dramatize U.S. interest and concern in the political situation there, while at the same time not involving the full force of the presidential office. Similarly, Vice-President Nixon was President Eisenhower's representative in the settlement of the steel strike of 1959.[40]

A President, it has been said, makes no new friends; he cannot afford to. The extent to which any President emphasizes loyalty depends on his own personality, yet he cannot function effectively in the absence of that crucial commodity, as President Jimmy Carter soon learned in his Presidency. Harry Truman's astute observation of the potential sharing of confidences between a President and the Vice-President sheds additional light on just how much loyalty a President might be able to demand. Noted Truman,

The President is the man who decides every major domestic policy, and he is the man who makes foreign policy and negotiates treaties. In doing these things it would be very difficult for him to take the second man in the government—the Vice President—completely into his confidence. The Presidency, by necessity, builds his [sic] own staff, and the Vice-President remains an outsider, no matter how friendly the two may be. There are many reasons for this, but an important one is the fact that both the President and the Vice-President are, or should be, astute politicians, and neither can take the other completely into his confidence.[41]

Because the Vice-President, like the President, is a political being, a pragmatic President knows full well that even the best-intentioned Vice-President might sometime be tempted to put his/her own interests above the President's.

Roosevelt had a "need for followers whose devotion was total," but he was not unusual in this respect. While it was Roosevelt who "started the evolution of the White House staff toward the large and powerful extra-constitutional institution that now exists,"[42] that evolution was inevitable, and with it the evolution toward an increasing emphasis on personal loyalty to the President. Presidents Johnson and Nixon placed demands of loyalty on their staffs, which may have been due in part to their individual makeups; but they could do so with greater ease as a result of the evolutionary trends in the institution of the Presidency.[43] Two case studies, focusing on the Johnson-Humphrey relationship and the Eisenhower-Nixon relationship, illustrate this point well.

THE IMPACT OF PERSONALITY: THE JOHNSON-HUMPHREY RELATIONSHIP

Lyndon Johnson described his relationship with John Kennedy as follows:

I served him loyally, as I would have wanted my Vice President to serve me. We did
not always see things in the same light. I did not always agree with everything that
happened in his administration. But when I did disagree with the President, I did so in
private, and man to man.[44]

Having experienced the frustration inherent in the vice-presidential office,
Johnson was, at least initially, determined to avoid having Humphrey suffer the
same fate.[45] Whatever Johnson's intentions, however, a combination of forces
worked to make Humphrey the frequently battered victim of the office.

In his psychohistorical study of American Presidents, James David Barber has
said of Lyndon Johnson, "The virtues were unquestioning loyalty, absolute
servitude; Johnson was not given to praising his men for independence of mind."
From the outset, Johnson had made clear to Humphrey that a precondition for
his vice-presidential nomination in 1964 was the promise of loyalty. Public
disagreements were taboo.

Barber notes that "from recruitment to subordination was a regular transition
for Johnson," and "Humphrey was no exception to the process," for "the crux
of Johnson's interpersonal style was the habit of turning occasions for mutuality
into occasions for domination."[46]

As Johnson threw himself into his Presidency with a vigor he had not exercised
since he had left the legislature for the relative impotence of the Vice-Presidency,
the true Johnson began to reassert himself. One observer noted that Johnson was
"oversize."[47] Johnson's aide, Walter Jenkins, said, "He drove his staff, but he
drove himself; he drove everyone around him,"[48] and former Secretary of State
Dean Rusk pointed out "one forgave him for that because he was hardest on
himself."[49] Said one confidential source, "People worked under LBJ in fear."
Frequently unable to delegate responsibility—not unlike his father figure in the
Presidency, Franklin Roosevelt—Johnson engulfed the Presidency, living and
breathing it inhumanly long hours of every day.

In describing the Vice-President's role, Humphrey said,

[T]he office is dictated pretty much by the fellow who occupies it, by the nature of the
man who is Vice-President—what's he like intellectually, mentally, genetically, his glan-
dular makeup, and his background and experience. Number two, the Constitution and
the public law that relates to the office. Number three, the relations—what the man
himself wants to make of the office. The man himself. And number four, what the
President permits—responsibilities he gives.[50]

President Johnson was willing to give as long as Humphrey obeyed the ground
rules, especially the one about loyalty. Continued Humphrey,

Now, my man, my President, the man that I worked for, Lyndon Johnson, gave me a
very active [role]. . . . I think he knew me well. . . . He knew that I would be restless if
I did not have duties. He knew that I had people that I could work with, that I had a
constituency. I didn't come to the Vice Presidency as just a parochial figure. I had actually

a national constituency—the labor movement, the civil rights movement, the education people that I had worked with. These were people that knew me, so he put me to work with these people, and I became sort of the eyes and ears of the President in many areas— without authority, without any great power, but reportorial. I reported; I coordinated; I was the President's spokesman to these groups.[51]

While Humphrey did indeed have an active Vice-Presidency, he endured many periods of uncertainty, resulting from what Albert Eisele, Humphrey's biographer, has called the "hot-and-cold Johnson treatment," during which Johnson "would praise Humphrey one day and damn him the next."[52] Johnson's unpredictability seemed to dominate the relationship; he was the President. The Vice-President was just that, nothing more, and certainly not an Assistant President.

Humphrey's flexibility fit in well with Johnson's unpredictability. And so Humphrey would be "chewed out" for getting too much publicity, or when in an ebullient moment, which was so inherently part of the Humphrey character and personality, for accidentally leaking information Johnson had preferred to remain confidential a while longer. As examples, Humphrey leaked information regarding minimum wage increases when talking with labor leaders; in July 1965 at the Governors' Conference, he pleaded for their backing in the decision to expand this nation's combat role in Vietnam (a decision Johnson had not yet made public);[53] and he made his exuberant call, also in 1965, for a "Marshall Plan" for the troubled cities.[54] This was the Humphrey who frequently got carried away in doing his job and who suffered the consequences.[55]

Johnson, not about to share the limelight and "out to use whatever technique would confirm his own power,"[56] was frequently enraged by some of Humphrey's slips and did not fail to tell him so. The result was a self-imposed restraint by Humphrey, during which time the Vice-President declined interviews and said little. The contrast was sufficiently apparent once to produce the remark that one could see the President more easily than his Vice-President.[57] Humphrey's friends perceived Johnson as "the great emasculator," but the Vice-President continued his unswerving loyalty.[58] From the time he assumed the Vice-Presidency, Humphrey was sure he would be able to survive the demands and frustrations of the Vice-Presidency and the particular problems of working under Lyndon Johnson.

Humphrey, however, began to diverge from Johnson on one grave and controversial point. At the February 10, 1965, meeting of the National Security Council, Humphrey, departing from his promise to avoid any public disagreements with the President, questioned the intelligence of bombing North Vietnam.[59] He followed this public expression of disagreement by a memorandum to Johnson. The President was furious. According to Eisele, "His secretive nature and absolute insistence on avoiding any public display bordered on an obsession, and he upbraided Humphrey for committing his thoughts to paper."[60] This break marked for Humphrey "a critical turning point in his vice presidency," and he was now excluded from the "Tuesday luncheons," meetings of Johnson's closest advisers who participated in making decisions on the war.[61]

Humphrey was lucky to have been left, at that point, with domestic chores. But Eisele astutely points out that "Humphrey's exclusion from Vietnam strategy sessions did not extend to matters relating to the impact of the war on the domestic front."[62] This fact represents one area in which the Vice-Presidency has come to be used a great deal, particularly since the first Eisenhower Administration. Humphrey described the role he was expected to play.

A Vice-President can [serve as] . . . a political spokesman for the Administration. President Johnson did not always want to get involved in all the campaigns and politics, so I was a political spokesman. I went to the party conventions. Obviously, he went to some— the biggest ones, but I was sent out to many of the state meetings, and I had to take on defending the Administration at the college campus level. The college campuses were [in turmoil during] my Vice Presidency—and went through a terrific upheaval, unbelievable, but I never once was ever driven from a platform. Most of the time despite all the heckling and all that it came off with a good reception.

Humphrey also mentioned the dilemma which this role posed.

The Vice-President *can* be a spokesman—because the President can always disavow you, you see, if you get too far out. He can always say, "Well, that's the Vice President speaking. He wasn't speaking for me." If he speaks well, and gets by, he was speaking for him, so it's really a no-win job, you know what I mean? It's really a no-win job. It's really being willing to do the Lord's work, you know. Whoever you are, I think that's the case.[63]

Humphrey defended policies he had no part in forging. He did so even after his relationship with Johnson had suffered a severe setback and the President, on many occasions, embarrassingly pulled the rug out from under him. Humphrey, for example, did not participate in the development of, nor was he given an advance copy of, Johnson's 1967 State of the Union message. And Johnson's abolition of the civil rights coordinating council, which in effect eliminated one of the Vice-President's jobs, came about in an abrupt, humiliating fashion.[64] As a result, Humphrey suffered a long-lasting setback with irremediable overtones, and perhaps "the full potential of Humphrey's vice presidency was never realized."[65]

Humphrey knew that his own personality and background, as that of all Vice-Presidents, helped shape his incumbency, both positively and negatively. The Minnesota senator was well aware that he brought with him his own constituency and the expertise of many years of governmental service. He knew a great deal about world affairs, and he had served as a United Nations delegate to the World Health Organization and UNESCO. He had attended the Geneva disarmament talks. He had met with Premier Nikita Khrushchev in 1958, during which time he had talked at length with the Soviet leader. Humphrey had served as chairman of the Senate disarmament subcommittee which performed preparatory work leading to the nuclear test ban treaty in 1963.[66] His expertise on civil rights and poverty issues, combined with his astute knowledge of the legislative process and close personal relationships with legislators, all served to condition his role as Vice-President. Moreover, he was highly knowledgeable regarding urban affairs, which became a principal concern of the Johnson Administration. As the former Secretary of Housing and Urban Development, Robert C. Wood, pointed out, "There was nothing like the focus of attention to urban affairs in the Kennedy time as was characterized in the Johnson era."[67]

Humphrey had a very long arm extended into the liberal camp—an arm Johnson would borrow to help him defend the administration's position on Vietnam and try to salve the alienated liberals.

The Vice-President's personality itself was a critical ingredient in his survival. Eager and grateful to be nominated for the office, and genuinely appreciative to Johnson for assistance in developing his political career as a legislator, Humphrey was eager to please. His gravest misfortune was that he was ultimately swallowed up by a war that the administration he served had inherited and enlarged. Because of his identification with Lyndon Johnson, Humphrey's abilities and potential were never fully realized or utilized by the American people.

As his Vice-Presidency progressed, Humphrey, fulfilling his pledge of loyalty, took on a hectic schedule of public appearances, speeches, political rallies, and legislative conferences. Throughout his Vice-Presidency, Humphrey was keenly aware that Johnson would make or break him politically. Humphrey knew that the President was his "constituency of one."[68] The Vice-President was stultified because he was at the time "almost totally dependent upon Johnson for his political future."[69] Yet, being subordinate to Johnson was not an unnatural role for him, for it was simply a continuation of their Senate relationship. Furthermore, his personality was far more flexible than Johnson's, and unlike Johnson, who rankled at his position under President Kennedy, total subordination to the President was not distasteful for Humphrey.

Johnson's domination of Humphrey gave rise to countless jokes in Washington. Allan Ryskind tells one story that circulated during the Johnson Presidency: "LBJ and Humphrey were attending a swank dinner affair when the President suddenly whispered into Humphrey's ear, 'Hubert, did I hear you belch?' To which Humphrey responded, 'No, Mr. President, was I supposed to?' "[70] And there was a great deal of truth behind these apocryphal tales. When Johnson criticized Humphrey for seeking publicity, Humphrey maintained a low profile; when Johnson criticized Humphrey for having a press secretary, Humphrey promptly fired him.[71] Throughout his Vice-Presidency, Humphrey followed Johnson's cue, snapping smartly into line when called to order, and strove to maintain a low profile. Humphrey's subordination contributed to his loss of identity and doubtless contributed to his defeat in the 1968 presidential race.

THE IMPACT OF PERSONALITY: THE EISENHOWER-NIXON RELATIONSHIP

In character and personality, Dwight Eisenhower represented the other end of the spectrum from Johnson. In stark contrast to Johnson, he not only was disinterested in politics, but also seemed to disdain politics and politicians. Among the few politicians in his entourage, the young Nixon rose rapidly as the politician par excellence.[72] Eisenhower was content to let Nixon take care of party politics, and the Vice-President made the most of the opportunity. Commentators have said of Eisenhower that party politics "was not congenial to him. There was a feeling of disorientation."[73] Despite the fact that the President never forgave or fully trusted Nixon after the "Checkers" debacle, Eisenhower pushed off political chores on Nixon.[74] It was advantageous to Nixon that Eisenhower never came to enjoy or appreciate the value of politics. Eisenhower went "all the way through feeling rather sorry for himself for having to deal with politicians; he felt demeaned by them."[75]

The Nixon Vice-Presidency was strongly conditioned by Eisenhower's reliance on the staff system which he had employed for so many years in the military. The dominant force of this staff system was the President's Chief of Staff, Sherman Adams, whom the *London Economist* referred to as "the most publicized hidden hand in Washington."[76] The Chief of Staff received briefings and decided what matters should be brought to the President's attention. He also made specific assignments to specific people, and unlike other administrations such as those of Roosevelt, Johnson, and Nixon, Adams made these assignments with very little overlap. These assignments helped isolate the President from members of his staff. Despite the limitations which this staff system had on the development of the vice-presidential office, Nixon survived and in many areas he even thrived, serving as a spokesman for the administration in foreign affairs, party affairs, and as chairman of the Committee on Government Contracts (the predecessor of the President's Committee on Equal Employment Opportunity). With the election of the popular Eisenhower, possibilities for Republican gains were ripe; the President, however, seemed unwilling to reap the harvest. Eisenhower's sweeping victory had carried his party with him. For the first time in years, the Republicans held control of both houses of Congress. New York's Republican Senator Jacob Javits recalls that at first there existed a very "reverential" sentiment toward the President and the hope that he would actively work for the party "to make it a living force in our country" and "to give it a greater status as the alternative in the two-party system."[77] The party was soon disappointed. Former New York Senator Kenneth Keating believed that Eisenhower

could have built the Republican Party to a position where it would have been hard to get them out. If he had taken that attitude, I'm sure Dick Nixon would have been elected when he ran, because it was close; any such little thing would have tipped the scales.[78]

Eisenhower, however, refused to work toward transferring his personal following into a party following.[79] As noted earlier, the task of being the party man fell to Nixon, who took on assignment after assignment, building an impressive reputation and acquiring a long list of political obligations upon which he would later collect.[80] In addition to his party role, Nixon himself estimated that he spent

more than 90 percent of his time on executive duties[81]—at National Security
Council meetings, Cabinet meetings, as chairman of the Cabinet Committee on
Price Stability, and as chairman of the Committee on Government Contracts.[82]

It was, nonetheless, in the field of party politics that Nixon was most outstanding. "Nixon was always a very strong party man," said Republican Leverett
Saltonstall.

> He also tried to help where he could, without getting in conflict with the President, on
> all patronage and things of that kind. Now for eight years I sat beside him at these morning
> weekly conferences. . . . Nixon didn't speak very much at those meetings, but when he
> did speak, it was generally to express a political point of view or the feelings in the
> country in a certain section, as he got it, and as Nixon always does, he spoke very well.[83]

And he got things done. Nixon was aware of his position as Vice-President,
and he was careful not to go too far. He ultimately maintained the President's
policy, and "in his first two years in office Nixon imposed a limited oath of
silence on himself."[84] Some observers feel that his maintenance of the Eisenhower policy caused a "conservative affection-disaffection syndrome" within
the Republican party.[85] Others have credited Nixon for being above all else
astutely political. As "a very effective member of the President's team . . . he
was careful not to try to assume any of the prerogatives of the Presidency in
carrying out functional responsibilities. . . . He didn't try . . . to go around the
President, or to build himself to the exclusion of somebody else."[86]

Nixon knew he could not, as some of his advisers had suggested, "stand up
to Ike"[87] and strike out on his own. His staunch party convictions and political
wisdom prevented such action.

When Eisenhower became President, the crusading senator from Wisconsin,
Joseph McCarthy, was riding high in his attempt to purge the country of the
"Red Menace." Little escaped his scrutiny. McCarthy's activities undoubtedly
contributed to the selection of Richard Nixon as the 1952 Republican vice-
presidential candidate. A nationally known figure as a result of his long fight
against the Communists within the United States, Nixon became the administration's spokesman on communism. While Nixon took no public posture on
McCarthy, as Vice-President he served as a buffer between McCarthy and the
administration.[88] In 1954, Nixon reluctantly responded to the President's order
that he reply to Adlai Stevenson's attack on the Eisenhower-McCarthy division
within the Republican party.[89]

Seeking to maintain his ambivalent ideological position in the party and to
avoid alienating its right wing, Nixon responded to his problem by utilizing a
speech form familiar to him, the innuendo. The Nixon formula was patterned
as follows: "Men who in the past have done effective work exposing communism
in this country have, by reckless talk and questionable methods, made themselves
the issue, rather than the cause they believe in so deeply." This led up to his
subtle attack on Stevenson whom Nixon did not name to avoid unnecessarily
alienating the left.

When they have done this . . . they have not only diverted the attention from the dangers of communism, but they have allowed those whose primary objective is to defeat the Eisenhower Administration to divert attention from its great programs to these individuals who have followed these methods.[90]

It was a brilliant speech, jabbing at McCarthy and Stevenson simultaneously. It touched on what needed to be covered without blatantly alienating, although it did little to quiet McCarthy.[91] In terms of its importance for the Vice-Presidency, Nixon's speech was symptomatic of a role that has developed during the modern Vice-Presidency, that of administration spokesman.

Nixon could do little more about McCarthy without making himself appear hypocritical. His record and his claim to fame as an avowed foe of domestic communism set the stage for his reactions to McCarthy. As long as possible, Nixon tried to remain on firm ground, balancing one move against another, playing to McCarthy and striving to keep the President from moving into a position apt to cause a party split.[92] Nixon's leitmotif seemed to be the unity of the Republican party, above and beyond all else, for as long as possible. Throughout this battle, Nixon played both sides against the middle. As administration spokesman, he served as a defender and buffer as he would be obliged to do throughout his incumbency; meanwhile, he continued to play the role of the party man.[93] "His effectiveness," noted one observer, "placed him in the line of fire," as it had in his successful 1953 confrontation with labor at the AFL Convention, a confrontation thrust upon him by the President.[94] Eisenhower even assigned Nixon and the Republican National Committee the task of dealing with Sherman Adams after the scandal involving gifts Adams received as Chief of Staff erupted; Adams eventually resigned. And, although Nixon ultimately worked toward the Senate's censure of McCarthy, Nixon's public reaction to the censure demonstrated "little policy and no principle . . . but there were displayed infinite adaptability and caution." He avoided any mention of what the censure meant to Eisenhower and the administration.[95]

Beginning in 1957, Nixon began to tone down his "hatchetman" role by utilizing a more subdued and moderate approach to political affairs. He doubtless was looking toward the next presidential election; the similarities in Nixon's behavior as a second-term Vice-President in 1957 and Spiro Agnew's in 1973 are striking.

Other developments helped make the Nixon Vice-Presidency an active one. Hubert Humphrey noted that Nixon was "propelled into responsibilities that were unusual for a Vice President."[96] Eisenhower's willingness, and sometimes preference, to have Nixon do the politicking for the party, his willingness to send Nixon on important diplomatic missions abroad, and especially his three illnesses gave Nixon immense exposure and prestige.[97] As acting chairman of the National Security Council and the Cabinet, he successfully focused attention on his role as Vice-President.

As Nixon's second term progressed, it seemed increasingly obvious that he would become the Republican presidential candidate in 1960. His Vice-Presidency set precedents for future occupants of that office. Although he was defeated in 1960, his titular leadership of the party continued,[98] and future Vice-Presidents would build on the precedents he had set, especially as administration spokesman and in foreign affairs.

ADMINISTRATION SPOKESMAN: THE JOHNSON INCUMBENCY AND A HIATUS

Nixon was well suited to the times of his Vice-Presidency. His willingness to take to the road and mount the podium, to sing the administration's praises and chastise its enemies, carved out a place for him in American politics virtually unknown to his vice-presidential predecessors.

In contrast, Vice-President Lyndon Johnson's personality was not well suited to the function of adminstration spokesman. Moreover, his position within the Kennedy Administration was far different from that of his predecessor, and he was neither called on nor inclined to fulfill his role as blatantly as Nixon. Some occasions did arise, however, notably within the delicate area of civil rights. Viewed initially with suspicion and sometimes outright hostility by liberals, Johnson was able to get involved in some areas that few others in the Kennedy Administration could approach. Through the civil rights arena, Johnson greatly enhanced his image as an effective administration spokesman.

Johnson's work as chairman of the President's Committee on Equal Employment Opportunity (PCOEEO) helped him rebuild his own image. While it seems quite obvious, as Tom Wicker has stated, that "Johnson had no political choice whatever but to commit himself to the civil rights bill Kennedy sent to Congress,"[99] the Vice-President had certain unique assets which rendered his support meaningful. He knew and understood the people whose minds had to be changed, especially within the legislature. As an astute politician, he knew that coercion was far less effective than persuasion. He also knew when and how to be forceful. Reflecting on the work of the PCOEEO in 1972, Johnson told Walter Cronkite,

We used all the power and all the authority we had. I don't think that we made a choice between what's hard-nosed and soft-nosed. I think we did everything that we had the implements to do. We created an awareness among the people in government that the minorities weren't getting a fair shake in employment in the government. We created an awareness in the employer groups in the country and the labor groups in the country that we had to move much farther in giving equal employment to all of our citizens. And we used every power that we had and some we didn't have. I don't think we had any compromise on it. We couldn't just go and wrestle with the fellow and say you've got to do this or we'll do something to you. We tried to lead them with persuasion because that's all the power we had.[100]

The Vice-President, Kennedy's elder in both years and government experience, was kept occupied by Kennedy, who was aware of Johnson's sensitivities. Kennedy well appreciated the need to insure "the care and feeding of Lyndon Johnson."[101] Arthur Schlesinger, Jr., recalls that during the Kennedy Administration "the problem remained of finding things for the Vice-President to do."[102]

In addition to attending the seldom-held Cabinet and National Security Council meetings, Johnson chaired numerous committees, including the PCOEEO and the Space Council. Kennedy used him extensively in the area of foreign travel, journeying not only to Europe but to Southeast Asia and the Middle East as well, visiting thirty-three countries.[103] The exposure which those foreign assignments gave him, coupled with his work in the civil rights field, provided valuable experience and filled many gaps in his background.[104] The experience he gained in his thirty-four months as Vice-President made him the best prepared man in the nation's history to assume the burdens of the Presidency upon the death of a predecessor. His vice-presidential incumbency continued the developmental trend in the Vice-Presidency begun under Nixon.

Former Johnson Press Secretary George Christian has noted that the comedown from the dominating position of Majority Leader to the "political limbo of being second man to John F. Kennedy for three years" was not an easy transition.[105] Despite Kennedy's sincere efforts to keep Johnson both active and informed, the Vice-President's negative relationship with the Kennedy staff and especially with the second most important individual in the administration, the President's brother, Attorney General Robert Kennedy, set the tone of frustration for his Vice-Presidency.[106] The relationship between Johnson and Robert Kennedy was at best one of tolerance. Robert Kennedy was more than staff, more than aide, more than Cabinet member. He was above all the President's alter-ego. His personal antagonism toward Johnson did not help Johnson's relations with the Kennedy staff. "Colonel Cornpone," as Johnson was derisively labeled by some members of the Kennedy staff,[107] did not fit the Kennedy image and "baiting the Vice President became the favorite indoor sport" of many Kennedy aides, as one high Johnson administration official confidentially recalled.

The emphasis of Kennedy's "New Frontier" was on youthful energy in the executive branch, and as the esprit de corps among the Kennedyites became almost visionary, the Vice-President, who had campaigned hard (and many felt unfairly) against Kennedy, was viewed as a throwback to another generation.[108] Johnson's aide, Walter Jenkins, described the difference succinctly: "Johnson was from Austin, not Boston."[109]

Although harmony was lacking, Johnson requested and received a major role in the space program, an area in which he had worked hard in the Senate.[110] This assignment pleased Johnson, and his association with the space program demonstrated President Kennedy's firm commitment to the program.[111] Future Presidents would also stress a particular issue or program by assigning the Vice-President to it. Richard Nixon, for example, assigned Vice-President Gerald

Ford to the Committee on Privacy, and President Ford assigned Vice-President Nelson Rockefeller to the committee to investigate the Central Intelligence Agency and to reorganize the Domestic Council. Similarly, President Reagan underscored the importance of de-regulation by assigning Vice-President Bush to the area.

Johnson deferred to the President and his men, avoided public disagreements, kept his opposition to administration policies private, and interjected his opinion "very quietly, unobtrusively."[112]

Johnson suffered the inevitable fate of Vice-Presidents vis-à-vis presidential staff, which in his case was particularly negative. Pierre Salinger describes Johnson's relations with the Kennedy staff as "distant and cool."[113] He was seldom asked to serve as administration spokesman as were his counterparts, especially Nixon, Humphrey, and Agnew.

THE VICE-PRESIDENT AS ADMINISTRATION SPOKESMAN: THE RISE OF SPIRO AGNEW

Perhaps the most striking utilization of the Vice-President as administration spokesman occurred during the Nixon Administration. Referred to frequently as "Nixon's Nixon," Agnew managed to draw audiences politicians only dream about, accumulating ardent fans and equally ardent enemies wherever he went and on whatever issues he pursued. Unlike his fictional predecessor Throttle-bottom, few could be unaware of, or neutral toward, Ted Agnew. The relatively obscure former governor of Maryland indeed fulfilled his campaign promise of becoming a household word. In a role comparable to that performed by Nixon during the 1954 congressional campaigns, Agnew took on the "unsavory political assignments" which the President shunned.[114]

Judging from his seemingly inept performance in the 1968 presidential campaign, Agnew seemed to be the last person one would expect to launch a frontal attack in behalf of the Nixon Administration. His tasteless ethnic references to "Fat Japs"[115] and the like had made him the butt of campaign ridicule. For awhile following the inauguration, the Vice-President was kept under wraps. Thereafter, he began to speak out as no Vice-President had before. In early May 1968, speaking before the Young President's Organization in Honolulu, Agnew's remarks foreshadowed the themes that would develop in the ensuing months. The Vice-President criticized the "continual carnival on the streets of . . . [the] cities and the campuses of the nation" that was taking place at the hands of "young adults hell-bent on 'non-negotiable' destruction," while college administrators stood by "confused and capitulating" and "sophisticated faculties" were "distraught and divided over issues as basic as the criminality of breaking and entering, theft, vandalism, assault and battery." Agnew had begun to take on the campus protest of the Vietnam War; subsequent speeches would build on these early remarks, and a theme which he had woven into this speech would gradually come to be the focus of the administration's attention: the "vast faceless majority of the American public in quiet fury over the situation." Agnew continued with an analysis of the "anatomy of violence" that had begun to pervade this nation, beginning with the civil disobedience of the civil rights movement, and cited as "prophetic" Supreme Court Justice Hugo Black's 1966 statement, "Once you give a nervous, hostile and ill informed people a theoretical justification for using violence . . . it's like a tiny hole in the dike . . . and violence becomes a normal, acceptable solution for a problem."

The Vice-President then, in the same speech, turned to a theme to which he would return repeatedly in the months ahead: permissiveness. This society, he said, had been entirely too tolerant: tolerant of "the new politics which campus radicals have pushed to the furthest extreme"; tolerant of "group[s] assert[ing] rights without commensurate responsibilities." Agnew was clearly echoing themes he had proclaimed as Maryland's governor. As Vice-President, however, he expanded this theme to appeal to the "majority . . . bewildered by present irrational protest."[116] The temper of the times caused Agnew's statements to strike a responsive chord among a vast segment of America frightened by the growth of crime and rioting in cities and disturbances on college campuses. In response to these fears, "law and order" had been the major issue of the 1968 presidential campaign. In this first speech as a spokesman for the Nixon Administration, Agnew attempted to find a resolution to the problem of "law and order." Responsibility, he asserted, fell to nongovernmental institutions to do their jobs better; the administrators and faculties who "capitulate before storm-trooper tactics" were creating the very environment of permissiveness that led to riots and disorders.[117]

The battleground had been determined. The permissiveness of the liberals, the permissiveness of the college environment, the permissiveness of the new politics would be the enemy. But before Agnew completed his speech, another enemy was identified, and the Vice-President charged that "the Fourth Estate, which would rise in righteous fury against any demagogue attacking freedom of the press, has been far more gentle with demagogues in the established order."[118] In a commencement address the next month, Agnew included florid statements in an otherwise moderate speech. To the graduates he said, "A society which comes to fear its children is effete. A sniveling, hand-wringing power structure deserves the violent rebellion it encourages. If my generation doesn't stop cringing, yours will inherit a lawless society where emotion and muscle displace reason."[119]

These initial speeches in May and June of 1969, after a long silence, portended the active role the new Vice-President was to play as administration spokesman. Opening his Ohio State University address with a quotation from Cicero, "Young men hear an old man to whom old men harkened when he was young," Agnew advised the assembly in Columbus that his purpose was "not to castigate youth nor discuss why the generations differ . . . [but] to point out the case for American democracy."[120]

In July 1969, an event occurred which was to have a profound effect and recurring repercussions for American politics. The last of the Kennedy brothers, viewed as the inevitable challenger to President Nixon in the 1972 presidential campaign, suffered a grave setback. His involvement in the tragic death of a former campaign worker for Robert Kennedy eliminated him as a presidential hopeful for the Democrats. The controversy surrounding the actual events and motives involved in the fatal accident still lingers, as does the controversy regarding the impact the event had on the Nixon Adminstration, particularly Agnew's role in the administration.

Agnew assumed a more vigorous and petulant role in the months following Chappaquiddick, which some have interpreted as a windfall of relief from political pressures for the White House. With Kennedy no longer a presidential threat, the path was opened for a stronger attack on the liberal segments of America championed by Kennedy. Some observers maintain that Agnew's new role was merely coincidental to the Chappaquiddick affair, This view is reinforced by the themes of Agnew's speeches made prior to Senator Kennedy's misfortune. Nonetheless, the Agnew crusade did not suffer as a result. As the Vice-President's crusade expanded, greater efforts were concentrated on the circumstances that had produced the Wallace vote, which had been so threatening in the 1968 campaign.

In response to the widely organized Vietnam Moratorium Day demonstrations on October 19, 1969, President Nixon declared that such manifestations would in no way influence his policies. This infuriated large segments of the press, to which Agnew responded four days later in a speech in New Orleans. "The young," said the Vice-President, "overwhelm themselves with drugs and artificial stimulants. . . . Life is visceral rather than intellectual, and the most visceral practitioners of life are those who characterize themselves as intellectuals." Slowly, over the course of several speeches, Agnew was polarizing the "majority," the masses, from those who disagreed with administration policy, "an effete corps of impudent snobs who characterize themselves as intellectuals."

Agnew was careful to note that not all the young were maliciously motivated; rather, they were "well-motivated young people, conditioned since childhood to respond to great emotional appeals, [who] saw fit to demonstrate for peace." They were misled, however, by the Moratorium leaders, "the hardcore dissidents and the professional anarchists within the so-called 'peace movement.' "[121]

Agnew then turned to the situation in Vietnam by first reviewing the progress that had taken place since Nixon took office, and then he resumed his attack on the enemy. "There's a constructive program [in Vietnam]. What do the marchers in the Moratorium offer in place of that? Nothing . . . except an emotional bath for the people of the United States." And then Agnew logically concluded that those who "prefer to side with an enemy aggressor rather than stand by this free nation" were less than patriotic.[122]

The "effete corps of impudent snobs" phrase established the kind of rhetoric that would typify the developing Agnew crusade. Criticism of the speech began to reverberate, and to many the comparative silence of the White House[123] signified tacit approval of Agnew's colorful new role. With Ted Kennedy out of the 1972 presidential picture, Agnew zeroed in on the many who now most threatened Nixon's reelection.

In the 1968 presidential campaign, Alabama Governor George Wallace's candidacy had greatly influenced the strategies of the two major party candidates, particularly in their decision to speak to the "law and order" issue that obsessed the country. As the presidential campaign continued, Wallace's potential strength became so formidable that some began to doubt whether either of the two major party candidates would receive the required majority of the Electoral College votes.[124] Wallace's strength with the electorate and the likelihood that Edward Kennedy would be the Democratic candidate in the next election forced the Nixon Administration to look forward prematurely to 1972. To some extent, perhaps "political schizophrenia" best characterized the reaction of the Nixon team, as they contemplated how to kill both the Wallace and Kennedy threats. After Chappaquiddick, however, factors bearing on the 1972 campaign were more limited, and only George Wallace remained a problem. Thus, the administration's strategy could be aligned with the Agnew crusade.[125] Several days following his grandiloquent New Orleans incursion, Agnew spoke in similar fashion at Jackson, Mississippi, saying "this Administration will never appeal to a racist philosophy. . . . However, a free government cannot impose rules of social acceptance upon its citizens. . . . The point is this—in a man's private life he has the right to make his own friends." The Vice-President continued with a disavowal of "the Southern Strategy"—that is, the administration playing to Southern issues in hopes of forging a new alignment. Despite this disavowal, Agnew proclaimed that "for too long the South has been the punching bag for those who characterize themselves as liberal intellectuals. Actually, they are consistently demonstrating the antithesis of intelligence."

The Jackson speech is an example of masterful rhetoric. Disclaiming any racist policy on the part of the administration, Agnew championed the right of the individual to remain unshackled by "rules of social acceptance." Calling for an ideological "alignment"—an exhortation to which he would give greater emphasis in his October 30 speech at Harrisburg, Pennsylvania—Agnew emphasized the need for a "positive polarization" from leftist adversaries. In subsequent speeches, Agnew denounced charges of a Southern Strategy in the administration and lashed out against the "Northeastern liberal community." The "liberal intellectuals with their admirers in Congress," said Agnew, are also the "arrogant ones" who "are bringing this nation to the most important decision it will ever have to make."

Agnew's cleverness with words enabled him to draw the battle lines against those who were "asking us to repudiate principles that have made this country great." The liberals who protested the war, he maintained, were "more comfortable with radicals." Stringing together words such as "the liberals," "Congress," "war protesters," the "New Left," the Democratic party, and "the media" had the effect of labeling them individually and collectively as "the enemy" of the country.[126] Agnew shortly became one of the most sought-after speakers in the country. Whenever he spoke, the public awaited the vituperative rhetoric which he was certain to deliver.

The "majority" of Americans of whom Agnew had spoken in his Jackson speech and whom Richard Nixon had mentioned in his acceptance speech at the 1968 Republican National Convention gradually made up the audience to whom Agnew's remarks and appeals were addressed. In his October 30 Harrisburg speech, Agnew defended his New Orleans speech and repeated his call for a polarization of political views, because "it is time for the preponderant majority, the responsible citizens of this country, to assert their rights. It is time to stop dignifying the actions of arrogant, reckless, inexperienced elements within our society."

The audience, Agnew assumed, was a "preponderant majority" composed of "the responsible citizens." The enemies, on the other hand, were the "arrogant, reckless, inexperienced," who engaged in "tantrums" that were destroying American society.

Taking advantage of the widespread fear of crime and violence in American society, Agnew labeled the activity of these "elements" as "unbridled protest," and suggested that our democracy was withering at its hands. The Vietnam protest, which had had its most recent expression in the Moratorium a few days earlier, he suggested, was a deception of the well intentioned by "political hustlers," an "evil cloaked in emotional disguises." In demanding the exposure of these "elements," Agnew again called for the polarization of the American people and utilized a "we/they" or "them/us" pattern of words in his speech: "*They* would have *us* believe that *they* alone know what is good for America; *they* would have *us* believe that *their* reflexive action is superior to *our* relfective action; that *their* revealed righteousness is more effective than *our* reason and experience. [italics added]"[127] The "them/us" pattern soon became Agnewism. What Agnew said seemed to strike a responsive chord with a large segment of America; the Vice-President's themes had become a belief system.

Agnew continued to polarize as he appealed to blue collar workers, saying of the critical unpatriotic: "most of them disdain to mingle with the masses who work for a living." "They mock the common man's pride in his work, his family and his country." Agnew further invoked the "masses" and the "common man," to form a "positive polarization" to obliterate those "avowed anarchists and communists who detest everything about this country and want to destroy it."[128]

In what came to be known as "The Media Speech," delivered on December 13 in Des Moines, the Vice-President unleashed an unprecedented torrent of criticism against the "Fourth Estate," a long-time Nixon "enemy." In December 1968, shortly after Nixon won the presidential election, an ironic account entitled "Will the Press Be Out to Get Nixon?" appeared.[129] On the contrary, as it turned out, Nixon's Vice-President was out to "get" the press. In response to the networks' negative reaction to the President's November 3 Vietnam speech in which Nixon had pleaded for the support of the "silent majority," Agnew asked Americans, "are we demanding enough of our television news presentations. ... Are the men of this medium demanding enough of themselves?"

The President's address, claimed Agnew, had its "words and thoughts characterized through the prejudice of hostile critics before they [could] even be digested." Referring to a "gaggle of commentators," Agnew attacked the media for being able to "elevate men from local obscurity to national prominence within a week." Pointing to the hidden persuasive power of the nation's commentators, the Vice-President noted, "A raised eyebrow, an inflection of a voice, a caustic remark dropped in the middle of a broadcast can raise doubts in a million minds about the veracity of a public official or the wisdom of a governmental policy." Not only do the media distort, claimed Agnew. Living and working in "the geographical and intellectual confines of Washington, D.C., or New York City...they...bask in their own provincialism, their own parochialism."[130]

The reaction, at least on the part of the media, was an uproar. Nonetheless, the Vice-President got considerable support. The "silent majority" had been aroused. Responding to the charge that he was nothing more than Nixon's mouthpiece, Agnew again invoked the silent majority theme: "I spoke out ... because, like the silent majority, I had had enough. ... It was not that I suddenly launched a spiritual crusade nor that I was handed the White House standard, but that I was speaking my thoughts and ... those thoughts abraded some revered dogmas of the Fourth Estate."[131] Thus, the "Fourth Estate" was the silent majority's enemy as well.

Whether or not the administration commanded Agnew to be its spokesman remains unclear. It is clear, however, that the White House did little to silence him. Perhaps Agnew did embark on his program of oratory on his own. It is possible that those elements in American society which he chose to take on as enemies happened by chance to correspond to the age-old Nixon enemies and to issues then besetting the administration. It is also possible that what Humphrey had to say about the relationship between a President and a Vice-President—"The President can always disavow ... if you get too far out"[132]—was on Nixon's mind as his Vice-President administered whiplashes in his behalf. It seems obvious that Nixon did not believe that Agnew had gotten "too far out," for the President did not disavow Agnew. Moreover, Agnew's role in the subsequent 1970 congressional campaign was at the explicit instruction of the White House.[133]

Agnew played a critical role as administration spokesman during the off-year campaigns, a role Nixon had played for Eisenhower. In undertaking that role, Agnew apparently took a cue from Nixon's commentary on the April 8, 1970, Senate defeat of his nomination of G. Harrold Carswell for a Supreme Court seat. Irate over the Senate's rejection of Carswell—following closely on the rejection of another Court nominee, Clement Haynsworth—Nixon told reporters, "I have recently concluded—with the Senate presently constituted—I cannot successfully nominate [individuals] from the South." Haynsworth and Carswell, claimed the President, "have been falsely charged with being racist."[134]

Agnew had a similar point tucked away in his Jackson, Mississippi, speech. The subsequent congressional campaign gave him the opportunity to assume the personification of a purifier. The President had expressed the belief that Congress, especially the Senate, would be cleansed ideologically. The White House seemed pervaded by the sense that ideology was more important than party.

A great deal of literature has been written depicting the rise of a new Republican party majority during the Nixon Presidency. Two tracts of the times are Kevin Phillips' *The Emerging Republican Majority* and Richard Scammon and Ben Wattenberg's *The Real Majority*. According to Phillips's analysis, a new majority coalition of voters "centered in the South, the West, and in the Middle American urban-suburban districts" would emerge in the 1970s.[135] This was the "silent majority" which claimed the close attention of both Nixon and Agnew despite denials from the White House of such a preoccupation. Moreover, this presumed new majority dictated the Republican campaign strategy for the 1970 elections and became the evolving theme of the Nixon Administration and the Agnew crusades.

Scammon and Wattenberg's study points out that the typical voter was not among any of the categories to which Democrats had appealed since FDR. In describing the so-called social issues, those writers identified the typical voter as being generally unyoung, unblack, unpoor, and one who felt very strongly about what was perceived as the upheaval of all that had been good and clean in America. This group of voters felt very strongly about law and order, violence on college campuses, what was viewed as America's new permissiveness, and the cost of social welfare programs. All these subjects had been touched on in Agnew's speeches, and the analysis of the "typical voter" provided an ideological framework for his political thrusts.

Committed to an ideological rather than a party majority, Agnew's congressional campaign crusades began. No one from either party was immune; the liberals had to be purged, especially those in the Senate. American politics had seen little of this type of vigilante politicking since Roosevelt's failed attempt in 1938 to purge the Democratic party. Few Presidents would be willing to undertake such a politically hazardous task. Richard Nixon found it unnecessary to do so until the very last weeks of the campaign, for his Vice-President was doing it for him. Agnew not only attacked but also suffered attacks. He campaigned vigorously for months, lashing out at critics within his own party as well as within the Democratic party. Striving for ideological purity, he stressed the necessity of polarization. One of his typical attacks backfired. Governor Nelson Rockefeller had appointed Charles Goodell senator to complete the term of the late Senator Robert F. Kennedy. The liberals attacked Rockefeller for the Goodell appointment because they regarded Goodell as a conservative. He turned out to be less conservative than had been expected, however, and the Nixon Administration soon came to regard him as a liberal threat.

In keeping with the White House technique in the 1970 campaign, Agnew was instructed to embark on a program that would make it clear to the voters that the conservative candidate, James Buckley, was far more appealing to the administration than Goodell. Apparently, the President told Agnew to attack Goodell at an opportune moment. Agnew was not slow in labeling Goodell a "radical liberal," a term that had emerged from and became part of the Vice-President's rhetoric.[136] Furthermore, he could not bring himself to support the senator from New York because Goodell posed a threat to Nixon's foreign policy and to the welfare of the nation as a whole. While Agnew did not come out openly in support of Buckley, he enhanced the conservative candidate's position as he continued his verbal attacks on Goodell.[137] In his most outlandish attack, he called Goodell "the Christine Jorgensen of the Republican Party."[138]

The administration chalked up Goodell's defeat as a victory of sorts but its immediate and longer range consequences for Agnew were ominous. The Vice-President's willingness to engage in the purge had alienated an important segment of his own party.

Agnew's Vice-Presidency was first and foremost a public one. There was a duality to his conduct of the office. As one observer pointed out, "when all his bureaucratic achievements are totaled, it is painfully obvious that he has not a great deal to show for his efforts—little, that is, beyond the public side of his Vice Presidency."[139] As Vice-President, Agnew was so public that by 1972 he had developed a large independent following, for "Agnewism," which embodied so many of the grave social issues troubling America, had had a notable impact. Agnew's place on the 1972 ticked seemed scarcely open to question, notwithstanding the widespread notion that President Nixon preferred the former Texas Democrat, Governor John Connally, as his successor.[140]

By the time the Nixon-Agnew Administration had entered its second term, speculation concerning Agnew's future as a presidential candidate in 1976 had grown. However, with the Vice-President's independent power base increased, Nixon chose to use him in the campaign less frequently.[141] Here again, Agnew seemed to suffer the fate of many of his predecessors in the office, subject, again, to the whims of the President. Understandably, the Vice-President became less abrasive than during his first term in order to broaden his acceptability over the next several years. For a time, Agnew found himself in a peculiarly advantageous position. As the President's Watergate-related problems increasingly engulfed the administration, Agnew, virtually alone, emerged unscathed. This image, coupled with his past reputation as a supporter of what was portrayed as right and good for America, would be of immeasurable help, it seemed, to an aspiring presidential candidate. Nor did his position seem to suffer when the White House cut his duties and staff. While the White House announced that new duties and responsibilities would replace them, little of anything new emerged. Rather than being a handicap, in this one instance the Vice-President's traditional lack of closeness with the President and his staff paid off. Agnew could point out convincingly that he had had precious little contact with the Watergate-implicated Bob Haldeman and John Erlichman.[142]

As a presidential hopeful looking to the 1976 national election, Agnew's task was twofold: to make the most of the experience and exposure gained from his role in the administration and to remain above the Watergate fray. Without the Watergate scandals, Agnew's position would have been little different from that of other incumbent Vice-Presidents who have aspired to the Presidency while at the same time being obliged to remain loyal to the President and his policies. One can only speculate what Agnew's political future might have been if no one had searched out his record in Maryland government service, with "kickbacks" going back to his days as a Baltimore County executive. His resignation, preceded by an admission to charges of guilt and his resort to plea bargaining to avoid further legal prosecution, abruptly ended a public career that might otherwise have led to the presidential nomination in 1976 and possibly the Presidency.[143]

Thus, the most "public" Vice-President in America's experience made his exit from the second highest office in the land. Time and future circumstances will determine whether Spiro Agnew enhanced that office by adding to its dimensions or whether he will be remembered merely as the thirty-ninth Vice-President of the United States, who resigned his office in ignominy.

PLENIPOTENTIARY: THE VICE-PRESIDENT AND FOREIGN AFFAIRS

As mentioned earlier, the Vice-Presidency is far more active than ever before, but, still, the Vice-President's agenda continues to depend on the inclinations of the President who, under the American constitutional system, alone must bear the responsibilities of "the supreme executive magistrate." As the Presidency has come to be dominated by foreign affairs, so too expansion into this arena has helped develop the role of the Vice-President.

Presidents have been willing to share certain functions with their constitutional heirs apparent, especially ceremonial duties and foreign travel.[144] Travel assignments and official representations abroad have often been regarded as mere exercises to preoccupy the prestigious and energetic men who have served as Vice-President, but not all their travels have been busy work. On the contrary, they relieve the President of excessive travel and at the same time enable the President to meet the demands of protocol by sending his Constitutional counterpart. A notable example, discussed previously, was Vice-President Johnson's Berlin trip in 1961, where he stood in for President Kennedy. Johnson's presence underscored the administration's concern without arousing the attention implicit in a personal presidential visit.[145]

Richard Nixon's travels were of immeasurable help to the Eisenhower Administration; they also focused national attention on the Vice-President himself, especially Nixon's South America trip when he and his wife were assailed by rocks and an angry crowd and his 1958 trip to Moscow where he engaged in a well-publicized confrontation with Premier Nikita Khrushchev in the famous "Kitchen Debates."[146] Nixon's keen mind and his ability to withstand an exhausting schedule, as well as Eisenhower's own distaste for travel and representative functions, made Nixon's own role all the more vital. Nixon soon became known as the most traveled Vice-President, journeying to the Soviet Union, Latin America, Africa, and Asia. One newsman said that Nixon "became a very good travelling ambassador. I followed him through Africa, and I think he did a good job in many respects."[147] In his 1953 trip to the Far East, "an assignment that changed the whole pattern of his life,"[148] the constitutionally elected Vice-President could speak and act with presidential authority and prestige. Parmet has pointed out that "Ike's purpose . . . was to dramatize that American foreign policy was aimed at putting Asia on a par with Europe,"[149] and Nixon's visit was intended to emphasize that point. Nixon buried himself in preparatory material, familiarizing himself with as many aspects as he could of the countries he would visit.[150] The trip was an overwhelming success. Nixon was the focus of attention, especially in his willingness, possibly even eagerness, to meet the common people in the huge crowds that greeted him. The reception upon his return home equaled the one he had received en route. A former Eisenhower associate said that in Nixon's report to the Cabinet the Vice-President had given a "very impressive performance."[151]

Nixon's observations and suggestions were transformed into administration policies,[152] and "the occasion was a landmark in Nixon's career. From that moment on he became a respected participant in the Administration."[153] As he approached the 1960 presidential nomination and election, Nixon could point to his proven activity and expertise in the field of foreign affairs. This background was crucial to his campaign strategy.[154]

By contrast, Nixon's own Vice-Presidents, first Spiro Agnew and then Gerald Ford, enjoyed few foreign assignments. Unlike Eisenhower, Nixon relished the Presidency's dominance in foreign affairs. He had chosen Agnew as his running mate in part to provide the domestic balance he thought necessary to a President who would concentrate on foreign matters; indeed, Agnew's few trips were largely "cosmetic."[155]

When Gerald Ford was appointed Vice-President, Nixon was even less willing to share his foreign affairs activities. Watergate upon him, Nixon sought to engulf himself more than ever in foreign relations since travel abroad could still bring him the cheering, excited, approving crowds at a time when he had little applause at home. In addition, Ford's background could not compete with Nixon's; Nixon, after all, had had the tutelage of Secretary of State John Foster Dulles.[156] Had Ford continued in the Vice-Presidency he would probably have been given few foreign affairs assignments in view of the dominant position of not only the President but also Secretary of State Henry Kissinger.

As discussed earlier, Vice-President Lyndon Johnson traveled extensively for Kennedy; some of his trips were more successful than others.[157] He journeyed to the Far East, to Southeast Asia, to Europe,[158] and to India, carefully reporting his findings and recommendations to the President, but he never evoked as much interest and fanfare as Nixon. This was not for lack of preparation, for the State Department briefed him thoroughly for these journeys and he was determined not to go on protocol visits, but rather to discuss matters of substance.[159] Perhaps the principal reason was "the excitement of the handsome era of Kennedy the King."[160]

President Kennedy, as would be true of President Nixon, became increasingly involved and fared far better in foreign relations than in domestic affairs. By sharp contrast, Johnson was much more adroit in domestic than in foreign affairs, and this remained true after he became President. It is understandable that Vice-President Johnson would regard foreign trips as "one great escape."[161]

As Johnson's Vice-President, Hubert Humphrey was given a role in foreign affairs that was linked to one of his most important domestic roles, that of administration spokesman, especially on Vietnam. In 1965, he made his first trip as Vice-President to Southeast Asia with Johnson watching closely.[162] But the real turning point in Humphrey's foreign affairs role came with his assignment to the funeral of India's Prime Minister Shastri and his second trip to Asia. These trips came in the wake of his outspokenness in the National Security Council criticizing the administration's Vietnam policies. Humphrey desperately needed to get back in Johnson's good graces, and these trips provided the opportunity. Humphrey's biographer Albert Eisele (who would later serve as Vice-President Walter Mondale's press secretary) points out that those trips "established his credentials in Johnson's eyes as an able roving ambassador who could hold his own in the high-stakes game of international diplomacy." Moreover, as an administration spokesman, Humphrey could "effectively present Johnson's Vietnam policies to America's allies and to critics at home."[163] Humphrey readily accepted both tasks. The Vice-President had learned an important lesson of the office.

Nelson Rockefeller had an extensive interest and background in foreign affairs, and he served a President who admitted little expertise in the area. At the same time, Rockefeller had a very harmonious relationship with Secretary Kissinger.

Following his departure from the Vice-Presidency, Walter Mondale engaged in a series of lectures in which he defended Carter's policies. Mondale repeatedly stressed the wisdom and necessity of the Carter human rights policy, saying, "The basic lesson of our experience and struggle to promote human rights is that the advance of our own moral concerns for humanity, democracy, freedom and justice is profoundly in our national interest."[164]

Throughout the Carter-Mondale Administration, the Vice-President was assigned a wide range of duties in his broader capacity as "trouble-shooter," a subject explored elsewhere in this work. Perhaps the most meaningfully utilized Vice-President in American history, Mondale had access to every major document received by the President.[165] Later, as a private citizen, Mondale emphasized that he was involved in every major decision made during the Carter years. Regarding his access to classified materials, Mondale said, "I believe we have broken new institutional ground."[166]

Mondale's access to the President, as well as the smooth working relationship between the two men, was unparalleled in the history of the second office. As part of this relationship, Mondale enjoyed weekly luncheon business meetings with the President, an opportunity afforded to only one other person in the White House, Rosalynn Carter.[167] The weekly breakfast meetings enhanced Mondale's role in foreign policy, for the meetings were held with the administration's top foreign policy advisers. Mondale's early assignment to African relations was expanded to other issues and areas.[168]

When George Bush assumed the Vice-Presidency, he was the beneficiary of Mondale's advice, especially to tell the President what he thought but to disagree in private. Bush has heeded this advice and has ungrudgingly accepted his supporting role.

Bush sees Reagan daily for national security briefings and has been the beneficiary of the Carter-Mondale weekly luncheon, a practice continued by Reagan.[169] Embracing the low profile necessary to survive in that office, Bush has been rewarded, most conspicuously by Reagan's announcement in late March 1981 that Bush would be in charge of the crisis management team. James S. Brady, Reagan's press secretary, made the announcement of March 24, saying,

The purpose of this team is to coordinate all appropriate Federal resources in responding to emergency situations both foreign and domestic. The type of incident that might be involved ranges from an isolated terrorist attack to an attack upon United States territory by a hostile power.

Bush would chair the team should the President be absent, and would be involved in advance planning for emergency situations, developing options to be presented to the President.[170] The assignment greatly upset Secretary of State Alexander M. Haig, Jr. Prior to Bush's appointment, Haig had already indicated that he was "not totally satisfied" with the administration's foreign policy arrangements. Initial rumors about the Bush appointment provoked Haig to suggest that it "would pose another set of problems."[171] Unlike Bush, Haig had maintained quite a visible profile, much to the consternation of many White House staffers. Perhaps the crisis management assignment for Bush was one way of getting the Secretary of State in line. Nonetheless, the assignment marked the continuing evolution of the Bush Vice-Presidency within the broader parameters of the office. Ironically, just six days following Bush's new assignment, an assassination attempt was made on President Reagan's life and George Bush's behavior during the ensuing days was exemplary as he deftly and smoothly worked with the White House entourage.

In addition to being named as head of the crisis management team, Bush steadily accrued foreign affairs assignments in other areas. During the campaign of 1980, Bush had made it clear that he would play a supporting role in all fields, if elected. As Director of the Central Intelligence Agency he had attended National Security Council meetings in 1975–76, where he was able to directly view Vice-President Rockefeller's actions. Observed Bush, "Rockefeller gave his advice and would speak up even if he disagreed with President Ford. He was strong, and Ford was impressed.'' Bush promised to add his own style to the strength of convictions Rockefeller represented. Continued Bush, ''If Reagan took a position that I disagreed with, I would not try to embarrass the President of the United States,'' but would present his views directly to the President.[172] As early as the campaign itself, Bush had a chance to act on his words and defer to the presidential prerogative. Perhaps there is no more poignant example than Bush's August 1980 restraint over a Reagan remark in which the presidential candidate had proclaimed favoring ''official'' relations between the United States and Taiwan. Bush, whose own credentials as a U.S. envoy to China (he had served as chief of the U.S. Liaison mission) certainly earned him respect in that area of foreign policy, happened to be in China at the time of the Reagan remark. While the vice-presidential candidate privately disagreed with the remark, his public stance was one of more positively reinterpreting what Reagan meant.[173]

Bush's former ambassadorial credentials were immeasurably useful to the administration throughout his incumbency. In a May 1982 trip to China, for example, Bush was referred to by Chinese leader Deng Xiaoping as ''an old friend of China,'' and in this respect perhaps the Administration had no more trustworthy spokesperson to deal with the delicate issue of the relationship between China and Taiwan.[174] Similarly, Bush's travels took him to Australia, where he undertook what turned out to be a successful effort to dispel potential areas of disagreement over future trade and commerce negotiations.[175] Just a year previous, in the summer of 1981, Bush had been given charge of preparations for the Canadian economic summit.

A Vice-President's role as administration spokesman also involves serving as the ''eyes and ears'' of the President. Bush's travel to seven African states during 1982 was designed to, as Bush himself noted, ''learn what key African leaders are thinking.''[176] So, too, would Bush attempt to get a head start on understanding the new leadership of the Soviet Union following the death of that country's leader, Leonid I. Brezhnev, in 1982. Vice-Presidents are often (and erroneously) depicted as merely attending funerals abroad in place of the President. Bush did indeed attend the Brezhnev funeral (which interrupted his African tour) but he lost no time in turning that symbolic and ceremonial activity into a substantive one, and made gestures of broadened cooperation toward the new Soviet leader, Yuri A. Andropov. In fact, Bush and Andropov met following the Brezhnev funeral in Moscow.[177] Bush would similarily meet with the new Soviet leader during the Soviet Union's next two leadership successions. (He met with Konstantin U. Chernenko following Andropov's death, and he met with Mikhail Gorbochev following Chernenko's death.) The foreign policy side of Bush's Vice-Presidency has thus been an active one. As in his domestic roles, the Vice-President clearly saw the advantage of being a team player, and he has consistently supported Administration policies.

NOTES

1. Hubert H. Humphrey, Interview held in a U.S. Senate reception room, March 1974.

2. Joseph Ernest Kallenbach, *The American Chief Executive* (New York: Harper & Row, 1966), pp. 232–33.

3. Speech File 63M143, Box XXII, 1952, The Papers of Alben W. Barkley, University of Kentucky Library, Lexington, Kentucky.

4. Ibid.

5. Kallenbach, *The American Chief Executive*, pp. 232–33. See also Sidney Hyman, *The American President* (New York: Harper, 1954), pp. 315–16; Michael Dorman, *The Second Man* (New York: Delacorte Press, 1968), p. 193; Harry S Truman, *Years of Decisions* (New York: Doubleday, 1955), p. 196.

6. Vice-President Statements, Container 3, Folder July 10, 1960, "Meet the Press," The Papers of Lyndon B. Johnson, Lyndon B. Johnson Library, Austin, Texas. See also "A Conversation with the Vice President," Vice-President Statements, Box 43, Interview, ABC News, March 26, 1963, Lyndon B. Johnson Library, Austin, Texas; Whitney M. Young, Jr., Oral History Interview, Lyndon B. Johnson Library, Austin, Texas, pp. 1–11, for a review of Johnson's views of the historical role of the office.

7. "Apprentice President," *Economist* 213 (December 26, 1964): 1423.

8. "A Conversation with the President."

9. "Apprentice President," p. 1423.

10. Ohio State University Speech, Vice-President Statements, Container 3, Folder: September 29, 1960, Lyndon B. Johnson Papers, Lyndon B. Johnson Library, Austin, Texas. See also "Apprentice President," p. 1423; Lyndon B. Johnson, *The Vantage Point: Perspectives of the Presidency* (New York: Holt, Rinehart & Winston, 1971), p. 2; Kenneth P. O'Donnell, Telephone Interview, Boston, Massachusetts, February 1974.

11. Albert Eisele, *Almost to the Presidency* (Blue Earth, Minnesota: Piper Co., 1972), p. 226.

12. As quoted by Rowland Evans and Robert D. Novak, *Nixon in the White House* (New York: Random House, 1971), p. 310.

13. President's Press Conference, May 31, 1955, Box 10 (SF) Fox, Folder: Vice-President. President's Press Conference May 31, 1955, Dwight D. Eisenhower Papers, Dwight D. Eisenhower Library, Abilene, Kansas. See also Dorman, *The Second Man*, p. 209.

14. Joseph Albright, *What Makes Spiro Run: The Life and Times of Spiro Agnew* (New York: Dodd, Mead, 1972), p. 227.

15. Dorman, *The Second Man*, p. 224.

16. "Nixon's Own Story of Seven Years in the Vice Presidency," *U.S. News* 48 (May 16, 1960): 98–106.

17. Birch Bayh, *One Heartbeat Away* (New York: Bobbs-Merrill, 1968), p. 87.

18. Ibid.

19. As cited by Evans and Novak, *Nixon in the White House*, p. 168. Vice-President Agnew concurred with this view; see "A New Kind of Vice President?" *U.S. News* 66 (March 17, 1969): 32–34.

20. Bayh, *One Heartbeat Away*, p. 87.

21. *Time* (July 2, 1973): 17.

22. *New York Daily News*, August 3, 1975.

23. *Time* (January 20, 1975).

24. "Walter Mondale," MacNeil/Lehrer Report, February 22, 1977.

25. Ibid.

26. *Christian Science Monitor* (March 3, 1981).

27. Hubert H. Humphrey, Interview, March 1974.

28. Vice-President Throttlebottom, a fictional character in the musical satire on the Presidency during the Franklin D. Roosevelt era entitled "Of Thee I Sing" was a nonentity who could not even obtain a library card because he lacked the requisite two references.

29. Harry S. Truman, *Years of Decisions*, p. 195ff. See also Frank McNaughton, *This Man Truman* (New York: McGraw-Hill, 1945), p. 191ff.; "Our Imaginary Vice," *American Scholar* 39 (Summer 1970): 387–94; Grant McConnell, *The Modern Presidency* (New York: St. Martin's Press, 1967), p. 59.

30. Alben W. Barkley, *That Reminds Me* (Garden City, N.Y.: Doubleday, 1954), p. 208.

31. Sidney Shalett, Interviews with Alben W. Barkley, Reel 6, side 1 (pp. 14–15; 18–23), Harry S Truman Library, Independence, Missouri. Also on file at the Franklin D. Roosevelt Library, Hyde Park, New York. See also Barkley, *That Reminds Me*, pp. 105–14.

32. Dorman, *The Second Man*, p. 193ff.

33. For more on the Truman-Barkley relationship, see Barkley, *That Reminds Me*; pp. 105–14; Shalett Interviews, passim, Susan M. Hartmann, *Truman and the 80th Congress* (Missouri: University of Missouri Press, 1971), p. 17; Jonathan Daniels, Oral History Interview, Harry S Truman Library, Independence, Missouri, p. 49ff.

34. For more on this point, see Patrick Anderson, *The President's Men* (Garden City, N.Y.: Doubleday, 1968), passim, who also notes the trend toward greater reliance on staff, especially at the expense of Cabinet officials who, claims Anderson, have been the victims of a "centrifugal force . . . pulling them away from the presidential orbit, making them prisoners of their bureaucracies, giving them priorities and loyalties that may not be identical with the President's." See also Kallenbach, *The American Chief Executive*, p. 256; Truman, *Years of Decisions*, p. 330.

Anderson adds that the White House staff has increasingly come to displace the influence and advice of so-called Distinguished Outsiders, the wise men of the party and business community who had traditionally been sources of advice (p. 2).

See also James Gaither, Oral History Interview, Lyndon B. Johnson Library, Austin, Texas, p. 8, for his account of the duties and responsibilities the presidential staff must assume because the President cannot possibly handle them.

For more on the Johnson staff, see Louis Heren, *No Hail, No Farewell* (New York: Harper & Row, 1970), passim.

35. Anderson, *The President's Men*, p. 10.

36. Ibid., p. 6.

37. Humphrey, Interview, March 1974.

38. Anderson, *The President's Men*, p. 9.

39. Ibid. See also McConnell, *The Modern Presidency*, p. 59ff.; Louis Clinton Hatch, *A History of The Vice-Presidency of the United States* (revised by Earl L. Shoup) (Westport, Conn.: Greenwood Press, 1934, 1970), p. 419.

40. "Nixon's Own Story."

41. Truman, *Years of Decisions*, p. 54. Herman Finer, *The Presidency: Crisis and Regeneration* (Chicago: University of Chicago Press, 1960), p. 294ff. echoed this point, pointing out that a President can only give his Vice-President a small amount of executive responsibilities. Jonathan Daniels, Oral History Interview, Harry S. Truman Library, Independence, Missouri, p. 50, talks of a President's heavy reliance on his personal staff, rather than on a Cabinet official or the Vice-President, because of political considerations.

42. Anderson, *The President's Men*, p. 7ff. See also Arthur Krock, Oral History Interview, John F. Kennedy Library, Columbia Point, Massachusetts, Part I, p. 28ff.

43. James David Barber, *Presidential Character* (Englewood, N.J.: Prentice-Hall, 1972), pp. 93–95; 129–40; 78–87; 347–442; 446–48.

44. Johnson, *The Vantage Point*, p. 2. Walter Jenkins said the same. Interview held at his Austin, Texas, office, April 1973.

45. "Apprentice President," p. 1423; see "Happy Understudy," *Saturday Review* 48 (May 8, 1965); 16–17,for additional material on Johnson's frustration in the Vice-Presidency. This point was made by former Secretary of State Dean Rusk. Interview held at his Athens, Georgia, office, May 1973.

46. Barber, *Presidential Character*, p. 79ff.

47. Francis Keppel, Oral History Interview, Lyndon B. Johnson Library, Austin, Texas, p. 28.

48. Walter Jenkins, Interview, May 1973.

49. Dean Rusk, Interview, May 1973.

50. Hubert H. Humphrey, Interview, March 1974.

51. Ibid. See also Allan H. Ryskind, *Hubert* (New York: Arlington House, 1968), p. 177ff. Bill Welch, in an interview held at his Washington, D.C., office in March 1974, talked about the lack of the Vice-President's followup power, no matter what his constituencies may be.

52. Eisele, *Almost to the Presidency*, pp. 251; 236.

53. Ibid., pp. 237–38; see also "Happy Understudy."

54. Ryskind, *Hubert*, p. 323ff.; Johnson, *The Vantage Point*, p. 342; Walter Jenkins, Interview, April 1973.

55. Humphrey demonstrated the wisdom Truman had regarding the Vice-Presidency. Truman had said that it is difficult for a President to always be open with his Vice-President:

A possible leak . . . every President realizes, need not be the result of an intentional act on the part of the Vice-President. But an unintentional leak can be as harmful as an intentional one, and, conceivably, might upset the whole program on which a President is working. (Truman, *Years of Decisions*, p. 54.)

56. Barber, *Presidential Character*, p. 83.

57. "I Enjoy It," *Newsweek* 65 (March 15, 1965): 28–29; Ryskind, *Hubert*, p. 320.

58. "The Bright Spirit," *Time* 87 (April 1, 1966): 21–25. See also "Foreign Policy—A New Strategy for Peace," *Vital Speeches* 35 (1968–69): 8–11—the much compromised speech in which presidential candidate Hubert Humphrey tried to sever his link with the adminstration's Vietnam policy.

59. Eisele, *Almost to the Presidency*, p. 231ff.

60. Ibid., p. 322.

61. George Christian, *The President Steps Down* (New York: Macmillan, 1970), pp. 148ff.; see also "Happy Understudy," for more on the question of Humphrey's role in Vietnam decision-making.

62. Eisele, *Almost to the Presidency*, p. 233ff.

63. Hubert Humphrey, Interview, March 1974.

64. Eisele, *Almost to the Presidency*, pp. 251; 237.

65. Ibid. See also "The Humphreys: Right Image for '68?" *U.S. News* 65 (September 9, 1968): 17–18; and "The Bright Spirit."

66. "The Bright Spirit."

67. Robert Wood, Oral History Interview, Lyndon B. Johnson Library, Austin, Texas, p. 10. For more on Humphrey's other areas of expertise, see Christian, *The President Steps Down*, p. 148ff.; Dorman, The *Second Man*, pp. 165–83; Eisele, *Almost to the Presidency*, p. 226ff.; Ryskind, *Hubert*, p. 320; "I Enjoy It"; and "Apprentice President."

68. "The Bright Spirit."

69. William V. Shannon, *The Heir Apparent* (New York: Macmillan, 1967), p. 285.

70. Ryskind, *Hubert*, pp. 319–320.

71. Eisele, *Almost to the Presidency*, p. 240; "I Enjoy It."

72. Richard Rovere, *The Eisenhower Years* (New York: Farrar, Straus & Cudahy, 1956), p. 15ff.; 195.; Ralph DeToledano, *One Man Alone: Richard Nixon* (New York: Funk & Wagnalls, 1969), p. 163ff.; Richard Rovere, Oral History Interview, Eisenhower Administration Oral History Collection, Columbia University, New York, New York, pp. 28–30, 35–36, 43; Sigmund S. Larmon, Oral History Interview, Eisenhower Administration Oral History Collection, Columbia University, New York, New York, p. 87; Robert Finch, Oral History Interview, Eisenhower Administration Oral History Collection, Columbia University, New York, New York, for a glimpse of Nixon's views on Eisenhower's lack of partisanship.

73. Jacob Javits, Oral History Interview, Eisenhower Administration Oral History Collection, Columbia University, New York, New York, p. 5.

74. Confidential interview with former member of the Eisenhower staff. The "Checkers debacle" referred to the Nixon difficulties during the 1952 campaign, during which he had to defend himself against charges of a questionable "slush" fund established by California businessmen. Nixon addressed the nation on television, during which speech he referred to his acceptance of only one gift in his political career, his dog Checkers. The speech has become widely known as the "Checkers" speech.

75. Rovere, *The Eisenhower Years*, p. 34.

76. "Washington's Rival Regents," *Economist* 185 (December 21, 1957): 1049–50.

77. Javits, Oral History Interview, pp. 3–4.

78. Kenneth Keating, Oral History Interview, Eisenhower Administration Oral History Collection, Columbia University, New York, New York, p. 14.

79. See Rovere, *The Eisenhower Year*, p. 122, for more on this point.

80. See "Washington's Rival Regents" for a word on Nixon's party popularity, especially in comparison to Sherman Adams.

DeToledano, *One Man Alone*, p. 162, takes the view that Eisenhower, contrary to the general characterization of a "bumbling refugee from the military life," was in reality "a consummate politician . . . , who respected Nixon's ability to grasp and synthesize issues—and he used that ability to the maximum. He was keenly conscious of Nixon's expertise, his knowledge of the nitty-gritty of day-to-day politics." Nevertheless, Nixon was still afforded the opportunity to expand the role and functioning of the Vice-Presidency.

Laurin Henry, *Presidential Transitions* (Washington, D.C.: Brookings Institution, 1960), p. 490, feels that Eisenhower would have made good his campaign talk of an increased role for Vice-President Nixon and would have given Nixon an even heavier assignment but that he had never forgotten or forgiven the 1952 slush fund scandal.

81. "Nixon's Own Story."

82. DeToledano, *One Man Alone*, p. 162ff.; OF 656 114–N, Folder: Cabinet Committee on Price Stability, Dwight D. Eisenhower Papers, Dwight D. Eisenhower Library, Abilene, Kansas; Frank McNaughton and Walter Hehmeyer, *Harry Truman, President* (New York: Whittlesey House, 1948), p. 215ff.; Box 31 (SF) Rogers, Folder: Nixon—VP. Correspondence Nixon to Jones, January 21, 1960, Dwight D. Eisenhower Papers, Dwight D. Eisenhower Library, Abilene, Kansas; Fred Lazarus, Jr., Oral History Interview, Eisenhower Administration Oral History Collection, New York, New York, p. 910.

83. Leverett Saltonstall, Oral History Interview, Eisenhower Administration Oral History Collection, Columbia University, New York, New York, pp. 140–41.

84. DeToledano, *One Man Alone*, p. 164. See also Rovere, *The Eisenhower Years*, pp. 296–97; Henry R. McPhee, Oral History Interview, Eisenhower Administration Oral History Collection, Columbia University, New York, New York, pp. 47–48.

85. DeToledano, *One Man Alone*, p. 164.

86. Mansfield D. Sprague, Oral History Interview, Eisenhower Administration Oral History Collection, Columbia University, New York, New York, pp. 47–48.

87. DeToledano, *One Man Alone*, p. 164.

88. Ibid., pp. 182–83; see also James R. Shepley, Oral History Interview, Eisenhower Administration Oral History Collection, Columbia University, New York, New York, pp. 29–30; OF 99B, Box 339, for an example of the Vice-President's speeches on communism; Earl Mazo and Stephen Hess, *Nixon: A Political Portrait* (New York: Harper & Row, 1968), p. 209, regarding Nixon and Fidel Castro, p. 333ff.

Prescott Bush, Oral History Interview, Eisenhower Administration Oral History Collection, Columbia University, New York, New York, pp. 328–37; 145–46; Emmet John Hughes, *The Ordeal of Power* (New York: Atheneum, 1963), p. 83ff., for more on Nixon and Joseph McCarthy; Jerry Voorhis, *The Strange Case of Richard Milhous Nixon* (New York: Paul S. Eriksson, 1972), pp. 17–18.

89. DeToledano, *One Man Alone*, pp. 183ff.

90. Ibid., pp. 186–87; see also Herbert S. Parmet, *Eisenhower and the American Crusades* (New York: Macmillan, 1972), pp. 347ff.

91. Ibid., p. 186ff., provides more on this point.

92. As cited byDeToledano, *One Man Alone*, p. 183; 190.
In a memorandum to DeToledano, Nixon said,

My theory as far as relations with McCarthy are concerned is that while the President would undoubtedly win in any head-on clash with McCarthy, he could not help but be hurt in the process. A controversy would cause a very decided split among Republicans and could well lead to defeat for us in the 1954 elections. There may be a time when as a matter of principle the President may have to become involved in such a fight. But I think it is the responsibility of all of us to avoid it as long as we possibly can. It will give aid and comfort to no one but the Democrats. It is interesting to note that many of the columnists who have been taking the President to task for not attacking McCarthy are neither friends of McCarthy nor of the President.

Nixon's leitmotif seemed to be the unity of the Republican party, above and beyond all else and for as long as possible. The memorandum to DeToledano explains the position he ultimately took in regard to McCarthy.

McCarthy and I broke when he attacked the Administration. I did my best to avoid this break, not only because I felt it would be harmful to the party and the Administration, but because I felt it would be harmful to the cause of those who had been engaged in the anti-communist fight. . . .

McCarthy's intentions were right, but his tactics were, frankly, so inept at times that he eventually did our cause more harm than good.

93. Parmet, *Eisenhower and the American Crusades*, p. 431; "Address of Vice President of U.S. Before Global Syndicate Press Awards Dinner," New York City, June 24, 1955, OF 339 99B, Dwight D. Eisenhower Papers, Dwight D. Eisenhower Library, Abilene, Kansas; "Washington's Rival Regents"; (SF) Hagerty Papers, Folder: Nixon—VP, Press Conference, June 30, 1954; "Responsibility for Delay in the Missile Program," *Congressional Record*, January 14, 1959, which includes Nixon's defense of the administration record; see William Knowland, Oral History Interview, Eisenhower Administration Oral History Collections, Columbia University, New York, New York, p. 9ff. See Parmet, *Eisenhower and the American Crusades*, p. 328ff., for a description of Nixon's role in relationship to labor and his delivery of presidential messages.

94. DeToledano, *One Man Alone*, p. 167.

95. Voorhis, *The Strange Case of Richard Milhous Nixon*, pp. 17–18. See Hughes, *The Ordeal of Power*, p. 83ff, for more on Nixon's role and Eisenhower's behavior in the struggle with Joseph McCarthy. See also Dwight D. Eisenhower, *Mandate for Change* (New York: Doubleday, 1963), chap. 13; DeToledano, *One Man Alone*, pp. 176–93; Henry, *Presidential Transitions*, p. 600ff.; Rovere, *The Eisenhower Years*, p. 297.; Bush, Oral History Interview, pp. 328–37.

96. Hubert W. Humphrey, Interview, March 1974.

97. Rovere, *The Eisenhower Years*, p. 319ff., provides more on this point.

98. This was underscored by President-elect Kennedy's November 14, 1960, visit to Nixon for the purpose of discussion. Paul T. David et al., *The Presidential Election and Transition, 1960–61* (Washington, D.C.: Brookings Institution, 1961), p. 326ff.

99. Tom Wicker, *JFK and LBJ* (New York: Morrow, 1968), p. 172.

100. Lyndon Johnson, Interview with Walter Cronkite, CBS News, December 12, 1972, Lyndon B. Johnson Papers, Lyndon B. Johnson Library, Austin, Texas.

101. Kenneth P. O'Donnell, Interview (telephone) conducted in Boston, Massachusetts, February 1975.

102. Arthur M. Schlesinger, Jr., *A Thousand Days* (Boston: Houghton Mifflin, 1973), p. 705.

103. Johnson, *The Vantage Point*, p. 52ff.

104. See Roy Wilkins, Oral History Interview, Lyndon B. Johnson Library, Austin, Texas, p. 5ff., for more on Johnson and civil rights.

105. Christian, *The President Steps Down*, p. 148.

106. For more on this point, see Schlesinger, *A Thousand Days*, p. 693ff.; Norbert Schlei, Oral History Interview, John F. Kennedy Library, Columbia Point, Massachusetts, p. 22; Donald E. Larrabee, Oral History Interview, John F. Kennedy Library, Columbia Point, Massachusetts, p. 10; Emmanuel Celler, Oral History Interview, Lyndon B. Johnson Library, Austin, Texas, passim.

107. Schlesinger, *A Thousand Days*, p. 693ff.; Charles Halleck, Oral History Interview, John F. Kennedy Library, Columbia Point, Massachusetts, p. 37; Theodore Sorensen, *Kennedy* (New York, Harper & Row, 1965), p. 267; Celler, Oral History Interview, p. 7; Donald Wilson, Oral History Interview, John F. Kennedy Library, Columbia Point, Massachusetts, pp. 27–28, for more on the JFK-RFK relationship.

108. See also Wicker, *JFK and LBJ*, p. 157.

109. Jenkins, Interview, May 1973.

110. Schlesinger, *A Thousand Days*, p. 705; Johnson, *The Vantage Point*, p. 278 ff.; see also Richard E. Neustadt to Bill Moyers, February 28, 1961, FG 440, John F. Kennedy Papers, John F. Kennedy Library, Columbia Point, Massachusetts, in which Neustadt expressed concern for the protection of the constitutional position of the Vice-President. Nicholas DeB. Katzenbach to Lyndon B. Johnson, April 18, 1961, provides the constitutional basis for the Vice-President's ability to serve as chairman of the National Aeronautics and Space Council, National and Aeronautics Space Council Microfilm, Reel 6, Lyndon B. Johnson Library, Austin, Texas.

111. Theodore C. Sorensen, Oral History Interview, John F. Kennedy Library, Columbia Point, Massachusetts, p. 1ff.; Sorensen, *Kennedy*, p. 525; Johnson, *The Vantage Point*, p. 278.

112. Dean Rusk, Interview, May 1973.

113. Pierre Salinger, *With Kennedy* (Garden City, N.J.: Doubleday, 1966), p. 333ff. See also "Happy Understudy."

114. Robert J. Sickels, *Presidential Transactions* (Englewood Cliffs, N.J.: Prentice-Hall, 1974), p. 52ff.

115. Albright, *What Makes Spiro Run*, p. 260ff.

116. As contained in Robert Curran, *Spiro Agnew: Spokesman for America* (New York: Lancer Books, 1970), p. 69ff.

117. Ibid., pp. 72–75.

118. Ibid., p. 75.

119. Ibid., p. 78.

120. Ibid., pp.78–79; see also Evans and Novak, *Nixon in the White House*, pp. 213–313.

121. Curran, *Spiro Agnew*, pp. 89–90.

122. Ibid., pp. 91–98.

123. For more on the effects of the "effete corps of impudent snobs" speech, see Evans and Novak, *Nixon in the White House*, p. 314ff.; Curran, *Spiro Agnew*, p. 17ff.; 85ff.; "Spiro Speaks," *Economist* (November 1, 1969): 233–50.

124. Richard M. Scammon and Ben J. Watternberg, *The Real Majority* (New York: Coward, McCann & Geoghegan, 1970), p. 211.

125. Judson L. James, *American Political Parties in Transition* (New York: Harper & Row, 1974), pp. 65–66, provides more on the potential Wallace candidacy in 1972; see also "Happy Warrior," *Economist* 233 (November 29, 1969): 51–52; Scammon and Wattenberg, *The Real Majority*, p. 208ff.

126. Curran, *Spiro Agnew*, pp. 107–20.

127. Ibid.

128. For further commentary on the Harrisburg speech, see Evans and Novak, *Nixon in the White House*, p. 314ff.

129. "Will the Press Be Out to Get Nixon?"

130. Curran, *Spiro Agnew*, pp. 121–30. For further commentary on the Des Moines speech, see Evans and Novak, *Nixon in the White House*, pp. 315–16, who claim that Pat Buchanan, a Nixon speechwriter, had focused on the idea and that Nixon knew about it from Buchanan. See also Voorhis, *The Strange Case of Richard Milhous Nixon*, pp. 254–56; and Albright, *What Makes Spiro Run*, p. 207ff.

131. Curran, *Spiro Agnew*, pp. 135–36.

132. Hubert H. Humphrey, Interview, March 1974.

133. Evans and Novak, *Nixon in the White House*, p. 315ff.

134. Barber, *Presidential Character*, p. 429.

135. Kevin Phillips, *The Emerging Republican Majority* (Garden City, N.Y.: Doubleday, 1969), p. 23.

136. Evans and Novak, *Nixon in the White House*, p. 332.

137. James, pp. 202–203; Evans and Novak, *Nixon in the White House*, p. 332.

138. Evans and Novak, *Nixon in the White House*, pp. 333–34.

139. Albright, *What Makes Spiro Run*, p. 246.

140. *New York Times Magazine*, June 24, 1973.

141. Albright, *What Makes Spiro Run*, p. 232ff.; see *Time*, April 23, 1973, for a sense of Nixon's reduction of Agnew's role; "The Nixon Watch—How It Works," *New Republic* (February 24, 1973); David Keene, Interview held at his Washington, D.C., office, March 1974.

142. *New York Times Magazine*, June 24, 1973; Albright, *What Makes Spiro Run*, p. 232ff.

143. Richard M. Cohen and Jules Witcover, *A Heartbeat Away* (New York: Viking Press, 1974), provides a good, thorough account of the Agnew investigation and scandal.

144. See also "A New Kind of Vice President?"; "The Bright Spirit"; White House File 192 FG440, Vice-President of the U.S., John F. Kennedy Papers, John F. Kennedy Library, Columbia Point, Massachusetts; DeToledano, *One Man Alone*, p. 160ff.; Evans and Novak, *Nixon in the White House*, p. 312; Louis W. Koenig, *The Chief Executive* (New York: Harcourt, Brace & World, 1964, 1968), p. 162ff.; Truman, *Years of Decisions*, p. 197ff.

145. Kenneth P. O'Donnell, Telephone Interview, February 1975.

146. For additional material on the Moscow trip, see OF 982. 225–D, Folder: Trip to Moscow. Nixon's Remarks in Poland, August 5, 1959, Dwight D. Eisenhower Papers, Dwight D. Eisenhower Library, Abilene, Kansas; OF 892. 225–D, Folder: Trip to Moscow. Nixon's remarks upon return from Moscow, August 5, 1959, Dwight D. Eisenhower Papers, Dwight D. Eisenhower Library, Abilene, Kansas; Hughes, *The Ordeal of Power*, p. 286ff.; Parmet, *Eisenhower and the American Crusades*, pp. 547–48; OF 99B, Box 399, Dwight D. Eisenhower Papers, Dwight D. Eisenhower Library, Abilene, Kansas.

147. Howard K. Smith, Oral History Interview, Eisenhower Administration Oral History Collection, Columbia University, New York, New York, p. 28ff.

148. DeToledano, *One Man Alone*, p. 170ff.

149. Parmet, *Eisenhower and the American Crusades*, pp. 359–60.

150. DeToledano, *One Man Alone*, p. 170ff.

151. Confidential observer. See also Person to Willis, December 12, 1953, OF 116–I–A, Box 584, Dwight D. Eisenhower Papers, Dwight D. Eisenhower Library, Abilene, Kansas.

152. Mazo and Hess, *Nixon*, p. 280ff.; "Nixon's Own Story."

153. DeToledano, *One Man Alone*, p. 173.

154. Robert Finch, Oral History Interview, Eisenhower Administration Oral History Collection, Columbia University, New York, New York, p. 65ff. See also OF 586. 116–J–7. Remarks re: S. A. Trip, Dwight D. Eisenhower Papers, Dwight D. Eisenhower Library, Abilene, Kansas; OF 586. 111–J–5. Nixon's Trip to Middle American Countries, Dwight D. Eisenhower Papers, Dwight D. Eisenhower Library, Abilene, Kansas; GF 52. ZZ. 3–A–2. 1956 (3): "The Vice Presidency in 1956"—Report by the Committee

for Young Men in Government. Dwight D. Eisenhower Papers, Dwight D. Eisenhower Library, Abilene, Kansas; OF 853. 161–B. Vice-President's Trip to Austria. WH Press Release, December 12, 1956, Dwight D. Eisenhower Papers, Dwight D. Eisenhower Library, Abilene, Kansas; OF 594. 116–NN. VP Report to Eisenhower on African Trip, April 8, 1957, Dwight D. Eisenhower Papers, Dwight D. Eisenhower Library, Abilene, Kansas; Mazo and Hess, *Nixon*, pp. 305–306; Parmet, *Eisenhower and the American Crusades*, pp. 273–74; Hughes, *The Ordeal of Power*; Prescott Bush, Oral History Interview, pp. 335–36; Milton S. Eisenhower, Oral History Interview, Eisenhower Administration Oral History Collection, Columbia University, New York, New York, p. 94; *New York Times*, May 15, 18, 1958; "Nixon's Own Story."

155. Albright, *What Makes Spiro Run*, p. 247; *New York Times Magazine*, June 24, 1973; *Time*, November 1, 1971, p. 20ff.; "A Look Inside the Nixon Administration," *U.S. News* 67 (October 6, 1969): 32–38.

156. Elie Abel, Oral History Interview, p. 48; Rovere, *The Eisenhower Years*, p. 56ff.; Roscoe Drummond, Oral History Interview, Eisenhower Administration Oral History Collection, Columbia University, New York, New York, p. 18; James R. Shepley, Oral History Interview, p. 29; "Nixon's Own Story."

157. Schlesinger, *A Thousand Days*, pp. 396–97; Jack Bell, Oral History Interview, John F. Kennedy Library, Columbia Point, Massachusetts, p. 5ff., who accompanied Johnson on the trip; Salinger, *A Thousand Days*, passim.; Sorensen, *Kennedy*, pp. 557; 594.

158. Sorensen, *Kennedy*, p. 653; Schlesinger, *A Thousand Days*, pp. 540–44; Wicker, *JFK and LBJ*, p. 199ff.; *The Vantage Point*, pp. 52ff.; 222ff; FG 440 August 22, 1962, Johnson's Mideast Trip, Lyndon B. Johnson Papers, Lyndon B. Johnson Library, Austin, Texas; Bundy to LBJ, May 8, 1961, FG 440, Lyndon B. Johnson Papers, Lyndon B. Johnson Library, Austin, Texas.

159. Dean Rusk, Interview, May 1973. For more on the Johnson trips, see White House File 192, FG 440, VP of U.S., January 18, 1961–March 31, 1961, Lyndon B. Johnson Papers, Lyndon B. Johnson Library, Austin, Texas, for a sense of Johnson's early role as a replacement for Kennedy on ceremonial trips abroad. See Clarence Mitchell, Oral History Interview, Lyndon B. Johnson Library, Austin, Texas, p. 22ff., and Roy Wilkins, Oral History Interview, p. 6ff., for the possible effects of Johnson's foreign travels on his domestic views.

160. Wicker, *JFK and LBJ*, p. 157.

161. Schlesinger, *A Thousand Days*, p. 705.

162. Eisele, *Almost to the Presidency*, p. 240; Johnson, the *Vantage Point*, p. 246; "Happy Understudy."

163. Eisele, *Almost to the Presidency*, p. 241; see also "The Bright Spirit."

164. *New York Times*, March 8, 1981.

165. Ibid., August, 1980.

166. Ibid.

167. Ibid.

168. Ibid.

169. *Christian Science Monitor*, March 3, 1981.

170. *New York Times*, March 29, 1981.

171. *New York Times*, March 25, 1981.

172. "Determined Second Fiddle," *Time* 116: (November 17, 1980) 38–39.
173. Ibid.
174. *Christian Science Monitor*, May 4, 1982.
175. Ibid.
176. Ibid., November 9, 1982.
177. *New York Times*, November 16, 1982.

6

The Post-Watergate Vice-Presidency: Trends and Prospects

"CARETAKER" GOVERNMENT: THE FORD-ROCKEFELLER ADMINISTRATION

The series of events now collectively known as Watergate was far reaching in both origin and effects. These events must be analyzed thoroughly here, for they profoundly affected the shape of the contemporary Vice-Presidency.

At the same time that the 1972 Democratic presidential candidate, Senator Goerge McGovern, was lambasting the Nixon Administration as the "most corrupt administration in history," the "Eagleton" scenario was unfolding and lessening the credibility of the populist presidential candidate. Nixon scored a landslide victory, but, ironically, that landslide victory coincided with the emergence of Watergate, both the break-in at Democratic National Headquarters in 1972 and the series of events following the break-in and continuing over a period of two years into 1974.

While not directly or literally connected to the Watergate break-in and coverup, the 1973 Agnew scandal nonetheless emerged as part of the total picture of an administration that was indeed perhaps "the most corrupt in history." As noted elsewhere in this work, once the disclosure of Vice-President Spiro T. Agnew's indiscretions as Baltimore County executive had been made, the White House hoped that Agnew's problems would take the heat off the President. As the history of the Vice-Presidency has demonstrated, the Vice-President must always be expendable to the President. The Agnew resignation provided President Nixon the opportunity to at least symbolically forge a "new beginning," and thus the appointment of Gerald Ford as Agnew's successor.

The period of time from 1972 to 1973 established a new framework within which the Vice-Presidency would be viewed. Symbolically, the Ford vice-presidential confirmation hearings, following President Nixon's use of the Twenty-fifth Amendment for the first time since its 1967 ratification, emphasized the need for a thorough scrutiny of vice-presidential candidates. (It should be recalled here that the Eagleton Affair and the Agnew resignation were the backdrops against which the Ford hearings were conducted.) The need for a thorough investigation of the candidate was further emphasized by the very real awareness that this particular Vice-President could well become President within a matter of months. It was widely expected that Nixon would be impeached and convicted, or resign.

Thus, Gerald Ford received an unprecedented screening for the job which the Vice-President is really all about: the Presidency. This formed the essence of the vice-presidential selection process from 1972 on; the 1973 Ford hearings simply gave greater intensity to this new concern. The hearings also helped focus increased public and political attention on the second office—not only in terms of succession to the Presidency (as, indeed, events since 1963 had already done), but also in terms of the functions of the second office itself.

Following his confirmation and inauguration as Vice-President, Ford was in the public eye almost incessantly, for he was so likely to succeed Nixon. Thus, the Ford Vice-Presidency brought even more awareness of the already visible Vice-Presidency. In a Nixon White House besieged by doubt and uncertainty, however, the duties assigned to Ford did not reflect any real change in the office.

By the time the Twenty-fifth Amendment was used again to fill a vice-presidential vacancy, the nation had become far more aware of the importance of the second office. Following the Nixon resignation, Ford became the first unelected President in American history. Since he carried no national mandate, he had to be extremely cautious about his own choice of Vice-President. He had to select someone who would give his "caretaker" administration as much credibility as possible. Thus, it was no accident that a figure as renowned as Nelson A. Rockefeller was selected. When the President first mentioned the office to Rockefeller in 1974, he did so with the heavy burden of having to establish legitimacy.

Rockefeller's prominence in national and international affairs gave the Ford Administration the tone of dignity and competence it needed. While some might have questioned Ford's credentials for the Presidency, none would challenge his Vice-President's.[1] Moreover, Rockefeller's reputation for attracting talented people was of enormous value to a President who had to rid himself of the past President's entourage. But by the time Rockefeller finally received congressional confirmation in December, circumstances had changed rather dramatically and the picture of the Vice-Presidency Ford had drawn for Rockefeller only in August took on a different image.

While Vice-President Rockefeller did enjoy a policymaking position in the Ford White House, the duties he had expected to perform following his August conversation with the President never materialized. By December 19, the day Rockefeller assumed the Vice-Presidency, a very different President and White House organization existed. Part of what had happened, of course, was that between August and December President Ford had become familiar and comfortable with the Presidency; thus, what he needed in a Vice-President had changed. Specifically, in August he had promised Rockefeller a domestic policy directorship with decision-making power. But while Rockefeller was responsible for the activities of the Domestic Council—the domestic counterpart of the National Security Council—his potential for utilizing the council as an implement of policymaking was not what he had expected it would be. This unanticipated difficulty arose precisely because of the changes that had occurred between August and December of 1974. Although Rockefeller's role as Vice-President needed redefinition, Ford never quite did so. Neither did the President tell his staff what relationship he thought Rockefeller would have with both the President and the staff.[2]

By the time Rockefeller came to office, the Ford staff had been operative for several months; Rockefeller appeared somewhat as an afterthought, but as one who expected to be a vital part of the policymaking process in domestic affairs, as Secretary of State Kissinger was in foreign affairs. Apparently, the Ford staff was unaware of the agreement (that the Vice-President would serve as a domestic policy director) that Ford and Rockefeller had reached during the summer.[3]

While the domestic policy role he came to play did not meet his initial expectations, Rockefeller was able to exert significant influence in this area. Rockefeller was so committed that he bluntly referred to himself as a "staff assistant" to the President,[4] causing the President's staff considerable irritation. They correctly judged that, while it would be difficult for *any* Vice-President to fulfill the role of a staff assistant—because the Vice-President is a constitutionally elected official—Rockefeller in particular would not be able to subjugate himself in that role.

To those staff people who jealously guard the perquisites of the Presidency, a Nelson Rockefeller would be considered dangerous. In fact, the President himself had pondered whether a Rockefeller Vice-Presidency would upstage him.[5] Ford need not have worried about being overshadowed, for no President is ever secondary to his Vice-President.

One of the early controversies of the Ford-Rockefeller Administration centered around the Domestic Council. Rockefeller eventually agreed to abandon the idea of personal leadership of the council and to vest such leadership in council staff directors, selected by the Vice-President himself. Rockefeller took this compromise directly to Ford, making clear that he intended to maintain a strong and active role in policymaking.[6]

Rockefeller was able to carve out a role for himself because of both his political savvy and his personal relationship with the President. In this regard, too, the President's own personality played a key role. Rockefeller immediately insisted that he hold weekly meetings with the President. The President agreed, thereby strengthening their relationship and, more importantly, creating an environment in which that close relationship would be sustained.

The second agreement between Ford and Rockefeller concerned the Vice-President's insistence that he be able to disagree publicly with the President. Rockefeller actually did so only once—on the issue of the New York City fiscal crisis—but the important point is that both men knew that open and honest disagreement was part of the ongoing relationship. Both demands demonstrate Rockefeller's basic approach to the Vice-Presidency: he was determined to be active and to seek out areas of policymaking. The achievements of his relatively short tenure in office are testimony to his initiative. In addition to his work with the Domestic Council, Rockefeller initiated proposals leading to the creation of a federal energy development finance corporation and gave Ford input for domestic policy options in the State of the Union Message. In addition, of course, Rockefeller inherited all of the statutory and ceremonial duties of the Vice-Presidency.

While short-lived, the Rockefeller Vice-Presidency was thus very active, but only because the Vice-President was conscious of forging a role for himself and because the President under whom he served gave him such latitude. Thus, personality and circumstances are key in understanding the relationship between the two offices. As has been amply demonstrated in this book, the Vice-President is subject almost entirely to presidential good favor and presidential needs. What happened to Rockefeller after Ford's July 1975 announcement that he intended to run for reelection in 1976 is a prime example of this. Ford's announcement immediately intensified liberal-conservative tensions within the Republican party, which now focused on whether Rockefeller would be Ford's running mate. In his initial statement, Ford expressed his "great admiration" for Rockefeller and his confidence that "both of us can convince the delegates that individually and as a team, we should be nominated." Shortly thereafter, the President's campaign manager, Howard Callaway, declared that Ford and Rockefeller would not run as a team.[7] Callaway said Ford approved of Rockefeller's performance, but in his words, "These are separate campaigns. Between now and the conventions next summer, I am not asking delegates if they will vote for Ford for President and Rockefeller for Vice President. I am asking them to vote for Ford for President, period."[8]

Why President Ford's *volte face* with regard to his future running mate? Ford was apparently concerned that Republican conservatives might abandon him and try to win the nomination for former California Governor Ronald Reagan. Shortly thereafter, Rockefeller indicated that he agreed with Callaway; he said disarmingly that "the nomination is for the President. When he's nominated, he decides who he wants to be his Vice-President." Rockefeller went on to say that he was "not a candidate" and facetiously asked, "Have you ever heard of anyone running for Vice President?"[9] Ultimately, even Nelson Rockefeller was beaten by the second office.

CARTER-MONDALE: A MODEL FOR THE VICE-PRESIDENCY

The Carter-Mondale Administration further demonstrates this point. To the extent that Walter Mondale was a viable part of the administration, it was because one man—Jimmy Carter—wanted him to be. The Mondale incumbency has served as a model for future administrations.

Mondale was a viable, though not visible, part of the administration from its outset—viable because of Carter's personality and political needs, and invisible because of Mondale's keen grasp of the Vice-Presidency and because of his own personality.

In the post-Watergate era, candidate Carter was acutely aware of the importance of conducting a careful vice-presidential search and of maintaining an open administration.

The circumstances of the Mondale selection clearly foretold the role he would play in the administration. As essentially the only Washington "insider" in the Carter camp, Mondale had knowledge that Carter desperately needed. Mondale also possessed links to interest and constituency groups which the President and his Georgia entourage lacked. As the protege of the much-respected Hubert Humphrey, Walter Mondale added a "legitimacy" to the relatively unknown administration. Of course, as the administration progressed, the President's needs inevitably changed, much as President Ford's needs changed vis-à-vis Rockefeller. As was true of all his predecessors, Mondale sometimes suffered the "ebb and flow" of the Vice-Presidency.[10]

Jimmy Carter was not unique when he promised an active role for his Vice-President; all Presidents since Harry Truman have at least paid lip-service to the need for a more active role for the Vice-President. On one occasion during the campaign, Carter discussed the prospective role of his Vice-President.

I have to be frank in telling you that the relative duties that would be accepted by me and by Senator Mondale if we are elected will have to be evolved as we get to know one another better and as we discern each other's particular strengths and weaknesses and particular interests in matters of public importance.

I am determined, beyond what has ever been done in this country, to put major responsibilities on the Vice President if I'm elected.

I can't give you now any better analysis than that, but I have discussed it enough with him to know that he and I will be searching for a way to let the Vice President be completely involved in our nation's affairs.[11]

The streets of Washington, D.C., were still littered with the confetti of the inauguration when Carter announced his intention to send Mondale on an important trip to Western Europe, to discuss issues of Middle East policy, economic policy toward the United States, and nuclear industrial technology with heads of government.[12] Mondale described this task as "unprecedented for a Vice President, going to the major allies and opening up our new relationship, discussing sensitive issues, laying the groundwork for the summit and many, many other concerns."[13] From the outset, however, Mondale worked quietly and behind the scenes.

While Mondale had learned much from his talks with Rockefeller and Humphrey, he chose to reject one bit of advice: to identify himself with one particular area of interest and responsibility. Instead, he chose to involve himself in a wide range of issues. While not becoming Carter's "chief staff person," which President-elect Carter had claimed Mondale would be,[14] the Vice-President took on a general trouble-shooter role. As noted more extensively elsewhere in this work, Mondale saw his role as that of the President's "adviser on critical, broad issues affecting government; to be the bearer of bad news."[15]

As a generalist in the Carter White House, Mondale was free to attend any meeting he chose. Statutorily, of course, Vice-Presidents are members of certain bodies, such as the National Security Council. Mere attendance at such meetings, however, does not mean that a Vice-President has a policymaking role. What was different, however, about the Mondale role was that he attended *working* meetings of the National Security Council. With his senatorial background as the second-ranking Democrat on the Church Committee (investigating intelligence abuses), Mondale thus had the qualifications necessary to oversee the President's intelligence operations study. In addition, Mondale had a role in reviewing major foreign policy positions, and he seemed to enjoy a good working relationship with national security affairs adviser Zbigniew Brezinski.[16]

As in all presidential-vice-presidential interactions, personalities played a crucial role in shaping the Carter-Mondale White House. President Carter was comfortable with his Vice-President and seemed to enjoy the close personal contact they shared. Indeed, much of Mondale's time was spent with the President, and the move of his office from the Executive Office Building to the West Wing of the White House, within a few steps of the Oval Office, illustrated the role of the Vice-President in this administration.

Mondale's easygoing, back-stage manner fit the vice-presidential job description well. Indeed, early on it had been conjectured that Mondale's cautiousness, willingness to accommodate, and reticence would round out the liberalism Carter so desperately needed. Mondale would know when to speak out and when to be silent. He did not disappoint the early speculators. Mondale himself has noted, "I think I'm a discreet person. In other words, when I have something I feel deeply about I go to the President, and I don't go out and talk about it."[17] Mondale preferred to limit himself to private disagreement, which Presidents have increasingly demanded. He also limited himself to the private influencing of policies and issues, a strategy which his mentor, Hubert Humphrey, had found most effective. Mondale pointed out that he found the wisest route was to say little at White House meetings. "If I speak up," said the Vice-President, "it kills discussion. A lot of people think I must be talking for the President. Secondly, if the President says something with which I disagree, I don't like to argue, in front of others. I'll go and tell him. Many times I've been very silent at these meetings and I'll go in right afterwards and tell him what I think."[18] His restrained public role has made it difficult to assess Mondale's full impact on the Carter White House.

Through his trouble-shooter role, Mondale was able to engage in a myriad of activities beyond that of the roving ambassador begun early in his incumbency.

Often serving as an administration spokesman, he served as a vital link to business groups.[19] He took on the steel industry for the Carter Administration, criticizing U.S. Steel in March 1978 for its price increase;[20] he vigorously defended the administration's SALT Treaty; and he severely criticized "the shameless attacks on people who voted their conscience" on the Panama Canal issue.[21] As other Vice-Presidents, Mondale often substituted for the President when the White House needed to lend credibility to an issue or an area but did not want to have the President himself make an appearance. For example, Mondale was asked to address the May 1978 United Nations special session on disarmament in Carter's place. Because Carter and Secretary of State Cyrus Vance were to deal with Soviet Foreign Minister Andrei Gromyko one week after the session, neither could politically make the address Mondale could.[22]

Mondale was well regarded within the Democratic party. This was increasingly important to the President as his own popularity sagged and then plummeted until the Iranian and Afghanistan crises temporarily resurrected him both in the public opinion polls and among fellow Democrats. In the interim, Mondale took to the political hustings and actively pursued the administration's party responsibilities. As one Democratic member of the House of Representatives put it, "Whatever people feel about Carter, they don't transfer it to Mondale. He knows how to campaign, he helps raise money, and he is also very popular here in the Midwest."[23] Mondale's extensive experience with this kind of politicking took enormous pressure off the President and a party worried that their titular leader might be an albatross. As the party and the administration approached the 1978 congressional elections, one vice-presidential adviser summed up the state of affairs: "Mondale is clearly going to be the one to do the party's work this year. Because of the problems Carter is having—and also because Fritz is simply better at this party stuff—he will have to be the main one trying to save . . . congressional seats. This year, Mondale is Carter's point man."[24]

As Mondale campaigned for congressional candidates in 1978, he coupled his party role with his role as administration spokesman and hinted at the administration's 1979–1980 presidential campaign strategy. Speaking in Dubuque, Iowa, in April 1978, Mondale faced head-on the criticisms of the Carter Presidency and the administration's record. Carter, said his Vice-President, was having difficulties because he was willing to face hard issues and refused to "duck and run." Said Mondale, "I predict before this is over that Jimmy Carter is going to be one of the most respected and popular Presidents in American history because he was man enough to do his job."[25] Once the Iran and Afghanistan crises intervened, Mondale quite effectively campaigned for the President in the 1980 renomination campaign, while Carter tended to the affairs of the world. The President rode to a comfortable victory in the early 1980 Iowa caucus.

During Carter's administration, when the President became too preoccupied with a trouble area, Mondale was asked to oversee much of the President's "normal" business. Such was the case during the fall of 1978 when Carter, engrossed in the Camp David talks with Egypt's Anwar Sadat and Israel's Menachem Begin, asked Mondale to handle most domestic business while the three executives were secluded at Camp David.[26] As presidential Press Secretary Jody Powell commented, ''The President's attitude is that he wishes the Vice President, in essence, to assume the responsibility for virtually all other activities of government and leave him free to the maximum extent possible to concentrate on his work at Camp David.''[27] In addition, since Mondale's background in the Mideast was more extensive than that of the President, Mondale shuttled to Camp David to attend some of the sessions. Similarly, he took over many presidential burdens during the long hostage ordeal in Iran and the subsequent invasion of Afghanistan by the Soviet Union.

With regard to the thorn of presidential staff, the Mondale experience was no exception. While both Carter and Mondale worked hard to lessen the inevitable tensions, nonetheless problems would arise. As noted elsewhere in this study, the White House staff even used the Vice-President as a sacrificial lamb when the President's popularity plummeted during the summer of 1979. They suggested that Mondale was lazy, and they hinted that he might be dropped from the 1980 ticket.

But Carter ended all speculation with the announcement that Mondale would indeed be his running mate. As the President's popularity in the polls climbed during the ensuing Iran and Afghanistan crises, Mondale assumed many commitments and activities the President had to forego, especially on the presidential campaign trail. Through his office Mondale also had a forum from which to serve as administration spokesman in a number of other areas. For example, he forcefully picked up on what the President had merely hinted at in his January 1980 remarks to the nation regarding the Soviet invasion of Afghanistan. Whereas the President had only hinted at a U.S. boycott of the summer Moscow Olympics, his Vice-President openly called for moving the games. This was a controversial point, but Mondale had heretofore taken on other controversial subjects in the name of the administration; in the natural gas filibuster, for example, as well as in his public defense of the SALT Treaty, an area in which Mondale had contributed substantively.[28]

All of Mondale's assignments were, of course, dependent entirely on what Jimmy Carter wanted. Mondale was acutely aware of this fact. ''My future in public life . . . depends upon the success of the Carter Presidency,''[29] Mondale said early in his incumbency.

TEAMWORK: THE REAGAN-BUSH ADMINISTRATION

George Bush's early years in the White House have witnessed the continuation of at least the symbolic change brought by the Carter-Mondale White House: the Vice-President's office remains in the White House, exactly where Mondale's was. With regard to the matter of the Vice-President's visibility, Bush remarked, ''It might work for awhile. But the President's staff will look at you differently.

I have a good relationship with the President's staff and my staff does, too. . . . If I'm out there with a high profile, holding press conferences, putting my spin on whatever it is, I won't have a [good] relationship with the President."[30]

Bush meets with President Reagan daily, when he attends a national security briefing; the two have a weekly luncheon to discuss "a range of issues."[31] Shortly after the 1980 election, Bush correctly speculated that he would have a role in foreign affairs and on the Hill, but he added, "I'm not going to be a lobbyist. I'll be talking to members of the Congress from time to time and on a selective basis."[32]

Regarding the role of his predecessor, Bush remarked:

Mondale had the best relationship with the President of any vice-president in history. . . . Mondale set a pattern—a mold—that I think is very good. It helped us start off—President Reagan and me—on what I hope will be for him a constructive way to go. Clearly it is constructive for me. Mondale persevered. The general feeling is that he was a useful vice-president.[33]

Bush observed that he could best fulfill his growth potential as Vice-President if he remembered the cardinal rule regarding viability and visibility. In all the statements he has made, Bush has consistently defended the President and has spoken forcefully in support of administration policies.[34] For example, Bush, who as a presidential candidate in the 1980 Republican primaries had opposed Ronald Reagan and labeled Reagan's economic program "voodoo economics," as Vice-President embraced that same program. In fact, Bush became a staunch spokesman for it. (Indeed, Bush had begun to play down his differences with Reagan as soon as he received the 1980 vice-presidential nomination.) Shortly after the beginning of the new administration, in a March 1981 interview with Godfrey Sperling, Jr. of the *Christian Science Monitor*, Bush was asked, "When you called the Reagan program 'voodoo economics,' what did you have in mind?" Bush responded, "That's not worth discussing anymore. . . . If I start pointing out even in a substantive way present differences (which there are none at this point)—well, that's not my concept of how you do something in my job— make something good happen." Then, in the same interview, Bush offered a defense of the program, "Whenever you chart an economic course in troubled economic seas like these, there is a certain amount of inexactitude in the science of prediction. But, having said that, I think that the need for acceptance of this program which is threefold—spending constraints, tax relief, and regulatory relief—is unarguable."[35]

Similarly, as President Reagan came under Democrats' charges—especially during the congressional campaigns of 1982—that he lacked compassion for the poor and less fortunate in America, his Vice-President took on a forceful defense of the President. In an appearance on the "Good Morning, America" show, Bush charged the Democrats with conducting a propaganda campaign, adding, "For these demagogues to accuse the President of having ice water in his blood"—

Bush was referring to a remark made by House Speaker Thomas ("Tip") O'Neill in a televised interview—"it gets my bile really moving."[36]

Bush's defense of the Reagan economic program and its effects upon various segments of Americans continued throughout his incumbency and it logically became a part of his role in the 1984 Reagan-Bush reelection campaign.[37] In his acceptance speech at the 1984 Republican Convention, Bush labeled the Democrats the party of "tax and spend, tax and spend." Said Bush, "Mr. Mondale calls [his] promise to raise taxes an act of courage. But it wasn't courage, it was just habit." Drawing a contrast between the Democratic and Republican conventions, Bush suggested the former was the "temple of doom," while he characterized his own party's message as "the American people want less spending and less regulation, not more taxes."[38]

Bush's defense of and deference and dedication to Ronald Reagan paid off. Reagan, who initially had misgivings over giving Bush the second place on the 1980 ticket, now frequently refers to Bush as the "best" Vice-President in history. Reagan said so throughout the 1984 campaign, and repeated this during the televised presidential debates with Walter Mondale (who himself had been quite an extraordinary and active Vice-President.) Meanwhile, Bush has even won the respect of some members on the Republican party's right; in 1980, the right had been enraged by the Bush selection. In a 1984 *Dallas Morning News* delegate poll, Bush received 48 percent support; New York Congressman Jack Kemp received 26 percent; former Senate Majority Leader Howard Baker received 16 percent. As 1988 nears, other Republicans will be eyeing the presidential nomination, especially if President Reagan can translate his personal popularity into a party popularity, and Bush will face some serious competition. Bush's proven abilities and loyalty and Ronald Reagan's adulation of his Vice-President certainly place Bush in an advantageous position as the heir apparent.

THE FUTURE OF THE VICE-PRESIDENCY: A CONCLUDING NOTE

The Founding Fathers provided for the presidential succession with the least possible delay to avoid any hiatus in the functioning of government. No sensitive person old enough to recall the tragic assassination of President John F. Kennedy in Dallas can fail to appreciate having had a Vice-President available and ready to assume the reins of government. Perhaps at no single moment before or since has the awesome importance of the Vice-Presidency been so apparent.

A different situation obtained with Watergate. As Watergate enveloped President Nixon, the need to fill the Vice-Presidency vacated by the resignation of Spiro Agnew became urgent. The extended period of time required to select candidates and to secure the necessary congressional confirmation of the appointee did not reassure the public of uninterrupted presidential leadership.

Critics of the vice-presidential office correctly maintain that it is not now a training ground for the Presidency, even though Vice-Presidents may be well versed in critical governmental areas and problems. This, however, need not be the case. The Rockefeller Vice-Presidency held promise for the development of the office in both domestic and foreign affairs, and Walter Mondale's function as adviser to the President—albeit with a low profile—marked the continuing preparation of an individual who had been considered for the Presidency when tapped for the number two spot. George Bush, who had been a contender for the 1980 Republican presidential nomination before accepting second place, masterfully dealt with the crisis imposed by the March 1981 assassination attempt on the President and would have been prepared to assume the presidential reins.

RESTRUCTURING THE VICE-PRESIDENCY

One approach to changing the structure of the Vice-Presidency would be to require Presidents to designate specific executive powers to the Vice-President. Such a change would require a constitutional amendment, as those engaged in the 1980 Republican vice-presidential talks with former President Gerald Ford were reminded. In that case, presidential candidate Reagan was severely criticized for not understanding the indivisibility of presidential power, and Ford's request for considerable presidential powers in exchange for running on the Reagan ticket was abandoned.

Perhaps Ford's suggestions, made several months later, should be given careful consideration. In offering a commentary on the Presidency itself, Ford noted the frustration of disregarded orders. As a possible source of aid in this regard, the former President suggested

using the Vice President as a real Chief of Staff, both to control the administrative bureaucracy and to see that Administration relations with the Congress really mesh. Having been the Vice President and having been the President, I know that there has to be a better delegation of responsibility between the two offices. . . . The President has always relied much more upon his own people. I believe you have got to take an elected official, a Vice President, and move him right into the West Wing of the White House as the Chief of Staff of the whole Administration.[39]

It can nonetheless be argued that an informal understanding that a President will assign his Vice-President major roles in either domestic or foreign affairs is both constitutionally feasible and a flexible enough mandate so as not to unduly harness a President. Any Vice-President incapable either intellectually or politically of being given such assignments should not be in line of presidential succession. Such an understanding would force presidential candidates to give even greater thought to the qualifications of the individual chosen as vice-presidential running mate.

These suggestions are aimed at strengthening rather than abolishing the Vice-Presidency. The recent history of the office has demonstrated that it can encompass significant functions. To abolish the Vice-Presidency and create a system of succession whereby a member of the legislature would act as President until a presidential election could be held, as suggested by Schlesinger, would only create new problems. Under such a plan, control of the White House might shift from one party to another abruptly. The public must have an understudy prepared and waiting in the wings; this individual must be someone chosen in the previous election rather than a member of the Congress who may be a relatively unknown figure and unprepared to assume the highest office in the land.

Perhaps much of the dissatisfaction and confusion concerning the office of the Vice-Presidency is misplaced and derives from the egregious flaws and ramifications of the Twenty-fifth Amendment. Its repeal or amendment is highly desirable. The need for such action should not be equated with abolishing the Vice-Presidency. Two separate issues are involved.

The Ford-Rockefeller Administration was an aberration that departed widely from a basic principle of American government, that is, that the President is elected by and represents all of the people. Such a deviation is not to be repeated. If the Twenty-fifth Amendment is to remain an operative part of the Constitution, it should be qualified by a further amendment providing for a special national election in the event an *unelected* Vice-President should succeed to the Presidency for a remainder of a presidential term exceeding two years. This would provide stability of succession via the Vice-Presidency and minimize the length of time a President by succession (who had not been elected to the Vice-Presidency in the previous election) would be apt to serve as the only national leader of the United States.

In his critique of the office, Schlesinger contends that the only function of the Vice-Presidency is as a jumping ground to the Presidency, or at least to the presidential nomination. While this is obviously true, what Schlesinger perceives negatively may be viewed alternatively as an already evolving solution to the challenging problem of the position of the Vice-Presidency: individuals capable of being President are indeed willing to spend several years in the second office, virtually at the mercy of the President's whim. Precisely because the Vice-Presidency provides a built-in advantage, the office has appealed to individuals of the stature of Hubert Humphrey, Nelson Rockefeller, Walter Mondale, and George Bush. Politicians of high calibre who show interest in the Vice-Presidency today are aware that the office has far more public interest and potential than it had a generation ago. Those who come to occupy the second-highest office, even though perhaps not destined to succeed to the Presidency, are much less likely to remain remote political figures than has often been characteristic in the past.

Whatever formal changes may be made by constitutional amendment, statutory elaborations, or presidential order, the evolution of the Vice-Presidency will be conditioned by the opportunities and challenges of future events. It may be said with some certainty that such developments as do occur in the foreseeable future will continue to depend in large measure on the person who occupies the Presidency and on what that person is willing to share with and assign to the Vice-President.

The contemporary Vice-Presidency has evolved considerably since Harry Truman struggled to overcome his inadequate preparation in that office. Public awareness of the office has increased both because of the strength of its incumbents and because of several disabilities and successions during this period. Since 1952 Presidents have made better use of the more prestigious incumbents, and these Vice-Presidents have become serious presidential contenders. The Vice-Presidency is no longer a "superfluous excellency." It is indeed a unique institution: it may be everything, as Hubert Humphrey pointed out, or it may be nothing. Which it is depends on both the President and the Vice-President, their likes and dislikes, their personalities and their understanding of the political realities. It is an office, Humphrey once said, that is ultimately "filled with all the uncertainties of human emotions."[40] Indeed, it is both prince and pauper.

NOTES

1. *Time*, November 19, 1975. Following Rockefeller's 1975 withdrawal from the nomination race, *Time* proclaimed that Rockefeller was even "overqualified" for the Presidency.

2. Michael Turner, "Finding a Policy Role for the Vice President: The Case of Nelson A. Rockefeller," unpublished Ph.D. dissertation, State University of New York at Binghamton, 1978, p. 320.

3. Ibid.

4. Ibid., p. 325.

5. *Newsweek* later reported the interaction between Ford and a "close associate" on this matter. Reportedly, the confidante had told Ford: "I have an idea that Nixon picked Spiro Agnew because he was insecure and didn't want anyone who would overshadow him. Don't *you* do anything like that! When you're President, you don't have to worry about being overshadowed by anyone." *Newsweek*, September 2, 1976; Turner, "Finding a Policy Role," identifies this "close associate" as Melvin Laird.

6. Turner, "Finding a Policy Role," pp. 314–15.

7. *Boston Globe*, July 10, 1975.

8. Ibid.

9. Ibid.

10. As Hubert Humphrey had termed it.

11. Carter news conference, New York City, July 15, 1976, quoted in U.S. Congress, House of Representatives Committee on House Administration, *The Presidential Campaign, 1976, Vol. I, Jimmy Carter*, 95th Congress, 2d Session, 1978, p. 317.

12. John Osborne, "Mondale at Work," *The New Republic* (April 23, 1977): 11–12.

13. "Walter Mondale," The MacNeil/Lehrer Report, WNET/WETA, February 22, 1977, p. 5.

14. Osborne, "Mondale at Work," p. 10.

15. "Walter Mondale," p. 5.

16. Osborne, "Mondale at Work," p. 12.

17. *Los Angeles Times*, September 5, 1978.

18. Ibid.

19. *New York Times*, May 18, 1978.

20. Ibid., March 31, 1978.

21. Ibid.

22. Ibid., May 19, 1978.

23. *Chicago Tribune*, April 5, 1978.

24. Ibid.

25. *Los Angeles Times*, April 4, 1978.

26. *The Sun*, September 2, 1978.

27. *The Detroit News*, September 6, 1978.

28. In stark contrast to the role as administration spokesman which his mentor, Hubert Humphrey, had been forced to assume on Vietnam, even though Humphrey had not participated in policymaking in that area.

29. "Walter Mondale," MacNeil/Lehrer Report.

30. *Christian Science Monitor*, March 3, 1981.

31. Ibid.

32. Ibid.

33. Ibid.

34. Ibid.

35. *Christian Science Monitor*, March 3, 1981.

36. *New York Times*, October 6, 1982.

37. Joel K. Goldstein, *The Modern American Vice Presidency* (Princeton, New Jersey: Princeton University Press, 1982), chapter 4 provides a useful discussion of the vice-presidential role in campaigns.

38. *New York Times*, August 24, 1984.

39. As quoted in *Time*, November 10, 1980, p. 30.

40. Hubert H. Humphrey, Interview, March 1974.

Bibliographic Essay

The archival materials on deposit at the presidential libraries are invaluable to the researcher on the American Vice-Presidency. This study made extensive use of both presidential and vice-presidential papers: the Papers of Franklin D. Roosevelt, Franklin D. Roosevelt Library, Hyde Park, New York (hereafter cited as FDR Lib.); the Papers of Harry S Truman, Harry S Truman Library (hereafter cited as HST Lib.); the Papers of Dwight D. Eisenhower, Dwight D. Eisenhower Library (hereafter cited as DDE Lib.); the Papers of John F. Kennedy, John F. Kennedy Library, Columbia Point, Massachusetts (hereafter cited as JFK Lib.); the Papers of Lyndon B. Johnson, Lyndon B. Johnson Library (hereafter cited as LBJ Lib.); the Papers of Henry Wallace, FDR Lib.; The Papers of Alben W. Barkley, University of Kentucky Library, Lexington, Kentucky; and the Papers of Hubert H. Humphrey, Minnesota Historical Society, Minneapolis, Minnesota.

In addition to the presidential and vice-presidential papers, collections of personal papers and records of presidential and vice-presidential aides, staff, and others abound with useful material on the subject. Specifically, on deposit at the Roosevelt Library are: the Papers of Harry L. Hopkins; the Papers of Henry Morgenthau, Jr.; the Papers of Eleanor Roosevelt; the Papers of Elbert D. Thomas; and the Papers of Samuel I. Rosenman. These collections offer fascinating reading and were of great use to this study.

On deposit at the Harry S Truman Library are the Files of the Democratic National Committee; the Papers of Richard H. Hansen (particularly on the subject of presidential disability); the Papers of Lou Holland; the Papers of Edward D. McKim; the Papers of Stephen A. Mitchell; and the Papers of Phileo Nash.

Among the extensive collection of papers available at the Dwight D. Eisenhower Library which were of greatest use to this study were: the Records of Sherman Adams; the Papers of Jack Anderson; the Records of John S. Beagdon; the Papers of Arthur F. Burns; the Papers of Frederick Fox; the Records of James Hagerty; the Records of Stephen Hess; the Records of James Lambie; the Records of Robert Merriam; the Records of Gerald Morgan; the Records of Don Paarlberg; the Papers of Merlo Pusey; the Republican National Committee Files; and the Papers of William Rogers.

Archival sources available at the Lyndon B. Johnson Library were useful from two perspectives, since Johnson had served as Vice-President and then had a Vice-President of his own. Papers there included: the Files of Horace Busby; the Files of Joseph Califano;

the Files of S. Douglas Cater; the Files of James Gaither; the Files of Harry McPherson; the Files of Mike Manatos.

An important dimension in the evolution of presidential materials has been the development of extensive oral history interviews. While they are *personal* recollections of individuals surrounding a President and/or his administration, these oral history interviews not only add invaluably to contemporary research by providing insights and interpretations of issues, individuals, and events, but often serve as seminal material that may spark research in initially unanticipated directions. Among the most useful to this study were the oral history interviews of: Elie Abel (DDE Lib.); Sherman Adams (DDE Lib.); Senator George Aiken (JFK Lib.); Carl Albert (JFK Lib.); George Allen (HST Lib.); Joseph Alsop (DDE Lib.); Alben Barkley (HST Lib.; FDR Lib.); Ross Barnett (JFK Lib.); Leo Beebe (LBJ Lib.); Jack Bell (JFK Lib.); Hale Boggs (JFK Lib.; LBJ Lib.); William J. Bray (HST Lib.); Samuel C. Brightman (JFK Lib.; HST Lib.); Edmund G. Brown (JFK Lib.); Herbert Brownell (DDE Lib.); Carter Burgers (DDE Lib.); James MacGregor Burns (JFK Lib.); Prescott Bush (DDE Lib.); Douglas Cater (LBJ Lib.); Anthony J. Celebrezze (JFK Lib.); Emmanuel Celler (LBJ Lib.); Wilbur J. Cohen (LBJ Lib.); Charles Daly (JFK Lib.); Jonathan Daniels (HST Lib.); Joseph F. Dolan (JFK Lib.); Paul H. Douglas (JFK Lib.); Roscoe Drummond (DDE Lib.); Mildred L. Dryden (HST Lib.); Dr. Milton Eisenhower (DDE Lib.); Allen J. Ellender (LBJ Lib.); Joseph G. Fenney (HST Lib.); Robert H. Finch (DDE Lib.); Edward Folliard (JFK Lib.); Stanley Fike (JFK Lib.); Thomas W. Fletcher (LBJ Lib.); James Gaither (LBJ Lib.); Edward Gallagher (JFK Lib.); Charles A. Halleck (JFK Lib.); Dr. Samuel Halperin (LBJ Lib.); Donald Hansen (HST Lib.); Arthur Harris (LBJ Lib.); Gilbert Harrison (JFK Lib.); Gabriel Hauge (DDE Lib.); Carl Hayden (LBJ Lib.); Rev. Theodore Hesburgh (LBJ Lib.); Stephen Hess (DDE Lib.); Edgard Hinde (HST Lib.); Carter Hodding, Jr. (LBJ Lib.); Luther Hodges (JFK Lib.); Claude E. Hooten (JFK Lib.); Ralph Horton (JFK Lib.); Harold Howe (LBJ Lib.); Jacob Javits (JFK Lib.; DDE Lib.); Mr. and Mrs. Randall Jesse (HST Lib.); Kenneth B. Keating (DDE Lib.); Joe G. Keen (LBJ Lib.); John H. Kelso (JFK Lib.); Francis Keppel (LBJ Lib.); William F. Knowland (DDE Lib.); Carroll Kilpatrick (JFK Lib.); Joseph Kraft (JFK Lib.); Arthur Krock (JFK Lib.); Sigmund S. Larmon (DDE Lib.); Donald R. Larrabee (JFK Lib.); Oscar M. Laurel (LBJ Lib.); William Lawrence (JFK Lib.); Fred Lazarus, Jr. (DDE Lib.); Barry Leithead (DDE Lib.); G. Gould Lincoln (JFK Lib.); Walter Lippman (JFK Lib.); Henry Cabot Lodge (JFK Lib.); Henry Loomis (LBJ Lib.); Judge J. C. Looney (LBJ Lib.); Henry R. Luce (JFK Lib.); Edward McCabe (DDE Lib.); Edward J. McCormack (JFK Lib.); Henry Roemar McPhee (DDE Lib.); Lester Maddox (LBJ Lib.); Mike Mansfield (JFK Lib.); Lowell B. Mason (HDT Lib.); Burke Marshall (JFK Lib.); Thurgood Marshall (JFK Lib.); George Meader (LBJ Lib.); George Meany (JFK Lib.); Wilbur Mills (JFK Lib.); Clarence Mitchell (LBJ Lib.); Maurine Newberger (JFK Lib.); Ethel Noland (HST Lib.); Claiborne Pell (JFK Lib.); Mike Peters (LBJ Lib.); William Proxmire (JFK Lib.); Wayne O. Reed (LBJ Lib.); J. Leonard Reinsch (JFK Lib.); Charles Roberts (DDE Lib.); Charles Roberts (JFK Lib.); A. William Robertson (LBJ Lib.); Richard Rovere (DDE Lib.); Harrison Salisbury (DDE Lib.); Leverett Saltonstall (DDE Lib.; JFK Lib.); Dr. Leonard Scheele (DDE Lib.); Norbert A. Schlei (JFK Lib.); David Seeley (LBJ Lib.); James R. Shepley (DDE Lib.); Hugh Sidey (JFK Lib.); John Singerhoff (LBJ Lib.); George Smathers (JFK Lib.); Howard K. Smith (DDE Lib.); Merriman Smith (DDE Lib.); Theodore Sorensen (JFK Lib.); Charles Spalding (JFK Lib.); Mansfield D. Sprague (DDE Lib.); A. J. Stephens (HST Lib.); James L. Sundquist (JFK Lib.); Herman E. Talmadge (JFK Lib.); Hobart Taylor, Jr. (JFK Lib.); Harry H.

Vaughan (HST Lib.); Ernest Warren (JFK Lib.); Robert C. Weaver (LBJ Lib.); Roy Wilkins (JFK Lib.); Donald Wilson (JFK Lib.); James Wine (JFK Lib.); Harris Wofford (JFK Lib.); Robert C. Wood (LBJ Lib.); and Whitney M. Young, Jr. (LBJ Lib.)

Personal interviews added a crucial depth and dimension to the findings of this work, and I sought a diversity of sources—incumbents of the second office itself; presidential and vice-presidential aides; U.S. senators (to garner a perspective on the Vice-President's constitutionally assigned job of presiding officer of the Senate); journalists; and individuals working with particular Vice-Presidents on various projects. Interviewees included: Frank Barber; Terry Barnett; Senator Glenn Beall; Senator Wallace Bennett; E. William Bohn; Lou Cannon; Liz Carpenter; George Christian; Clark Clifford; Jack Corman; Senator Carl Curtis; John Damgard; Marty Donovan; Vice-President Gerald R. Ford; James L. George; Bill Heckman; Senator Hubert H. Humphrey; Walter Jenkins; David Keene; Senator Gale McGee; Senator Frank E. Moss; Kenneth P. O'Donnell; Courtnay Pace; Donald Paarlberg; Governor Endicott Peabody; Senator Claiborne Pell; Floyd Riddick; Gordon Roberts; Dean Rusk; Senator John Sparkman; Senator Herman Talmadge; Hobart Taylor, Jr.; Robert Troutman, Jr.; Elbert Tuttle; Agnes Waldron; Jack Warner; Bill Wesch; and Jules Witcover.

Secondary sources abound on each of the presidential administrations within the time frame of this study. These were principally useful in two ways: as background material on each of the administrations involved; and for (usually quite scattered) material on the roles performed by each Vice-President. Underscoring the neglect suffered by the office of the Vice-Presidency was the fact that the indexes of many secondary sources did not include a subject heading ''Vice-President.'' (This has begun to change noticeably, especially since 1973 and the resignation of Vice-President Agnew.) Included in the secondary sources are a myriad of general works on the subject of the Presidency; works confined to one administration or an aspect of one administration; works on political parties; biographical, autobiographical, and quasi-biographical works on individual incumbents of the Vice-Presidency. Particularly useful in this last category were: Joseph Albright, *What Makes Spiro Run: The Life and Times of Spiro Agnew* (Garden City: Doubleday, 1972); Robert Curran, *Spiro Agnew: Spokesman for America* (New York: Lancer Books, 1970), which is one of the few sources providing a chronological ordering and background material on the Agnew speeches while he was in the Vice-Presidency; Albert Eisele, *Almost to the Presidency* (Blue Earth, Minnesota: Piper Company, 1972), a candid, well-thought-out source on Hubert Humphrey; and Allan H. Ryskind's *Hubert* (New York: Arlington House, 1968), a similarly useful work.

Presidential and vice-presidential memoirs also aided this study: Dwight D. Eisenhower, *Mandate for Change 1953–1956* (New York: Doubleday and Company, 1963) and *The White House Years: Waging Peace 1956–1961* (New York: Doubleday, 1963); Lyndon Baines Johnson, *The Vantage Point: Perspectives of the Presidency* (New York: Holt, Rinehart & Winston, 1971); Richard M. Nixon, *Six Crises* (New York: Doubleday, 1962); Harry S. Truman, *Mr. Citizen* (New York: Random House, 1955), *Years of Decisions* (Garden City, N.Y.: Doubleday, 1955), and *Years of Trial and Hope* (Garden City, N.Y.: Doubleday, 1956).

Works on or more closely related to the Vice-Presidency are few and far between and less than comprehensive. Greenwood Press is responsible for an early work on the Vice-Presidency, Louis Clinton Hatch's *History of the Vice Presidency of the United States* (Westport, Conn.: 1934; revised by Earl L. Shoup, 1970). But specific works on the subject during the modern Vice-Presidency, while sometimes useful and interesting, have often dealt with only a part of the picture or have taken a biographical approach rather than offering a comprehensive statement on the generic nature of the office. Specific works include: Leonard Baker, *The Johnson Eclipse: A President's Vice Presidency* (New York: Macmillan, 1966); Richard M. Cohen and Jules Witcover, *A Heartbeat Away* (New York: Viking Press, 1974); Michael Vincent Di Salle, *Second Chance* (New York: Hawthorne Books, 1966); Michael Dorman, *Second Man* (New York: Delacorte Press, 1968); Earl Mazo, *Richard Nixon: A Political and Personal Portrait* (New York: Harper, 1959); Irving G. Williams, *The American Vice-Presidency: New Look* (Garden City, N.Y.: Doubleday, 1956) and *The Rise of the Vice-Presidency* (Washington, D.C.: Public Affairs Press, 1956); Jules Witcover, *White Knight: The Rise of Spiro Agnew* (New York: Random House, 1972); Donald Young, *American Roulette: The History and Dilemma of the Vice Presidency* (New York: Holt, Rinehart and Winston, 1965); Klyde H. Young and Lanar Middleton, *Heir Apparent: The Vice Presidency of the United States* (New York: Books for Libraries Press, 1948, 1969). Two more recently published works are worth examining: Paul C. Light's *Vice Presidential Power: Advice and Influence in the White House* (Baltimore: Johns Hopkins University Press, 1984), which principally provides a view of the administrative side of the Rockefeller and Mondale Vice-Presidencies (although offering some interesting remarks regarding the Bush Vice-Presidency) and Joel E. Goldstein's *The Modern American Vice Presidency* (Princeton, N.J.: Princeton University Press, 1982), which comes closer to providing a more global, although not comprehensive, perspective on the office. Both of these latter works need to incorporate greater use of archival sources. Several of my own earlier works on the Vice-Presidency have appeared in issues of the *Presidential Studies Quarterly*, beginning in 1976.

A useful bulk of secondary works exist on the specific topics of presidential disability and vice-presidential succession. These include: Bernard Asbell, *When F.D.R. Died* (New York: Holt, Rinehart and Winston, 1961); John D. Feerick, *From Failing Hands* (New York: Fordham University Press, 1965); Richard Hansen, *The Year We Had No President* (Lincoln: University of Nebraska Press, 1962); Michael Harwood, *In the Shadow of Presidents: The American Vice-Presidency and Succession System* (Philadelphia: Lippincott, 1966); Louis Heren, *No Hail, No Farewell* (New York: Harper and Row, 1970); Cabell Phillips, *The Truman Presidency: The History of a Triumphant Succession* (New York: Macmillan, 1969; Robert Sherrill, *The Accidental President* (New York: Grossman Publishers, 1967); and Ruth C. Silva, *Presidential Succession* (Ann Arbor: University of Michigan Press, 1951).

Index

Adams, John, 4, 7, 133
Adams, Sherman, 125 n.44, 147; resignation, 147; role during Eisenhower disability, 93–95, 101 n.79; role in Eisenhower Administration, 145
Administration spokesman, 139; Agnew as, 119, 150–58; Ford as, 84–85; Humphrey as, 142, 144, 150; Johnson as, 150
Afghanistan, 179, 180
Agnew, Spiro T., 85; as Administration spokesman, 119, 150–58; as Administration spokesman, compared to Nixon as Vice-President, 155; as Administration spokesman regarding Vietnam, 152; attacks on Congress, 153; attack on "enemies," 153–54; attack on liberals, 151, 152, 153–54; attacks on Senator Charles Goodell, 157; campaign blunders, 150; and civil rights leaders, 67–68; civil rights views, 65–66 (Appendix A); compared with Edmund Muskie, 112; Congressional purge: campaign of 1970, 156; controversy surrounding, 119; criticism of Humphrey, presidential campaign of 1968, 127 n.52; criticism regarding college campuses, 150; defense of Nixon's Vietnam speech, 154–55; defense of the South, 153; electoral constituency, 24, 45; foreign travel as Vice-President, 159; Harrisburg, Pennsylva-

nia, speech, 153; as "heir apparent," 105, 119–21, 156–58; and "ideological alignment," 153; Jackson, Mississippi, speech, 153, 155; law and order, 151; law and order record, 28–30; regarding "majority" of Americans, 154; media attack by, 119, 151, 152; media's reaction to Agnew's attack, 155; "Media Speech," 154–55; "Mr. Clean" image, 119–20, 131 n.111; negative image, 1968 presidential campaign, 112, 150; New Orleans speech, 152–53; nomination as vice-presidential running mate, 21, 26–27, 28–30; "Northeastern liberal community," attack on, 153; regarding permissiveness, 151; polarization, call for, 152, 154, 156; as President of the Senate, 8–9; presidential plans, 120, 147; reactions to, 119, 152; realignment of the electorate, 119; relations with Nixon Administration, 121; relations with Nixon, 119, 157; resignation, 50–51, 83–84, 121, 136, 158, 173, 182; review of Nixon's Vietnam policy, 152; rhetoric of, 119, 150–58, passim.; rise to national prominence, 119–20; role in 1968 presidential campaign, 129 n.79; role in 1970 congressional campaigns, 155–56; roles as Vice-President, 119–20; scandal preceding resignation, 139; silenced by Nixon, 150; silent majority theme,

About the Author

MARIE D. NATOLI is Associate Professor of Political Science at Emmanuel College in Boston and is a member of the Editorial Board of the *Presidential Studies Quarterly* as well as the John F. Kennedy Library Academic Advisory Committee.